A Practitioner's Guide to Powers of Attorney

D
L

1

This boo
stampe
if it is n

First published in 1991

A Practitioner's Guide to Powers of Attorney

by **John Thurston LLB, Solicitor**
Associate with Thurston & Co Solicitors
Fifth edition

LexisNexis™ UK

Members of the LexisNexis Group worldwide

United Kingdom	LexisNexis UK, a Division of Reed Elsevier (UK) Ltd, Halsbury House, 35 Chancery Lane, LONDON, WC2A 1EL, and 4 Hill Street, EDINBURGH EH2 3JZ
Argentina	LexisNexis Argentina, BUENOS AIRES
Australia	LexisNexis Butterworths, CHATSWOOD, New South Wales
Austria	LexisNexis Verlag ARD Orac GmbH & Co KG, VIENNA
Canada	LexisNexis Butterworths, MARKHAM, Ontario
Chile	LexisNexis Chile Ltda, SANTIAGO DE CHILE
Czech Republic	Nakladatelství Orac sro, PRAGUE
France	Editions du Juris-Classeur SA, PARIS
Germany	LexisNexis Deutschland GmbH, FRANKFURT, MUNSTER
Hong Kong	LexisNexis Butterworths, HONG KONG
Hungary	HVG-Orac, BUDAPEST
India	LexisNexis Butterworths, NEW DELHI
Ireland	Butterworths (Ireland) Ltd, DUBLIN
Italy	Giuffrè Editore, MILAN
Malaysia	Malayan Law Journal Sdn Bhd, KUALA LUMPUR
New Zealand	LexisNexis Butterworths, WELLINGTON
Poland	Wydawnictwo Prawnicze LexisNexis, WARSAW
Singapore	LexisNexis Butterworths, SINGAPORE
South Africa	LexisNexis Butterworths, DURBAN
Switzerland	Stämpfli Verlag AG, BERNE
USA	LexisNexis, DAYTON, Ohio

© John Thurston 2003

Crown copyright material is reproduced with the permission of the Controller of HMSO and the Queen's Printer for Scotland. Any European material in this work which has been reproduced from EUR-lex, the official European Communities legislation website, is European Communities copyright.

While every care has been taken to ensure the accuracy of this work, no responsibility for loss or damage occasioned to any person acting or refraining from action as a result of any statement in it can be accepted by the authors, editors or publishers.

A CIP Catalogue record for this book is available from the British Library.

First published in 1991

ISBN 0 75452 087 0

Typeset by Kerrypress Ltd, Luton, Bedfordshire

Printed and bound in Great Britain by The Cromwell Press, Trowbridge, Wiltshire

Visit LexisNexis UK at www.lexisnexis.co.uk

Preface

Powers of attorney are granted frequently in various situations – the grantor may be going abroad for a prolonged period, or may be elderly. In the case of an elderly person, enduring powers, which are not revoked by the subsequent mental incapacity of the donor, are particularly useful. Powers of attorney are also found in commercial transactions, for example in mortgage and partnership agreements.

Powers of attorney may be granted to lay persons as well as to professionals, and I hope this book will serve its purpose and be of use not only to legal practitioners, but also to anyone who is asked to act as an attorney. Throughout this book I have referred to the donor or donee of the power as 'he' or 'him' – it is nothing more than a way of avoiding the slightly clumsy alternative of 'he/she' and 'him/her', and I apologise to female readers for any offence caused.

Since the last edition, there have been some amendments to the Court of Protection Rules 2001 and the Court of Protection (Enduring Powers of Attorney Rules) 2001, which have been incorporated in the text where appropriate. The opportunity has also been taken to include a chapter comparing the tests for capacity to grant an enduring power of attorney, to make lifetime gifts and to make wills. Some sections have been rewritten or expanded.

I acknowledge Crown copyright for the Acts of Parliament, statutory instruments, and orders and rules quoted or referred to in the text. Law Commission reports are reproduced with the permission of the Controller of Her Majesty's Stationery Office.

John Thurston

Contents

Table of Cases

Table of Statutes

Table of Statutory Instruments

Chapter 1

Introduction

What is a power of attorney?

1.1 A power of attorney is a deed by which a person confers power on another to act on behalf of the person granting the power. The person granting the power is called the donor, grantor, or principal, and the person on whom the power is conferred is called the donee, grantee, agent, or attorney. The power can be general or limited. If it is general, the donee, grantee, agent or attorney will be authorised to do anything which the donor, grantor, or principal could have lawfully done; if it is limited, the donee, grantee, agent, or attorney may have authority only to deal with one particular transaction, for example the sale of a house. The power may also be limited in time; it may expressly state that it is to remain in force for a specified period, or whilst the donor is abroad. As soon as the specified period expires, or the donor returns to the United Kingdom, the power will terminate.

For the sake of simplicity, in this book the person granting the power is usually called the donor, and the person to whom the power is granted is usually called the donee or attorney.

Typical uses

1.2 Powers of attorney are frequently granted when a person is about to go abroad for a prolonged period and may be difficult to contact. They are also granted in respect of short absences abroad, for example a holiday, if it is likely that action will have to be taken on behalf of the donor whilst he or she is away.

Elderly persons also appoint attorneys so that they do not have to deal with their business affairs. It is particularly appropriate for those persons who are confined to the house or are in care, who cannot get out to visit the bank or otherwise attend to their affairs. It is also appropriate for elderly persons to grant enduring powers of attorney, which will not be revoked by their subsequent mental incapacity.

Younger persons may also grant enduring powers of attorney. This may be because they are concerned about what will happen if they are rendered mentally incapable by an accident or illness, in which circumstances it might be difficult for a partner to access money in bank or building society accounts, or deal with other assets without application to the Court of Protection for the appointment of a receiver.

In addition, a power of attorney may be incorporated into other transactions. In a mortgage, the mortgagor or borrower may give the mortgagee or lender a power of attorney to enable the mortgagee or lender to sell the property should the mortgagor or borrower default. A power of attorney is also often found in partnership agreements; the partners appoint each other their attorney so as to enable them to deal with partnership matters on behalf of each other. This power is particularly useful if a partner has left the partnership, perhaps because he has been expelled, and is not prepared to co-operate with the other partners. He may refuse to sign documents connected with the partnership; the continuing partners can sign the documents on his behalf if they have a power of attorney. Powers of attorney are also used in conveyancing transactions, for example where a house is purchased by a home relocation company.

Types of power of attorney

1.3   It is always open to the donor of a power to specify in detail the powers conferred on the attorney. These can merely authorise the attorney to enter into one transaction, or they can be so wide as to permit the attorney to do anything the donor or principal could have done. In the latter situation, before 1971 the power was usually very long (for example, see *Midland Bank Ltd v Reckitt [1933] AC*).

Since the Powers of Attorney Act 1971, if a donor or principal wants to confer a general authority on the attorney, it has not been necessary to set out at great length the powers conferred on the attorney. Instead, use can be made of the general form of attorney set out in Schedule 1 to the Act, which gives the attorney authority to do any act which the donor could have lawfully done (s 10 Powers of Attorney Act 1971). The donee under this power will be able to operate bank or building society accounts on behalf of the donor, sell any house or other property belonging to the donor, and invest money on behalf of the donor. This power is reproduced at A2.1 below, and it should be used if the donor or principal intends to grant a general power.

Frequently powers of attorney are granted by elderly donors, perhaps about to enter residential or nursing homes, to adult children to enable the children to operate bank and building society accounts and deal with investments on behalf of their parents. The basic rule is that a power of attorney is revoked by the supervening mental incapacity of the donor, so that if a parent who has given a child a power of attorney becomes incapable of managing his or her affairs, the power of attorney terminates, and the child cannot continue to act under the power. In this situation the only way of dealing with the assets of the parent is to apply to the Court of Protection under the Mental Health Act 1983. Usually, the Court of Protection appoints a relative to be a receiver to manage the assets of the patient. The disadvantages of applications of this nature are the procedural requirements and the fees (for a further discussion, see page 9 of the Law Commission's report on *The Incapacitated Principal* (Law Com No 122 Cmnd 8977)).

The recommendations of the Commission were enacted in the Enduring Powers of Attorney Act 1985 ('EPAA 1985'). This authorises the creation of enduring powers of attorney which are not revoked by the subsequent mental incapacity of the donor.

Operation of enduring powers of attorney

1.4   This is dealt with in more detail in CHAPTER 7. In outline, the donor grants a general or limited power of attorney to the donee or attorney, using a prescribed form. The power is operated as an ordinary power, until the donee or attorney has reason to believe that the donor is or is becoming mentally incapable, whereupon the attorney must make application to the court for the registration of the power. Notice of application must be given to specified relatives, who can object to the registration on various grounds. Once the power is registered, the attorney continues to act, but the court has various supervisory powers. Thus an enduring power is not revoked by the supervening mental incapacity of the donor, although an ordinary power would be revoked in that situation. Enduring powers are accordingly very useful in the case of elderly donors as they enable the attorney to continue to act after the donor has become mentally incapable, provided they are registered.

Joint powers and joint and several powers

1.5   Frequently a donor will appoint one person to act as attorney. However, the donor does not have to appoint a sole attorney; he or she can appoint two or more persons to act as attorney.

If two or more persons are appointed, they will either have a joint power, or a joint and several power. The instrument creating the power should state which power is being created, and in the case of an enduring power, must clearly state, because there is a difference between joint authority and joint and several authority.

If it is a *joint power*, all the attorneys must join in making any decision, so that one joint attorney cannot bind the others. If one joint attorney dies, the power terminates. On the other hand, if it is a *joint and several power*, all the attorneys do not have to join in making decisions, and one can bind the others. If one joint and several attorney dies, the others can continue to act.

Apart from the general importance of the distinction between joint powers and joint and several powers, the EPAA 1985 lays down different rules for these types of powers.

Who should be appointed as attorney?

1.6   A donor of a power should always appoint as donee or attorney a person he or she can trust. However, there may be situations where it will cause offence if a person the donor distrusts is not appointed the attorney. For example, if there are several children living near a parent, it may cause offence if all of them are not appointed attorneys, even though the parent may distrust one of them. One way round this problem is for the donor to appoint joint attorneys so that they can act as a check on each other, as a joint attorney will not be able to deal with the property or money of the donor without the consent of the other attorney. The disadvantage of appointing joint attorneys is that if one dies, then the power automatically terminates.

PD Lewis in *The Law Society's Gazette* (26 November 1986 at page 3568) poses the problem of a donor who has two children, neither of whom he wishes to alienate, but does not want to entrust sole management of his affairs to one. He suggests that the donor could grant two enduring powers – one appointing the donor's solicitor and one child, and the other appointing the solicitor again, and the other child.

Joint and several powers should be conferred when it is expected that one or more of the attorneys will sometimes be unable to act, for example because he or she goes abroad frequently, or because one or more of the attorneys is elderly, and may predecease the donor.

There is doubt as to whether a joint or joint and several appointment of three persons on the basis that only two of them could act is valid.

Is a power of attorney necessary?

1.7   If it is intended that the power should continue despite the supervening incapacity of the donor of the power, an enduring power must be granted. However, if there is little possibility of the donor becoming mentally incapable, so that an enduring power of attorney is not appropriate, it may be that a power of attorney is not essential, and that the donee can do all that is required on behalf of the donor under a written or even an oral authority.

The grant of a power of attorney creates an agency relationship between the donor and the donee of the power. The basic rule is that no formalities are required for the appointment of the agent, and an oral appointment can be effective, although it is highly desirable that any appointment should be in writing in order to prevent disputes later, and to protect the donee against allegations that he or she has exceeded his or her authority. However, there are a few transactions where a power of attorney will be required. These are considered next.

Transactions which require a deed

1.8   Certain transactions require a deed for their validity. Examples of transactions requiring a deed are:

   (i)   a conveyance of land. This must be made by deed under s 52(1) Law of Property Act 1925, and under s 205(1)(ii) 'conveyance' is defined as including a mortgage, charge, and a lease;

   (ii) leases for more than three years (s 54(2) Law of Property Act 1925);

   (iii) transfers or registered land (Land Registration Act 2002 and Sch 9 Land Registration Rules 2003).

The Law of Property (Miscellaneous Provisions) Act 1989 ('the 1989 Act'), the relevant provisions of which came into force on 31 July 1990, altered the rules about deeds. Section 1(3) provides that a deed must be signed by the person making it, or alternatively it can be signed by an agent at the direction and in the presence of the maker of the deed and in the presence of two witnesses who each attest the signature.

Section 1(1)(c) of the 1989 Act abolishes any rule of law which requires that a deed must be used to confer authority on another person to deliver an instrument as a deed; s 1(3)(b) provides that the deed must be delivered by the person making it or by a person authorised to do so on his behalf.

The effect of these provisions is that no authority by deed is necessary for an agent to sign a deed in the presence of the maker of the deed, or to deliver it whether or not the maker is present. However, a deed will normally have to be used to confer authority on the agent to sign a deed in the *absence* of the principal. A power of attorney is therefore essential if a donor is going abroad and wishes to confer authority on an agent to enter into a transaction which will require the execution of a deed whilst the donor is abroad.

Transactions which do not require a deed

1.9   Under s 2(1) of the 1989 Act a contract for the sale or other disposition of an interest in land can only be made in writing, and under s 2(2) the contract must be signed by or on behalf of each party to the contract. However, there is no requirement of writing for the appointment of an agent to sign such a contract.

Section 1 of the Stock Transfer Act 1963 requires a transfer of shares to be executed by the transferor. Article 23 of Table A in the Companies (Tables A to F) Regulations 1985 (SI 1985 No 805) states that a transfer must be in any usual form or other form which the directors may approve, and must be executed by or on behalf of the transferor. There does not appear to be any requirement that a person executing a transfer on behalf of another should be authorised to do so by a power of attorney, but it is clearly desirable that this should be done in order to take advantage of the protection offered by ss 5 and 6 Powers of Attorney Act 1971. These sections are discussed in CHAPTER 12.

If the only assets of the prospective donor are money in a bank or building society account, the donee can be authorised in writing to operate the account, and most banks and building societies have a standard form of authority for this purpose. However, any such authority will be revoked by the subsequent mental incapacity of the donor, although most banks and building societies do not make enquiry about the mental state of the donor.

It is also possible for a person to be appointed as an agent or appointee in order to collect social security benefits for another person.

Thus an oral or written authority will often suffice, apart from the situations where the agent will be required to sign a deed in the absence of the principal. However, if it is intended that the authority should continue after the donor has become mentally incapable of managing his own affairs, an enduring power of attorney should be granted.

The donee

1.10   The question of capacity is discussed in CHAPTER 9. In most cases, it will be appropriate to appoint from amongst the following:

(a)   relatives;

(b)   friends;

(c)   solicitors;

(d)   accountants.

The donor and the donee are often related. A person going abroad for a prolonged period may wish to appoint his spouse, or a parent, or a child as his attorney; an elderly donee may wish to appoint a child or a friend as attorney. In these situations the attorney will frequently not expect to be paid for the work he or she does in pursuance of the power. However, if there is no suitable relative or friend, a solicitor or accountant or other professional person may be appointed, and they will expect to be paid for the work they do as attorneys.

As will be seen later, there are few restrictions on who can be appointed attorney, but he or she should be a person whom the donor considers he or she can trust. There is always the risk that relatives or friends may use the power to benefit themselves rather than the donor of the power, and although they can be made to account for any misuse of money or property belonging to the donor, such right is of little use if the donee has no assets. If professional persons such as solicitors or accountants are appointed, it is unlikely that the power will be exercised otherwise than for the benefit of the donor. However, as mentioned earlier, professional persons will expect to be paid for their services, and if the assets of the donor are not very valuable, the expense may not be justified.

The Public Trustee will not accept an appointment as attorney (PD Lewis, *The Law Society's Gazette* (28 October 1987) at page 3083).

(The Public Trustee is an office created by the Public Trustee Act 1906. Fees are chargeable for the services provided by the Trustee, and he is not bound to act if appointed. However, he cannot refuse to act on the ground that the estate is too small.)

Summary

1.11

- A power of attorney may be desirable if a person is about to go abroad, or is elderly.

- A power of attorney can be general or limited in time or to a particular transaction.

- If a donor of a power of attorney is elderly, he or she should grant an enduring power, which will not be revoked by the supervening mental incapacity of the donor.

- More than one person can be appointed attorney; the authority conferred can be joint or joint and several.

- A power of attorney may not be necessary as an agent can be authorised orally or in writing to carry out many transactions.

Chapter 2

Powers of attorney and the elderly

When should an enduring power be granted?

2.1   This chapter is concerned with the practical aspects of when an enduring power should be granted. The question of when a donor has capacity to grant an enduring power is considered in more detail at 9.17–9.29 below. Whilst a donor should have a general understanding of what is being created, it is not necessary for the donor to have a complete understanding of what is happening. However, the donor must be able to understand the following:

(a)   that the donee will be able to assume complete authority over the donor's affairs, if the power is unrestricted;

(b)   that the donee will be able to do anything with the donor's property which the donor could have done, if the power is unrestricted;

(c)   that the authority will continue if the donor should be or become mentally incapable;

(d)   that if he should be or become mentally incapable, the power will be irrevocable without confirmation by the court.

(*Re K; Re F [1988] 1 All ER 358* at page 363.)

It could be argued that as soon as a person attains 70, or even 60, he should grant an enduring power to any children. On the other hand, many people retain their faculties well into their seventies or eighties or nineties or even beyond, and they may not be very happy about entrusting the management of their affairs to their children. It is clearly an issue which may need tactful handling, although many people will readily grant such a power. They may also be reluctant to entrust all their affairs to a particular child, in which situation it may be best to grant a joint or a joint and several power – a joint power could be granted to two or more children – the effect of this would be that all the attorneys would have to agree to any action. For a discussion of joint and several powers, please see 1.5 above.

Of course, the donor can continue to manage his own affairs despite the grant of an enduring power, and so it may be a good idea for a person to grant an enduring power on the understanding that it will not be exercised whilst the donor retains his faculties. Indeed, it is possible for the power to expressly state that it will not come into effect until some event occurs, for example the making of an application for registration of the power (see below).

It is also clear that an enduring power can still be granted even though the donor is showing signs of mental incapacity. Thus it is possible to wait, but at the first signs of mental incapacity, an enduring power can be granted. Most people do not suddenly become incapable; it is usually a gradual process. On some days they will be fully capable; on other days they will not.

When should an enduring power be registered?

2.2   The duty to register an enduring power arises if the attorney has reason to believe that the donor is mentally incapable (s 4(1) EPAA 1985). As it could be difficult to decide precisely when a donor becomes mentally incapable, the section also provides that the duty arises when the attorney has reason to believe that the donor is becoming mentally incapable.

Many donors become incapable gradually, and it is best to register as soon as it becomes clear that the donor will not recover his mental capacity. It should be noted that once the duty to register has arisen, application for registration must be made as soon as practicable (s 4(3)).

Whilst the attorney is under a duty to register the power if the attorney has reason to believe that the donor is mentally incapable, this does not always happen, and the attorney may continue to act under the unregistered power.

Procedure for registration

2.3   In outline, the procedure is that the attorney must give notice to the donor and to various relatives of the donor. The attorney then has to apply to the Public Guardianship Office for registration of the enduring power.

The relatives to whom notice must be given are specified in Sch 1 Pt I para 2(1) EPAA 1985. The first four specified are:

(a)   the donor's spouse;

(b)   the donor's children;

(c)   the donor's parents;

(d)   the donor's brothers and sisters, whether of the whole or half blood.

Notice does not have to be given to more than three persons, but if one person in a class is entitled to notice, then notice must usually be given to all the other members of the class (para 2(4)). This means that if the donor has a spouse and four children, it will be necessary to give notice to the spouse and all the children. It is more than likely that the attorney will be one of the children, but he does not have to give notice to himself (para 3(1)).

Notice must also be given to the donor, but the court has power to dispense with this requirement in certain circumstances (para 4(2)).

Form EP1 must be used to give notice to the relatives and the donor.

Rule 7 Court of Protection (Enduring Powers of Attorney) Rules 2001 (SI 2001 No 825) requires that an application to register an enduring power of attorney shall be made in Form EP2. It must be lodged with the Court of Protection office not later than ten days after notice has been given to the donor and every relative entitled to receive notice and every co-attorney. A new form of EP2 has been introduced, and must be used for all applications for registration made after 1 March 2003.

Effect of registration of the power

2.4   The effect of registration of a power is to freeze the power. This means that the donor cannot revoke the power unless the revocation is confirmed by the court. In addition, the donor cannot extend or restrict the scope of the authority conferred by the instrument, and the attorney cannot disclaim the power without giving notice to the court.

Duties of the attorney

2.5   The duties of an attorney are varied, but they can be summed up very simply. An attorney must show the utmost good faith to the donor. This means that the attorney must keep accurate accounts, and if he wants to purchase property belonging to the donor, he must disclose all relevant facts. If the attorney is a solicitor, further duties may be imposed. Similar rules apply to other dealings with the property of the donor. However, once the power has been registered, the court has power to consent to transactions of this nature.

Summary

2.6

- People in their sixties or older should consider granting an enduring power of attorney.

- An enduring power should be registered as soon as the donor becomes mentally incapable.

- Once a power has been registered, the donor cannot revoke, extend or restrict the operation of the power.

Chapter 3

Going abroad and powers of attorney

3.1   Although postal services are often quick, it may be considered desirable for anyone living or working abroad to grant a power of attorney. It may also be desirable that a person going abroad for an extended holiday should grant a power of attorney. The purpose of this chapter is to highlight some of the issues involved in connection with such powers.

Ordinary power or enduring power?

3.2   It seems that a donor living abroad can grant an enduring power, and thus it is clear that a donor resident in England and Wales, but contemplating a trip abroad, can grant an enduring power.

If the donor is young or middle aged, an ordinary power is often appropriate, although there is no reason why an enduring power should not be granted; particularly if the donor is concerned about possible mental incapacity due to accident or illness. On the other hand, if the donor is elderly, there is considerable merit in the grant of an enduring power in case the donor becomes mentally incapable; this would otherwise revoke the power.

Delegation by trustees

3.3   It may be that a person who is *a trustee and is* going abroad may wish to appoint a person to act on his behalf whilst he is abroad. This is possible under s 25 Trustee Act 1925 as amended by s 9 Powers of Attorney Act 1971, and as substituted by s 5 of the Trustee Delegation Act 1999 in relation to powers of attorney created after the commencement of the Trustee Delegation Act (1 March 2000). The delegation must be by power of attorney, and it must be for a period not exceeding twelve months. The delegation can be very wide; the attorney can be authorised to execute or exercise all or any of the trusts, powers and discretions vested in him as trustee either alone or jointly with any other person or persons. Note that the person appointed attorney may include a trust corporation and, if the power was granted after the commencement of the 1999 Act, and there are two trustees, the other trustee. However, s 7 preserves the 'two trustees' rule (see 9.6 below).

Various formalities must be satisfied; these are discussed in more detail in CHAPTER 9.

Section 1 of the Trustee Delegation Act 1999 provides that the donee of a power of attorney can exercise trustee functions in respect of:

(a)   land;

(b)   capital proceeds of a conveyance of land; or

(c)   income from land,

provided the donor has a beneficial interest in the land, proceeds or income. This Act came into force on 1 March 2000.

Section 1 was intended to help co-owners to delegate their powers as trustees, but it is still necessary for at least two persons to sign any transfer or conveyance.

The Trustee Act 2000, which came into force on 1 February 2001, contains wide-ranging provisions permitting trustees collectively to delegate most of their functions. Broadly, the functions which cannot be delegated are decisions about the distribution of assets.

Section 9 Trusts of Land and Appointment of Trustees Act 1996 provides that trustees can delegate any of their functions to any beneficiary or beneficiaries of full age and beneficially entitled to an interest in possession in land. The delegation can be for a set period, or indefinitely, but it cannot be done by an enduring power.

Grants of powers of attorney by co-owners

3.4   This situation is of course very common as the majority of houses are vested in the names of both spouses or cohabitants, who are trustees of the legal estate. If one co-owner is going abroad, he may want to delegate his powers, and often he will want to grant a power of attorney to his spouse or cohabitant. What provisions can be used depends on whether the power was granted before or after the Trustee Delegation Act came into force.

Situation prior to 1999 Act

3.5   Section 10 Powers of Attorney Act 1971 forbids the use of the general power of appointment for this purpose. Under s 25 Trustee Act 1925 a trustee could not delegate to another trustee. However, although the position was not without doubt, it seems that it was possible to use an enduring power to appoint another co-owner as attorney. Section 3(3) EPAA 1985 authorised an attorney under a general or limited enduring power to execute or exercise without obtaining any consent, all or any of the trusts, powers or discretions vested in the donor as trustee. Also without the concurrence of any other person, the attorney could give a valid receipt for capital or other money paid.

Situation now the 1999 Act is in force

3.6   Section 3(3) EPAA 1985 does not apply to enduring powers created after the commencement of the Trustee Delegation Act 1999 (s 4(1) Trustee Delegation Act). There are also transitional provisions dealing with powers created before the commencement of the Act.

Trustees who are co-owners could make use of s 25, which permits delegation by one trustee to the other where there are only two trustees. However, s 7 preserves the two trustee rule, so that delegation to a sole co-trustee will not be effective in situations where a minimum of two trustees is required, for example receipts for capital money arising on a sale of land. In addition, delegation can only be for twelve months under s 25.

It may also be possible to make use of s 1, but again s 7 preserves the two trustee rule so that if spouses or cohabitees grant enduring powers of attorney to each other, and one becomes mentally incapable, the one retaining mental capacity will not be able to sign any transfer in their own capacity and as attorney for the mentally incapable spouse or cohabitee. However, the capable spouse or cohabitee can appoint another trustee.

For a fuller discussion, see 9.21–9.23.

Extent of the power

3.7   The power of attorney may authorise the attorney to do anything with regard to the property of the donor which the donor could have done. Alternatively, it may merely authorise the attorney to deal with a particular transaction, for example the sale of a house.

In the case of an elderly person, it is desirable that the power should be unlimited, and that an enduring power should be granted. If the donor becomes mentally incapable, the power will not then be revoked. If the power is limited, then should the donor become mentally incapable, the attorney can only deal with property that is the subject of the power. If there is any other property, then an application will have to be made to the Court of Protection for the appointment of a receiver to deal with the assets not included in the power.

On the other hand, if the donor is relatively young, it may be that only a limited power will be granted.

The power of delegation contained in s 9 Trusts of Land and Appointment of Trustees Act 1996 is wide, but very little use is made of the section.

Summary

3.8

- If a young donor is going abroad, an ordinary power may be appropriate; otherwise use an enduring power.

- Trustees can delegate under various provisions: s 25 Trustee Act 1925, s 1 Trustee Delegation Act 1999 and s 9 Trusts of Land and Appointment of Trustees Act 1996.

Chapter 4

Powers of attorney and professional persons

4.1   Solicitors and accountants are frequently appointed as attorneys. This chapter is aimed at highlighting some of the aspects which professional persons appointed as attorneys should consider.

Duties

4.2   Generally an attorney is not under a duty to act. However, if a client appoints a solicitor or an accountant as an attorney, it is probable that there is a contractual obligation on the attorney to act.

There is a general duty imposed on attorneys to keep accounts, and of course solicitors must comply with the Solicitors' Accounts Rules.

There is also a duty to take care and be skilful, and in the case of attorneys who are professionally qualified the duty is higher than that imposed on an unqualified person.

Is an attorney who is a solicitor entitled to benefit himself at the expense of the donor? The rule applying to all attorneys is that they must disclose all relevant facts. Is a higher duty imposed on attorneys who are solicitors and accountants? *The Guide to the Professional Conduct of Solicitors 1999* at page 318 states that a solicitor who is appointed an attorney must not use that power so as to confer a benefit on himself which 'he would not be prepared to allow to an independent person'. However, a solicitor should advise the donor of a power to take independent advice before exercising the power so as to enter into a transaction which benefits the attorney. If the attorney is acting under an enduring power which has been registered, application should be made to the court for directions as the court has power to authorise the donor to enter into transactions benefiting the donor of the power (s 8(2) EPAA 1985; see CHAPTER 7).

Rights

4.3   An attorney is entitled to be indemnified for all acts within the limits of the power; on the other hand, if he exceeds the limits of the power, he is not entitled to any indemnity.

As regards remuneration, there may be an express term as to remuneration. If not, an attorney will have to rely on an implied contractual term if he is to be paid. It is submitted that if a client appoints a solicitor or an accountant as attorney, there will be an implied right to reasonable remuneration.

If an enduring power has been registered, s 8(2)(b)(iii) EPAA 1985 empowers the court to give directions with regard to the remuneration or expenses of the attorney, whether or not in default of or in accordance with any provision made by the instrument, including directions for the repayment of excessive remuneration, or the payment of additional remuneration.

Financial services

4.4   The Financial Services Authority became the regulator for solicitors' firms on 1 December 2001. A small minority of firms are be regulated directly by the new authority, but the great majority are not. These firms may carry on certain regulated activities without being regulated by the Financial Services Authority. However, they must comply with the Solicitors' Financial Services (Scope) Rules 2001. Rule 3 prescribes certain prohibited activities, and rule 4 states that a firm which carries on any regulated activities must ensure that:

(a)   the activities arise out of, or are complementary to, the provision of a particular professional service to a client;

(b)   the manner of the provision by the firm of any service in the course of carrying on the activities is incidental to the provision by the firm of professional services;

(c)   the firm accounts to the client for any pecuniary reward or other advantage which the firm receives from a third party;

(d)   the activities are not of a description, nor do they relate to an investment of a description, specified in any order made by the Treasury under s 327(6) of the Financial Services and Markets Act 2001;

(e)   the firm does not carry on, or hold itself out as carrying on, a regulated activity other than one which is allowed by these rules or one in relation to which the firm is an exempt person;

(f)   there is not in force any order or direction of the Financial Services Authority under s 328 or s 329 of the Act which prevents the firm from carrying on the activities; and

(g)   the activities are not otherwise prohibited by these rules.

Rule 5 prescribes other restrictions. A firm must not manage assets belonging to another person in circumstances which involve the exercise of discretion except where the firm or a partner, officer or employee of the firm is a trustee, personal representative, donee of a power of attorney or receiver appointed by the Court of Protection, and either:

(a)   all routine or day-to-day decisions, so far as relating to that activity, are taken by an authorised person with permission to carry on that activity or an exempt person; or

(b)   any decision to enter into a transaction, which involves buying or subscribing for an investment, is undertaken with the advice of an authorised
person with permission to give advice in relation to such an activity or an
exempt person.

Rule 8 defines 'authorised person' by reference to the definition in s 31 of the
Act. It also defines 'exempt person'.

Readers are also referred to article 38 of the Financial Services and Markets Act
2000 (Regulated Activities) Order 2001, and the Law Society guidance on
Financial Services and Solicitors dated August 2001.

Miscellaneous points for solicitors

4.5   (Readers are referred to *The Guide to the Professional Conduct of
Solicitors 1999*, pages 451 and 452 and the Law Society Policy Directorate
'Enduring Powers of Attorney – guidelines for solicitors' (last revised Septem-
ber 1999 and reproduced in APPENDIX 5)).

It is understood that claims for negligence arising out of the use of powers of
attorney are rare; when they do arise, they are often caused by the use of
out-of-date forms. Solicitors acting for the donor of a power, or dealing with the
attorney, should ensure that the correct forms have been used. It is to be hoped
that this cause of action will to a large extent disappear as it is believed that most
solicitors use computerised precedents which are updated regularly.

The guidelines for solicitors, prepared by the Mental Health and Disability
Committee of the Law Society, is essential reading for any solicitor engaged in
this type of work; some of the points raised are considered below.

A donor contemplating granting an enduring power of attorney may approach a
solicitor directly, but frequently the approach is through a relative concerned
about the declining mental and physical disabilities of a parent or another close
relative. It should always be remembered that the client is the donor of the
power, and that if the instructions come through a third party the solicitor should
check to ensure that the proposed donor really does want to grant an enduring
power of attorney, and is not reluctant to do so. At the very least, the solicitor
should obtain written confirmation that the donor does want to grant an
enduring power of attorney to the proposed attorney. In the opinion of the writer,
the solicitor should always see the prospective donor when the instructions
come through a third party in the absence of the third party to ensure that the
donor is acting of his or her own free will.

The solicitor should also ensure that the proposed donor has capacity to grant an
enduring power of attorney. The test for capacity to grant an enduring power of
attorney was considered in *Re K, Re F [1988] 1 All ER 358* (see para 16.2).
Whilst many enduring powers of attorney are granted when the donor clearly
has capacity to grant such a power, others are granted when the donor is

beginning to show a decline in mental abilities. Unless a donor suffers some major event like an accident, donors do not become mentally incapable overnight. There is usually a gradual decline into mental incapacity, and a donor in the early stages of the decline clearly has the capacity to grant an enduring power of attorney. If the solicitor has any doubt about the capacity of the donor to grant an enduring power of attorney, the solicitor should obtain a report from the donor's doctor as to the mental capacity of the donor.

Assuming that the donor has the mental capacity to grant an enduring power of attorney, the solicitor should ensure that the donor understands the nature of an enduring power of attorney, and that it will continue to operate even if the donor becomes mentally incapable. The prescribed form requires the explanatory notes to be read to the donor if the donor has not been able to read them himself.

There are various matters on which the solicitor needs instructions in order to draft the enduring power of attorney.

(a)   Firstly, there is the issue of whether one person is to be appointed attorney, or whether two or more persons are to be appointed. If the donor only has one child, then the issue may be clear cut – that child should be appointed as attorney. However, if the donor has two or more children, then the issue is not so clear cut. The donor may not trust all the children, but it may cause friction if one child is appointed as attorney but not another. The great advantage in having more than one attorney is that they can keep a check on each other.

If the donor wishes to appoint more than one attorney, then the next question is whether the authority should be joint or joint and several. This is discussed in more detail in paragraphs 1.5–1.6. Joint authority means that all the attorneys must sign all documents, whereas if the authority is joint and several, then one attorney can bind the others. The major disadvantage of joint authority is that if one attorney dies, the authority of the other attorney terminates.

(b)   Secondly, the solicitor also needs to obtain instructions as to whether the power is to apply to the whole of the donor's property, or part of it. It is not desirable for the power to be restricted – if the donor becomes mentally incapable, the attorney will be able to deal with the property the subject of the enduring power, but not the property excluded from it. It would be necessary for a receiver to be appointed by the Court of Protection to deal with the property not included in the enduring power of attorney. At the very least, this will be inconvenient, and may add to the costs.

(c)   If there is nothing to the contrary on the enduring power of attorney, then the power will be effective as soon as it is granted. Some donors are content to grant enduring powers of attorney, but do not want them to come into effect until they are becoming mentally incapable or have become mentally incapable. Such a condition can be imposed.

(d)   Instructions should also be sought on the question of gifts. An attorney has very limited powers to make gifts, and the donor may wish to extend these powers or possibly restrict them.

(e)   Instructions should also be sought on the question of attorney's power to delegate. It is clear that the attorney can delegate administrative acts, but not managerial decisions. If the attorney is likely to be managing valuable investments, consideration should be given to extending the powers of delegation by the attorney if the attorney does not want to take such decisions himself.

(f)   If the solicitor is to be the attorney, it may be desirable to include a charging clause in the power of attorney. It is the opinion of the author that a solicitor appointed as attorney has an implied contractual right to charge, but there can be no doubt if there is an express charging clause in the power. It may also be desirable to notify the donor about the method of charging and the charging rate.

(g)   Where the solicitor is to be the sole attorney, it may be desirable to specify that the charges to be made by the solicitor are to be approved by a third party.

(h)   When taking instructions, it may be desirable to obtain the consent of the donor to obtaining medical evidence from the donor's doctor as to the mental capacity of the donor, in case of a challenge to the capacity of the donor to grant the power, or a doubt as to whether the power should be registered.

(i)   If the power does have to be registered, then it is necessary to give notice to various relatives. It can be helpful to obtain a list of the names and addresses of the relatives who may have to be served when taking instructions for the power. This is particularly appropriate in the case of an elderly donor who has no children, but several brothers and sisters and nephews and nieces.

(j)   A solicitor may draft a will for a donor, and the attorney, who may be a relative and possible beneficiary under the will, may ask to see it. If the donor is of full capacity, the permission of the donor for disclosure must be obtained. If the donor is not of full capacity, and the attorney is acting under an enduring power which has been registered because of the incapacity of the donor, the advice of the Public Guardianship Office should be sought unless the power permits disclosure. Solicitors should consider whether the power should contain an express power to disclose the contents of a will.

If a solicitor is instructed by an attorney, the question may arise as to who is the client. Usually it will be the donor of the power, but once the power is operative, instructions can be accepted from the attorney.

An attorney under an enduring power cannot consent to medical treatment on behalf of the donor.

A solicitor may be instructed by an attorney acting under an unregistered power. The attorney should be reminded about capacity, and that if the donor lacks capacity, the power should be registered. The attorney should also be advised that an enduring power will be invalid if it has not been registered when it should have been. It may be that the attorney should be asked to give a written assurance, and if there is anything giving rise to suspicion, the instructions of the donor of the power should be sought.

Once the power is in operation, a solicitor appointed as attorney owes the same duties to the donor as a lay person appointed as attorney. However, the solicitor attorney is under a higher duty of care than a lay attorney, and must display the level of competence displayed by a reasonable solicitor in dealing with this type of work.

In many cases the donor of the power will have few assets. Frequently all that the attorney will be administering is the proceeds of sale from the house the donor lived in, and a few thousand, if that, in bank and building society accounts Also, the amount of the estate will be decreasing very rapidly if the donor is in a care home. In this situation, there may be no alternative but to keep the money invested in a bank of building society accounts where it can be accessed easily. However, if the solicitor is administering large sums of money, or an investment portfolio, the solicitor should take advice at regular intervals from a financial adviser who is qualified to advise about investments. The duties of attorney with regard to investment are considered at paragraphs 10.17-10.19.

For the purposes of the Solicitors' Accounts Rules, the donor is the solicitor's client where the solicitor is acting under a power of attorney. This means that any money received by the solicitor must be paid into client account. On the other hand, if the solicitor operates the donor's bank account, that is not client's money.

Further guidance can be obtained from the Professional Ethics Division of the Law Society telephone number 020 7242 1222.

Summary

4.6

- There may be a contractual duty to act.

- Usually there will be an implied right to remuneration.

- Solicitors must comply with the Financial Services and Markets Act 2001 and regulations made thereunder.

- Solicitors must ensure that the proposed donor of an enduring power of attorney has the capacity to grant such a power.

- Solicitors must ensure that they use the correct form.

- Before drafting the enduring power of attorney, solicitors should take instructions on various aspects – whether the authority is to be joint or joint and several, whether it is to extend to all the donor's assets or only part.

- It may be desirable to include a charging clause in the power of attorney.

- It may be desirable to obtain the consent of the donor to obtaining medical evidence if there is any doubt about the capacity of the donor to grant an enduring power of attorney.

- Solicitors who are appointed as attorneys may owe a higher duty of care to the donor and the donor's relatives than lay attorneys.

- Solicitor attorneys who are managing large funds may need to take advice from persons qualified to advice about investments.

Chapter 5

Formalities

5.1   The Powers of Attorney Act 1971 as amended contains provisions dealing with the formalities required for an ordinary power of attorney. The formalities required for an enduring power of attorney are set out in the Enduring Powers of Attorney Act 1985 ('EPAA 1985'), and the regulations made under that Act. It is therefore necessary to deal separately with the requirements for enduring powers and other powers.

I. Ordinary powers of attorney

Individuals

A deed is required

5.2   Section 1(1) Powers of Attorney Act 1971, as amended by s 1(8) and Sch 1 Law of Property (Miscellaneous Provisions) Act 1989 ('the 1989 Act') which came into force on 31 July 1990, requires that a power of attorney must be executed as a deed.

Section 1(2) of the 1989 Act provides that an instrument shall not be a deed unless:

(a)   it makes it clear on the face of it that it is intended to be a deed by the person making it or, as the case may be, by the parties to it (whether by describing itself as a deed or expressing itself to be executed or signed as a deed or otherwise); and

(b)   it is validly executed as a deed by that person or, as the case may be, by one or more of those parties.

Execution of the power by the donor

5.3   Section 1(3)(a)(i) of the 1989 Act provides that an instrument is validly executed as a deed by an individual if it is signed by him in the presence of a witness who attests the signature.

Execution of the power by a person on behalf of the donor

5.4   It is permissible for the power to be signed by another person, but this must be done at the direction of the donor of the power, and also in his presence.

In this situation, two other persons must witness the signing, and they must attest the instrument (s 1(3)(a)(ii) of the 1989 Act).

Under s 1(4) of the 1989 Act 'sign' includes making a mark.

Delivery

5.5   Whether the donor of a power signs it himself or not, the power must be delivered by him or a person authorised on his behalf to do so (s 1(3)(b) of the 1989 Act). 'Delivered' in this context means that the donor of the power has shown an intention by acts or words to be bound by the deed. Usually the donor of a power will intend that it should come into effect immediately. If the power is delivered by another person, the authority for this need not be given by deed (s 1(1)(c) of the 1989 Act).

Companies

5.6   A company granting a power of attorney must use a deed to do so. The law governing the execution of documents by companies was amended by s 130 Companies Act 1989 which inserted a new section into the Companies Act 1985. This new section, s 36A, which came into force on 31 July 1990, provides in subs (2) that a document is executed by a company by the affixing of its common seal. However, subs (3) provides that a company need not have a common seal, and subs (4) provides that a document signed by a director and the secretary of the company, or by two directors, and expressed to be executed by the company has the same effect as if executed under the common seal of the company.

Section 36A(5) provides that if a document makes it clear on the face of it that it is intended to take effect as a deed, it will take effect as a deed on delivery, and there is a rebuttable presumption that it will be delivered on execution.

Section 36A(6) provides that in favour of a purchaser a document will be deemed to have been duly executed by a company if it purports to be signed by a director and the secretary of the company, or by two directors of the company, and, where it makes it clear on its face that it is intended by the person making it to be a deed, to have been delivered upon its being executed. 'Purchaser' is defined as the purchaser in good faith for valuable consideration and includes a lessee, mortgagee or other person who for valuable consideration acquires an interest in property. Thus a purchaser who knows or suspects that the execution is defective will not be protected.

If the company affixes its seal to a power, s 74(1) Law of Property Act 1925 provides that in favour of a purchaser a deed will be deemed to have been duly executed by a company if its seal is affixed to it in the presence of and attested by its clerk, secretary or other permanent officer or his deputy, and a member of the board of directors, council or other governing body of the company. Furthermore, where a seal purporting to be the seal of the company has been affixed to a deed, attested by persons holding those offices, the deed will be deemed to have been executed in accordance with the requirements of the section, and to take effect accordingly. 'Purchaser' is defined in s 205(1)(xxi) Law of Property Act 1925 as a purchaser in good faith for valuable consideration and includes a lessee, mortgagee or other person who for valuable consideration acquires an interest in property. Again a purchaser who suspects or knows that the execution is defective will not be protected.

II. Enduring powers of attorney

5.7   Unlike other powers of attorney, an enduring power of attorney can survive the mental incapacity of the donor, and as a consequence the EPAA 1985 lays down special rules for enduring powers.

Section 2(1) EPAA 1985 requires an enduring power to:

(a)   be in a prescribed form;

(b)   be executed in a prescribed manner by the donor and the attorney; and

(c)   incorporate at the time of execution by the donor the prescribed explanatory information.

Form

5.8   The Lord Chancellor is empowered to make regulations as to the form and execution of instruments creating powers of attorney, and s 2(2)(a) EPAA 1985 requires these regulations to contain whatever provisions are appropriate to ensure that every enduring power of attorney contains information in a prescribed form explaining the general effect of creating or accepting an enduring power. Section 2(2)(b) EPAA 1985 provides that the power must also contain statements:

(i)   by the donor, that he intends the power to continue in spite of any intervening mental incapacity;

(ii)   by the donor that he read or had read to him the information explaining the effect of creating the power;

(iii)   by the attorney that he understands the duty of registration imposed by the Act.

The Enduring Powers of Attorney (Prescribed Form) Regulations 1990 (SI 1990 No 1376) ('EPR'), replacing regulations made in 1987 which had in turn replaced regulations made in 1986, came into force on 31 July 1990. Regulation 2(1) EPR provides that an enduring power must be in the form set out in the Schedule to the regulations. Printed forms can be obtained from law stationers, but they can be typed, or produced by word processor. Readers are referred to the form, and their attention is drawn to the following points, some of which are raised in articles by PD Lewis in *The Law Society's Gazette* (26 November 1986 at page 3566 and 29 April 1987 at page 1219):

(a)   The enduring power must contain all the explanatory information headed 'About using this form' in Part A of the Schedule and all the relevant marginal notes to Parts B and C. It may also include such additions (including paragraph numbers) or restrictions as the donor may decide (reg 2(1) EPR). The explanatory information may be bound up with the power, or stapled to it. (See Practice Direction [1989] 2 All ER 64.)

   Section 2(5) EPAA 1985 provides that an instrument in the prescribed form purporting to have been executed in the prescribed manner will be taken, in the absence of evidence to the contrary, to be a document which incorporated at the time of execution by the donor the prescribed explanatory information. There is thus a rebuttable presumption that the explanatory notes were attached to the power in the prescribed form.

(b)   Although it is clearly desirable that the full name of the donor should be inserted, it is not fatal to an application for registration of the power that the donor's middle name or names have been omitted. Affidavit evidence will be required.

(c)   The omission of the donor's date of birth, or the insertion of an incorrect date, will not normally be fatal to an application for registration. An affidavit exhibiting the donor's birth certificate will be required.

(d)   Regulation 2(2)(a)(i) EPR provides that where the donor appoints only one attorney, everything between the square brackets on the first page of Part B will be excluded either by omission or deletion.

(e)   It is possible to appoint joint attorneys, and the senior partner in a firm of solicitors; these possibilities are discussed later in this chapter.

(f)   Where there are alternatives, one and only one of any pair of alternatives must be excluded, again either by omission or deletion (reg 2(2)(a)(ii) EPR).

(g)   If two or more attorneys are appointed, either the words 'jointly' or 'jointly and severally' must be deleted. If one is not deleted, the power will not be an enduring power because of s 11(1) EPAA 1985.

(h)   'all my property and affairs' and 'the following property and affairs': omission of both these alternatives is a material difference, and will render the power invalid as an enduring power.

(i)   The omission of the statement by the donor that he or she intends the power to continue even if he or she becomes mentally incapable is a material difference.

(j)   Regulation 2(2)(b) EPR provides that there may also be excluded either by omission or deletion:

(i)   the words on the second page of Part B 'subject to the following restrictions and conditions', if those words do not apply;

(ii)   the attestation details for a second witness in Parts B and C if a second witness is not required; and

(iii)   any marginal notes which correspond with any words excluded under the provisions of this paragraph and the two notes numbered 1 and 2 which appear immediately under the heading to Part C.

It is permissible for an enduring power to be produced on a word processor leaving out the alternatives.

Execution

Execution by donor and attorney

5.9   Regulation 3(1) EPR provides that an enduring power of attorney must be executed:

(a)   by both the donor and the attorney; and

(b)   in the presence of a witness, who

(c)   must sign the form and give his full name and address.

The signature can be typed, in block capitals or made by means of a rubber stamp (see PD Lewis in *The Law Society's Gazette* (26 November 1986 at page 3567)).

The donor and the attorney need not sign at the same time, and they need not sign in the presence of the same witness. But reg 3(2) EPR provides that a donor and an attorney must not witness the signature of each other nor one attorney the signature of another.

Execution by a person on behalf of donor

5.10   Regulation 3(3) EPR permits the power to be executed at the direction of the donor, provided the following requirements are satisfied:

(a)   it must be signed in the presence of two witnesses who must each sign the form and give their full names and addresses; and

(b)   a statement that the enduring power of attorney has been executed at the direction of the donor must be inserted in Part B;

(c)   it must not be signed by an attorney or any of the witnesses to the signature of either the donor or an attorney.

Under reg 2(3)(b) EPR the form of execution by the donor may be adapted where the enduring power of attorney is executed at the direction of the donor.

Execution by a person on behalf of donee

5.11   Regulation 3(4) EPR permits an enduring power to be executed at the direction of an attorney, provided the following conditions are satisfied:

(a)   it must be signed in the presence of two witnesses who must each sign the form and give their full names and addresses; and

(b)   a statement that the enduring power of attorney has been executed at the direction of the attorney must be inserted in Part C;

(c)   it must not be signed by either the donor, an attorney or any of the witnesses to the signature of either the donor or an attorney.

If a trust corporation is appointed attorney, the form of execution by an attorney may be adapted to provide for execution by a trust corporation.

The following points should also be noted:

(a)   The donor must execute the power before the attorney.

(b)   The attorney should execute the power as soon as possible after it has been executed by the donor in case the donor becomes incapable of managing his or her affairs in the meantime, or the power is registered. Execution by the attorney would then be too late. (See page 18 of *Enduring Powers of Attorney* published by the Public Guardianship Office.)

(c)   If the attorney's signature was not witnessed when he or she first signed it, there is doubt about whether the attorney can re-execute the document; in any event if the donor has become mentally incapable, any re-execution will be ineffective. If the only defect is that the witness failed to give his or her name, address or occupation, this can be cured by means of an affidavit.

(d)   Although a spouse can witness the signature of the donor, it is suggested that this is not desirable as it may not be possible to compel a spouse to give evidence in proceedings relating to the power, and may lead to family friction.

(e)   It is not a material difference to omit the address or occupation of a witness.

(f)   It is not a material difference to omit the dates when the donor or attorney signed.

These points are discussed by PD Lewis in *The Law Society's Gazette* (26 November 1986, page 3566 and 29 April 1987, page 1219); see also Chapter 7.

Alterations and deletions do not have to be initialled: PD Lewis, *The Law Society's Gazette* (28 October 1987 at page 3084) and *Enduring Powers of Attorney* published by the Public Guardianship Office.

Blind or physically handicapped donors

5.12   Blind or physically handicapped donors or attorneys can make a mark, and reg 2(3) EPR provides that the form of execution by the donor or by an attorney may be adapted in such a case. Additional words should be added to the attestation clause to show that the notes in Part A of the prescribed form have been read to the donor and that he or she understood them. The attorney may become under a duty to apply for registration of the power (this is discussed in CHAPTER 7). If this is the case, the court will require an explanation of how notification was given to the donor of the intention to apply for registration (see PD Lewis, *The Law Society's Gazette* (26 November 1986, page 3567 and 29 April 1987, page 1220) and *Enduring Powers of Attorney* published by the Public Guardianship Office).

Joint powers and joint and several powers

5.13   It is possible to appoint more than one attorney under an enduring power, but they must be appointed to act jointly or jointly and severally (s 11(1) EPAA 1985). A joint power means that all the attorneys must join in making decisions, whereas if the power is joint and several, one attorney can bind the others.

In the case of joint and several powers, at least one of the attorneys must execute the power, but if the power is registered (see CHAPTER 7), or the donor becomes mentally incapable, only those attorneys who have executed the power can act (reg 4 EPR). One attorney cannot witness the signature of another (reg 3(2) EPR). If it is a joint power, then all the attorneys should execute the power as the power will be invalid as an enduring power if it has to be registered.

As mentioned earlier in this chapter, if two or more persons are appointed attorneys, either the words 'jointly' or 'jointly and severally' in the prescribed form must be deleted.

Section 11(4), which applies to joint and several powers (s 11(3)), provides that a failure, as respects any one attorney, to comply with the requirements for the creation of enduring powers, will prevent the instrument creating such a power in his case without, however, affecting its efficacy for that purpose as respects the other or others or its efficacy in his case for the purpose of creating a power of attorney which is not an enduring power. Thus if one joint and several attorney fails to comply with the rules for enduring powers, the power can still be an enduring power as regards those attorneys who do comply, and it can operate as an ordinary power for those who do not comply.

Alternative appointments

5.14   It is doubtful if it is permissible to appoint one person with the proviso that if he or she does not act, another person is to be the attorney. Section 11(1)

EPAA 1985 provides that an instrument which appoints more than one person to be an attorney cannot create an enduring power unless the attorneys are appointed to act jointly or jointly and severally. Page 11 of *Enduring Powers of Attorney* issued by the Public Guardianship Office suggests that a donor could grant an enduring power to a spouse, and another to a child or children. That second power will only come into operation if the power in favour of the spouse becomes ineffective; and s 2(9) EPAA 1985 provides that a power of attorney which gives the attorney, or if it is a joint attorney, any attorney, the right to appoint a substitute or successor cannot be an enduring power (Sch 3 Pt I para 2 EPAA 1985).

Alterations to the prescribed form

5.15   It is essential to be very careful about alterations to the prescribed form of an enduring power.

Section 2(6) EPAA 1985 provides that an enduring power will be treated as sufficient in point of form and expression if it differs only in an immaterial respect from the prescribed form.

Regulation 2(1) EPR provides that all the explanatory information headed 'About using this form' in Part A of the Schedule and all relevant marginal notes to Parts B and C must be included.

Regulation 2(2) EPR permits certain omissions and deletions, including the omission or deletion of one and only one of any pair of alternatives, and reg 2(2)(b)(iii) provides that any marginal notes corresponding with any words excluded under the provisions of that paragraph may also be excluded.

What else constitutes an immaterial difference? In articles in *The Law Society's Gazette* (26 November 1986 at page 3566 and 29 April 1987 at page 1219) PD Lewis, Assistant Public Trustee, offered some guidance, although the rules were then contained in regulations made in 1986. According to the articles, the following differences are considered to be immaterial:

- omission of the donor's date of birth;
- omission of the address of a witness;
- omission of the dates when the donor or attorney signed;
- omission of donor's middle names;
- donor's signature witnessed by wife of attorney;
- explanatory information bound up with the power or stapled to it.

It may be necessary to file affidavit evidence about these omissions.

According to PD Lewis, the following differences are material:

- not deleting 'jointly' or 'jointly and severally';

- omission of both alternatives 'all my property and affairs' and 'the following property and affairs';

- omission of the statement by the donor that he intends the power to continue in spite of his supervening incapacity.

Regulation 2(4) states that, subject to paras (1), (2) and (3) of reg 2 and to reg 4, an enduring power of attorney which seeks to exclude any provision contained in the Regulations is not a valid enduring power of attorney.

It is clearly best to amend, omit or delete parts of the prescribed form as little as possible, and in any event any alteration should be within the limits of the EPAA 1985 and the EPR.

Miscellaneous points

5.16

- It is in order to appoint 'the senior partner in the firm of . . .'.

- An attorney living out of the jurisdiction can be appointed, but if this caused problems when the power was registered, the court might appoint a receiver.

- It is probable that a donor living abroad can grant an enduring power.

See PD Lewis, *The Law Society's Gazette* (26 November 1986 at page 3568).

Non-compliance with formalities

5.17   Section 9(6) EPAA 1985 deals with the situation where an instrument has failed to create a valid enduring power, and the power has been revoked by the donor's mental incapacity. In his article in *The Law Society's Gazette* (26 November 1986) PD Lewis states at page 3567:

'A power which has not been executed by the attorney cannot be an enduring power but may be used as an ordinary power unless and until the donor loses capacity.'

It would thus seem to be clear that an invalid enduring power can take effect as an ordinary power. However, RT Oerton in an article in the *Solicitors' Journal* (11 December 1987 at pages 1645 and 1646) has argued that an invalid enduring power can only take effect as an ordinary power in very limited circumstances. The author argues that most enduring powers will be general powers, and that the donee will have the powers conferred by s 3 EPAA 1985. If the enduring power is invalid, the donee cannot have these powers. Furthermore, the author argues that the invalid enduring power cannot take effect as an ordinary power within s 10 Powers of Attorney Act 1971, because it is not in the form prescribed by that section. Additionally, it is argued that it cannot take effect as a general power outside s 10 Powers of Attorney Act 1971 because it was necessary to use a much longer form of power of attorney to confer general powers on an attorney before the passing of the 1971 Act. There is also the question of intention: the donor intends to create an enduring power, not an ordinary power. In the light of all these factors, the author concludes that an invalid limited enduring power may be valid as an ordinary power, but not an invalid general enduring power.

There is clearly considerable force in these arguments. However, it is submitted that although, in the past, powers of attorney were long, it may be that they were unnecessarily lengthy, and that a shorter version would have sufficed. Thus an enduring power which is invalid under s 3 EPAA 1985 can perhaps operate outside the Powers of Attorney Act 1971.

As there is clearly some doubt about whether an invalid enduring power can take effect as an ordinary power, the wisest course of action is to assume that it cannot.

Summary

Ordinary powers of attorney

Individuals

5.18

- The power must be signed by the donor of the power in the presence of a witness who attests the signature.

- Alternatively, it can be signed by another individual at his direction and in his presence and the presence of two witnesses who each attest the signature.

- The power must be delivered as a deed by him or a person authorised to do so on his behalf; this authority can be given orally, although it is desirable that it should be in writing.

Companies

5.19

- A company can affix its seal to a power. The secretary and a director must be present and attest the power.

- A company need not affix its seal to a power. A director and the secretary of a company or two directors can execute a power of attorney on behalf of the company, provided it is expressed to be executed by the company.

- The power should make it clear on its face that it is intended to be a deed; the easiest way of achieving this is to indicate that it is executed or signed as a deed at the place where the seal of the company is affixed, or the document is signed.

Enduring powers of attorney

5.20

- The prescribed form must be used.

- Comply strictly with the explanatory notes; it is unwise to alter the prescribed form.

- The power must be executed by both the donor and the donee in the presence of a witness who must sign the form and give his or her full name and address.

- The form can be executed at the direction of the donor and the donee provided it is signed in the presence of two witnesses who must each sign the form and give their full names and addresses. The donor and donee cannot sign for each other, and the witness cannot sign for either. The form must be amended to indicate that it has been signed at the direction of the donor or attorney.

Chapter 6

Duration and termination of powers of attorney

6.1   This chapter deals with the circumstances in which a power of attorney will come to an end. It is necessary to distinguish between ordinary powers of attorney and enduring powers of attorney as although the rules are similar, there are substantial differences in some areas.

I. Ordinary powers of attorney

Expiry

6.2   Many powers of attorney are granted without any limitation as to time. However, a power of attorney may be granted for a specified period, and once that period has expired, the donee's authority ceases. If the period is specified by reference to months, s 61 Law of Property Act 1925 provides that 'month' means calendar month unless the context otherwise requires.

A power may also expire even though no time limit is specified. In *Danby v Coutts & Co (1885) 29 Ch D 500* the donor appointed two attorneys. Although there was nothing in the main part of the power about its duration, a recital stated that the donor was about to return to South Australia, and that the donor wanted to appoint attorneys to act for him whilst he was abroad. It was held that the recital controlled the main part of the document, and that the power was exercisable only whilst the donor was abroad.

It should be noted that s 25(1) Trustee Act 1925 as amended by the Powers of Attorney Act 1971, as substituted by the Trustee Delegation Act 1999, permits trustees to delegate the powers and discretions vested in them for a period not exceeding twelve months. In addition, s 9(1) Trusts of Land and Appointment of Trustees Act 1996 (which came into force on 1 January 1997) and s 1 of the Trustee Delegation Act 1999 (which came into force 1 March 2000) permit delegation by trustees of land to beneficiaries for any period or indefinitely. The capacity of trustees to delegate is discussed in CHAPTER 9.

Performance of purpose of power

6.3   Although powers of attorney frequently give the donee a wide author-ity to act for the donor of the power, often to do anything the donor could have lawfully done, the power may be limited, and may give authority to the donee to complete only one transaction. For example, the authority may be limited to the acts necessary to complete the sale of a particular property. As soon as the sale of that property has been completed, the authority of the donee of the power ceases.

An example of the termination of an ordinary agency by the performance of the purpose is provided by the case of *Gillow & Co v Aberdare (1892) 9 TLR 12*. The plaintiffs were agents, and they were instructed to let a house furnished or unfurnished, or to sell the ground lease. The plaintiffs successfully negotiated the letting of the property to a Mr Tooth, and were paid commission. Mr Tooth then bought the ground lease, but he conducted the negotiations through another agent. It was held that the plaintiffs were not entitled to any commission on the sale of the ground lease as their agency had terminated on completion of the letting to Mr Tooth.

A power of attorney authorising the donee to let or sell a property may thus terminate if the donee lets the property. If it is intended that the donee should have the power both to let and sell the property after letting, it should be clearly stated in the power that this is the case.

Express revocation

6.4   In *Bromley v Holland (1802) 7 Ves 3* Lord Eldon LC stated at page 28 that a power of attorney was a 'revocable instrument', and so the donor can revoke it at any time, unless it is an irrevocable power. The revocation can be oral, in writing or by deed (*The Margaret Mitchell (1888) Swab 382, 166 ER 1174*), but it is ineffective until it is received by the donee (*Re Oriental Bank Corporation, ex parte Guillemin (1884) 28 Ch D 634*). Notice to one joint attorney is effective (*Bristow and Porter v Taylor (1817) 2 Stark 50, 171 ER 568*).

If it is an irrevocable power, the donor will not be able to revoke it without the consent of the donee. Irrevocable powers are usually granted in commercial transactions, and are discussed later in this chapter and in CHAPTER 12.

Often the donee of the power is a solicitor; if the solicitor is given a power which is expressed to last for a specified period, can the donor terminate it before the end of that specified period? The answer is yes, but if there was a contract not to terminate it for the specified period, the solicitor might be able to sue for damages for breach of contract. Whether the solicitor can sue depends on the terms of the contract with the client; usually it is only the express terms which can be considered as the courts are very reluctant to imply any terms into the contract. In *Hamlyn & Co v Wood & Co [1891] 2 QB 488 CA* Lord Esher MR said:

'I have for a long time understood that the Court has no right to imply in a written contract any such stipulation, unless on considering the terms of the contract in a reasonable and business manner, an implication necessarily arises that the parties must have intended that the suggested stipulation should exist. It is not enough to say that it would be a reasonable thing to make such an implication.'

If no period for the duration of the contract is specified, the courts will be reluctant to imply any term that the contract is to last for a set term, and it will usually be terminable by, at the very most, reasonable notice. In *Martin-Baker Aircraft Co Ltd v Canadian Flight Equipment Ltd [1955] 2 QB 556* the subject matter of the dispute were contracts with no or limited provision for termination. It was held that they were terminable on notice. McNair J, at pages 577 and 578, said:

'Accordingly, it appears to me that I have to approach the determination of this question not with any presumption in favour of permanence; and, indeed, if there is any presumption at all, it would seem to me to be a presumption the other way . . .

The common law, in applying the law merchant to commercial transactions, has always proceeded on the basis of reasonableness in filling up the gaps in a contract which the parties have made on the basis of what is reasonable, so far as that does not conflict with the express terms of the contract, rather than on the basis of rigidity . . .

It is, of course, true that this kind of consideration can in many cases be excluded by express provision; but where the contract leaves the matter open, I think that the common law approach would be to provide a solution which is reasonable.'

Thus, whether or not the duration of the power of attorney is specified, in the absence of any specified agreement between the solicitor and the client as to how long the solicitor is to operate the power, the client will usually be able to terminate both the power and the contract, at the most on giving reasonable notice, without breaking the contract, unless it is one of the few situations when the court would be prepared to imply a term as to the duration of the contract.

It is essential that notice that the power has been revoked should be given to anyone who might rely on it. This is because s 5(2) Powers of Attorney Act 1971 provides that where a power of attorney has been revoked and a person, without knowledge of the revocation, deals with the donee of the power, the transaction between them shall, in favour of that person, be as valid as if the power had then been in existence. It is not good enough to destroy the original, or to note on it that it has been revoked, as a copy can be used to prove the contents of an instrument under s 3(1) Powers of Attorney Act 1971. (See *Powers of Attorney* (Longman, 9th edition, 2000, at page 60) by Aldridge.)

A donee acting under a power of attorney warrants that he had authority to act under the power, and if that authority does not exist, the donee may be liable in damages to anyone who suffers loss as a result of relying on that warranty (*Starkey v Bank of England [1903] AC 114 HL*). However, s 5(1) Powers of

Attorney Act 1971 may protect an attorney in this situation. It provides that a donee of a power of attorney who acts in pursuance of a power at a time when it has been revoked will not, by reason of the revocation, incur any liability (either to the donor or to any other person) if at that time he did not know that the power had been revoked. These matters are discussed further in CHAPTERS 11 AND 12.

The donee is also liable to the donor if he continues to act knowing that a power has been revoked (*Pearson v Graham (1837) 6 A & E 899, 112 ER 344*).

Implied revocation

6.5   Any act by the donor inconsistent with the continuance of the power will have the effect of revoking the power, unless it is irrevocable. For example, if a donee is given a power of attorney authorising the sale of a particular property at a specified price, and the donor signs a contract for the sale of the property at a higher price, this is an act inconsistent with the power of attorney, and has the effect of revoking it (*Smith v Jennings Lane 97, 145 ER 329*). However a donee is entitled to assume that the power of attorney is still in existence until the donor does some act inconsistent with the power (*Re Oriental Bank Corporation ex parte Guillemin (1884) 28 Ch D 634*).

As with express revocation, a person dealing with the donee without knowledge of the revocation is protected by s 5(2).

A donee acting under a power which has been revoked will be liable in damages for breach of warranty of authority. However, s 5(1) Powers of Attorney Act 1971 protects the donee of a power who acts in pursuance of a power at a time when it has been revoked if at that time the donee did not know that the power had been revoked.

A donee who continues to act under a power knowing that it has been impliedly revoked will be liable to the donor.

Bankruptcy

The donor

6.6   The bankruptcy of the donor of a power of attorney revokes the power (*Markwick v Hardingham (1880) 15 Ch D 339 CA*) unless it is irrevocable, but the donee will still have authority to complete the formalities of a transaction entered into before the bankruptcy (see *Halsbury's Laws of England*, 4th edition, volume 1(2) paragraph 199).

At what stage in the bankruptcy is the power revoked? Section 284 Insolvency Act 1986 provides that any disposition made during the period beginning with the day of the presentation of the petition and ending with the vesting of the bankrupt's property in a trustee is void except to the extent that it is or was made with the consent of the court, or is or was subsequently ratified by the court. Under s 284(2) a similar rule is applied to a payment whether in cash or otherwise.

As any disposition of property by a bankrupt is void in the period beginning with the presentation of the bankruptcy petition, any power of attorney granted by the bankrupt will terminate on the presentation of the petition.

Section 284(4) provides that 'the preceding provisions of this section do not give a remedy against any person –

(a)   in respect of any property or payment which he received before the commencement of the bankruptcy in good faith, for value and without notice that the petition had been presented, or

(b)   in respect of any interest in property which derives from an interest in respect of which there is, by virtue of this subsection, no remedy.'

Presumably this section would operate to protect a purchaser from the attorney of a donor who has become bankrupt, provided the purchaser acted in good faith and without notice that the petition had been presented.

It is also possible for debtors to enter into voluntary arrangements with their creditors (ss 252–263 Insolvency Act 1986). It is submitted that if a donor of a power enters into a voluntary arrangement with his creditors, it will not cause the power of attorney to terminate unless the continuance of the power is inconsistent with the voluntary arrangement. For example, if the debtor grants a general power of attorney, a voluntary arrangement providing that the debtor's business should not be sold would revoke the power as far as the business was concerned.

There is further protection in the Powers of Attorney Act 1971 for persons dealing with the attorney without knowledge of the revocation. As mentioned earlier, under s 5(2) a person dealing with the donee of the power without knowledge of the revocation will be protected, but the donee may be liable for breach of warranty of authority, although he or she may be able to claim the protection of s 5(1).

The donee

6.7   The bankruptcy of the donee of a power of attorney does not automatically terminate the power. It will do so if the continuation of the power is inconsistent with the bankruptcy (*Bailey v Thurston & Co Ltd [1903] 1 KB 137 CA*). The situation is the same if the donee enters into a voluntary arrangement with his creditors.

Insolvency of a company

The donor company

6.8   If a company grants a power of attorney, and is then wound up, the power will be revoked. However, the donee of the power will still be able to complete the formalities required for a transaction entered into before the revocation.

Section 86 Insolvency Act 1986 provides that 'a voluntary winding up is deemed to commence at the time of the passing of the resolution for voluntary winding up', and s 87(1) provides that as from the commencement of the winding up the company shall cease to carry on business, except so far as may be required for its beneficial winding up. It could be argued that a power of attorney granted by a company could be exercised for the limited purpose specified in s 87(1), but, having regard to s 127, it is unwise to rely on this argument.

Section 127 deals with a winding up by the court, and provides that in such proceedings 'any disposition of the company's property . . . made after the commencement of the winding up is, unless the court otherwise orders, void'. Section 129(1) provides that 'if, before the presentation of a petition for the winding up of a company by the court, a resolution has been passed by the company for voluntary winding up, the winding up of the company is deemed to have commenced at the time of the passing of the resolution; and unless the court, on proof of fraud or mistake, directs otherwise, all proceedings taken in the voluntary winding up are deemed to have been validly taken'. Subsection (2) provides that 'in any other case, the winding up . . . is deemed to commence at the time of the presentation of the petition for winding up'.

Thus it seems that a power of attorney cannot continue once a resolution for winding up the company has been passed, or a petition for the winding up of the company has been presented to the court.

Action short of winding up may be taken against a company in financial difficulties. Under the Insolvency Act 1986 the following courses of action are available in respect of such a company:

(i)   a voluntary arrangement (ss 1–7 Insolvency Act 1986);

(ii)   an administration order (ss 8–27 Insolvency Act 1986);

(iii)   the appointment of a receiver or administrative receiver (ss 28–72 Insolvency Act 1986).

Will these events revoke the power? It is submitted that the power will be revoked only if the continuance of the power is consistent with the consequences of any of the actions which can be taken by or against the company.

Entering into a voluntary arrangement, or making an administration order, or appointing an administrative receiver is not necessarily inconsistent with the continuance of a power of attorney granted by the company. However, in so far as it is inconsistent, any power will be revoked; for example, if a voluntary arrangement provided that certain property should not be sold, any power of attorney authorising the attorney to sell it would be revoked to that extent.

If the power of attorney is coupled with an interest, it may not be revocable. In *Sowman v David Samuel Trust Ltd [1978] 1 WLR 22* the company granted a debenture in favour of two banks, which authorised them to appoint a receiver, and appointed the banks and any person appointed by them attorney for the company. The banks appointed a receiver, and the company then went into liquidation. Subsequently, the receiver agreed to sell a property to the second plaintiff. The conveyance was executed by the banks and the receiver. It was held that the conveyance was effective. Goulding J said at page 30:

> 'Winding-up deprives the receiver, under such a debenture as that now in suit, of power to bind the company personally by acting as its agent. It does not in the least affect his powers to hold and dispose of the company's property comprised in the debenture, including his power to use the company's name for that purpose, for such powers are given by the disposition of the company's property which it made (in equity) by the debenture itself. That disposition is binding on the company and those claiming through it, as well in liquidation as before liquidation, except of course where the debenture . . . is otherwise invalidated by some provision of law applicable to the winding-up.'

It was also held that the power of attorney had not been revoked. Goulding J said at page 30:

> 'It is clear law that in their hands it was not revoked by the winding-up of the company. The conclusion rests on a double foundation: first, the common law rule tritely expressed in the phrase that "an authority coupled with an interest is irrevocable" and, secondly, the statutory enactment in section 4 of the Powers of Attorney Act 1971. By the conveyance of March 4, 1977, the debenture holders used their power of attorney to execute the assurance required to complete a sale validly effected by the receiver for the purposes of the security.'

Section 4 Powers of Attorney Act 1971 is discussed in CHAPTER 12.

Section 5(2) Powers of Attorney Act 1971 protects any person dealing with the donee of the power without knowledge of its revocation, and s 5(1) may protect the donee.

The donee company

6.9   If a company is a donee, it is submitted that the power is revoked as soon as a resolution for the winding up of the company has been passed, or a petition for the winding up of the company has been presented to the court, because s 87(1) Insolvency Act 1986 provides that the company must cease to carry on business as from the commencement of the winding up, except in so far as may be required for its beneficial winding up; this provision is discussed above. If a donee company enters into a voluntary arrangement, or an administration order is made, or a receiver is appointed, the power of attorney will terminate if its continuance is inconsistent with the effects of any of these events.

Death

6.10   The death of the donor or donee of a power terminates a power of attorney, unless it is irrevocable. However, the personal representatives of a deceased donor may be able to ratify a contract entered into after the death of the donor (*Foster v Bates (1843) 12 M & W 226*).

If two or more attorneys are appointed jointly, the death of one will cause the power to terminate (*Adams v Buckland (1705) 2 Vern 514, 23 ER 929*); but if the authority of the attorneys is joint and several, the death of one attorney will not affect the authority of the other(s) who can continue to exercise the power.

Section 5(2) Powers of Attorney Act 1971 applies to protect any person dealing with the donee without knowledge of the death of the donor, and s 5(1) may protect the donee.

Disclaimer of power

6.11   The donee of a power of attorney can disclaim the power. The donee must give notice to the donor, and the notice will be ineffective until received by the donor (*Re Oriental Bank Corporation, ex parte Guillemin (1884) 28 Ch D 634*). The notice can be written or oral (*The Margaret Mitchell (1888) Swab 382, 166 ER 1174*). However, it may be that there is a contractual relationship between the donor and the donee, for example if the donee is a solicitor or accountant, and an unjustified disclaimer might amount to a breach of contract.

Mental incapacity

6.12   The mental incapacity of the donor or donee of a power terminates the power (*Drew v Nunn [1879] 4 QBD 661 CA*), unless it is an irrevocable power or a third party dealing with attorney is not aware that the donor has ceased to have mental capacity.

Section 5(2) Powers of Attorney Act 1971 protects the person dealing with the donee without knowledge of the revocation, and s 5(1) may protect the donee.

Illegality

6.13   If the performance of a power of attorney necessarily involves the commission of an illegal act, the power will terminate. For example, if the donor of the power becomes an enemy, the authority conferred by the power may cease. According to Cozens-Hardy MR in *Tingley v Muller [1917] 2 Ch 144 CA* at page 156:

> '. . . "enemy" means any person resident or carrying on business in an enemy country, but does not include persons of enemy nationality who are neither resident nor carrying on business in the enemy country.'

Thus even if the donor and donee become 'enemies', the power of attorney will not terminate if neither resides nor carries on business in the enemy country.

Even if the donor has become an enemy as defined above, a transaction authorised by a power granted before the donor became an enemy may be valid. In *Tingley*, the defendant, a German by birth, executed an irrevocable power of attorney in May 1915 whilst he was resident in this country. He then travelled to Germany under a government permit. It was held that the power was still valid even though the defendant had become an alien enemy. The attorney could complete the transaction without consulting the defendant, and the proceeds of sale would be retained in this country.

In *Hangkam Kwintong Woo v Lin Lan Fong [1951] 2 All ER 567* the donor of a power of attorney lived in Hong Kong, which at the time was occupied by the Japanese. He left Hong Kong, and went to live in Free China. The donee of the power sold a house belonging to the attorney. It was held that the power was still in existence as it did not involve any trading with the enemy.

Irrevocable powers

6.14   It may be that the donor and donee will want to create a power of attorney which cannot be revoked. Irrevocable powers are usually found in commercial arrangements. For example, mortgages sometimes give the mortgagee a power of attorney authorising the mortgagee to deal with the mortgaged property. A vendor may also give a purchaser a power of attorney to transfer property if the purchaser does not intend to take a conveyance of the property, for example if it is a sale to a home relocation company. A mortgagee or purchaser in these situations would not want the power to be revoked. The Powers of Attorney Act 1971 recognises this, and contains special provisions dealing with powers which are part of a commercial arrangement and which are intended to continue in spite of events which would normally cause a revocation.

Section 4(1) Powers of Attorney Act 1971 provides:

'Where a power of attorney is expressed to be irrevocable and is given to secure –

(a)   a proprietary interest of the donee of the power; or

(b)   the performance of an obligation owed to the donee, then, so long as the donee has that interest or the obligation remains undischarged, the power shall not be revoked –

   (i)   by the donor without the consent of the donee; or

   (ii)   by the death, incapacity or bankruptcy of the donor or, if the donor is a body corporate, by its winding up or dissolution.'

This subsection is clearly wide enough to cover all the situations mentioned above. Furthermore, the section protects subsequent owners of the proprietary interest. Section 4(2) states:

'A power of attorney given to secure a proprietary interest may be given to the person entitled to the interest and persons deriving title under him to that interest, and those persons shall be duly constituted donees of the power for all purposes of the power but without prejudice to any right to appoint substitutes given by the power.'

Section 4 and the protection available to third parties are discussed in CHAPTER 12.

II. Enduring powers of attorney

Expiry

6.15   The principles appear to be the same as for ordinary powers of attorney. Section 3(1) Enduring Powers of Attorney Act 1985 ('EPAA 1985') states that an enduring power may be conferred subject to conditions and restrictions, and reg 2(1) Enduring Powers of Attorney (Prescribed Form) Regulations 1990 (SI 1990 No 1376) provides that the prescribed form may include such additions or restrictions as the donor may decide.

Under s 4(1) EPAA 1985, if the attorney has reason to believe that the donor is becoming mentally incapable, the attorney must as soon as practicable make an application to the court for the registration of the instrument creating the power (for details of the provisions relating to registration of enduring powers, see CHAPTER 7).

Section 8(4)(d) EPAA 1985 provides that the court will cancel the registration of an enduring power on being satisfied that the power has expired. The procedure for cancelling the registration of enduring powers is discussed in CHAPTER 7.

Performance of purpose of power

6.16   The principles are the same as for ordinary powers. Section 3(1) EPAA 1985 and the prescribed form permit a general or limited authority to be conferred; if authority is given for one transaction, the authority conferred by that power will terminate when that transaction has been completed.

Section 8(4)(d) EPAA 1985 applies to this situation (see above), and so the court must cancel the registration of a power on being satisfied that the purpose has been fulfilled.

Express revocation

6.17   The principle that a power of attorney can be revoked at any time still applies, but the EPAA 1985 has in effect modified this rule.

Under s 7(1) EPAA 1985, once a power is registered, any revocation of the power by the donor must be confirmed by the court. However, until registration, no confirmation by the court is necessary. Under s 8(3) the court must confirm the revocation of the power if satisfied that the donor has done whatever is necessary in law to effect an express revocation of the power, and was mentally capable of revoking the power of attorney when he did so (regardless of his mental capability when the court considers the application). Under s 8(4)(a) the court must cancel the registration on confirming the revocation. The procedure for cancelling a power is discussed in CHAPTER 7. Whilst in theory a registered power can be revoked by the donor, in practice it is unlikely to happen as the power can only be registered if the donor has become mentally incapable, and in the great majority of cases will remain mentally incapable. A registered power can only be revoked if the donor has capacity.

Subsections 5(1) and 5(2) Powers of Attorney Act 1971 may operate to protect the donee and person dealing with the donee. These provisions are discussed in more detail above and in CHAPTER 12.

Implied revocation

6.18   Until registration, any act by the donor inconsistent with the power will revoke it, but after registration ss 7(1) and 8(3) and (4) EPAA 1985 apply, so that once the power is registered, any revocation must be confirmed by the court. Section 8(3) and (4) apply only to express revocation; thus after registration of an enduring power, the donor must expressly revoke the power.

Section 5(1) and (2) Powers of Attorney Act 1971 may protect the donee and persons dealing with the attorney.

In *Re E, X v Y [2000] 3 All ER 1004*, E executed an enduring power of attorney in 1992. This appointed two of her daughters, Y and Z, as attorneys. It was subject to a restriction preventing the attorneys from selling, charging or leasing any land in which E had an interest. In 1997 E executed another power of attorney in the form prescribed for an enduring power. This power was not subject to any restriction. It appointed Y and Z, and in addition E's third daughter, X, as joint attorneys. The words 'save that any two of my attorneys may sign' were added by E's solicitor. These words rendered the power invalid as an enduring power, and at most it took effect as an ordinary power. E became mentally incapable and that incapacity revoked the 1997 power. Y and Z applied for the 1992 power to be registered. X opposed the application on the grounds that the 1997 power had revoked the 1992 power, and also that Y and Z were unsuitable as attorneys. The Master registered the power.

On appeal, the decision of the Master was upheld. Arden J held that the earlier power could be revoked only by unambiguous inconsistent conduct, and that the onus was on the appellant to show that the 1992 power had been revoked. He held that the 1997 power was not inconsistent with the 1992 power.

Arden J also held that the objection to Y and Z as attorneys failed. X did not get on with her sisters, and the main area of dispute was over a tax planning scheme. On reviewing the evidence, he decided that Y and Z were not unsuitable attorneys.

Bankruptcy

6.19   As with ordinary powers, the bankruptcy of the donor of the power will revoke the power. Although in the case of ordinary powers the bankruptcy of the donee may not necessarily revoke the power, under s 2(10) EPAA 1985 the bankruptcy of the donee of an enduring power will revoke the power whatever the circumstances of the bankruptcy.

If it is a joint power, the bankruptcy of any attorney will revoke the power (Sch 3 Pt I para 2 EPAA 1985), but if it is a joint and several power, only the bankruptcy of the last remaining attorney under the power will cause a revocation. The bankruptcy of any other attorney under a joint and several power causes that person to cease to be an attorney whatever the circumstances of the bankruptcy (Sch 3 Pt II para 7 EPAA 1985).

Section 8(4)(d) EPAA 1985 provides that the court will cancel the registration of the power if it is satisfied that the power has been revoked by the bankruptcy of the donor or donee of the power. Section 11(7), which applies to joint and several attorneys, provides that the court or the Public Trustee will not cancel the registration of an instrument under s 8(4) for any of the causes vitiating registration specified in that subsection if an enduring power subsists as respects some attorney who is not affected thereby, but will give effect to it by the prescribed qualification of the registration. Thus if one joint and several attorney becomes bankrupt, the court will not cancel the registration, but will amend it. Readers are referred to CHAPTER 7 for a discussion of the procedural requirements for cancellation.

A voluntary arrangement may have the effect of revoking a power; the EPAA 1985 does not deal specifically with what happens in this situation, but presumably it takes effect as an implied revocation of the power.

Section 5(1) and (2) Powers of Attorney Act 1971, may operate to protect the donee and persons dealing with the attorney.

Insolvency of a trust corporation appointed as attorney

6.20   As with ordinary powers, the winding up or dissolution of a trust corporation will revoke any power of attorney given to the company, and s 8(4)(d) EPAA 1985 provides that the court will cancel the registration of an enduring power of attorney on being satisfied that a body corporate appointed as an attorney has been wound up or dissolved. For a discussion of the procedural requirements, see CHAPTER 7.

If the trust corporation was appointed jointly with another attorney, Sch 3 Pt I para 6 EPAA 1985 applies. This provides that in s 8(4) references to 'the attorney' will be read as including references to any attorney under the power. Thus the mere fact that there is another attorney will not prevent the revocation of a joint power if one attorney is a trust corporation which is insolvent.

If the trust corporation was appointed jointly and severally with another attorney, s 11(7) applies with the effect that the registration will not be cancelled on the winding up or dissolution of the trust corporation if there is one attorney who is still able to act. However, the authority of the trust corporation will terminate.

Entering into a voluntary arrangement, the making of an administration order or the appointment of a receiver may all have the effect of revoking the power; the EPAA 1985 does not deal specifically with these situations, but it is submitted that any such revocation will take effect as a disclaimer of the power.

Section 5(1) and (2) Powers of Attorney Act 1971 may operate to protect the donee and persons dealing with him.

Death

6.21   As with ordinary powers, the death of the donor or donee of the power revokes the power, and the court must cancel the registration of an enduring power if it is satisfied that the power has been revoked by the death of the donor or donee of the power (s 8(4)(d) EPAA 1985). The procedure for cancelling the registration is discussed in CHAPTER 7.

If joint attorneys have been appointed, Sch 3 Pt I para 6 EPAA 1985 provides that in s 8(4) references to 'the attorney' will be read as including references to any attorney under the power. The effect of this is that if one joint attorney has died, the court must confirm the revocation of the power, even though another joint attorney is still alive.

However, if more than one attorney has been appointed, and their authority is joint and several, s 11(7) applies, with the effect that on the death of one attorney the registration remains in force as regards the surviving attorneys.

Section 5(1) and (2) Powers of Attorney Act 1971 may operate to protect the donee and persons dealing with the attorney.

Disclaimer of power

6.22   The donee of an enduring power can disclaim at any time, but under s 2(12) EPAA 1985 the disclaimer is invalid unless and until the attorney gives notice to the donor.

If the attorney is under a duty to apply for registration under s 4 EPAA 1985, s 4(6) provides that no disclaimer will be valid unless and until the attorney gives notice to the court. In the case of joint and several attorneys, this restriction applies only to those attorneys who have reason to believe that the donor is or is becoming mentally incapable (Sch 3 Pt II para 8).

Once the enduring power has been registered, under s 7(1)(b) EPAA 1985 no disclaimer of the power is valid until the attorney gives notice to the court. Under s 8(4) the court must cancel the registration of an instrument on receiving notice of disclaimer. If one joint attorney disclaims, the registration must be cancelled completely (Sch 3 Pt I para 6), but if a joint and several attorney disclaims, the registration remains valid as regards the other attorney(s).

Rule 10(7) Court of Protection (Enduring Powers of Attorney) Rules 2001 (SI 2001 No 825) provides that the disclaimer takes effect on the day on which the notice of disclaimer is received at the court.

Mental incapacity

6.23   The mental incapacity of the donor of the power will not cause its revocation (s 1(1)(a) EPAA 1985) but, apart from some limited exceptions, the donee cannot do anything under the power until the instrument creating the power is registered (s 1(1)(b) EPAA 1985). The exceptions are contained in s 1(2), and permit the attorney to maintain the donor or prevent loss to his estate, or to maintain himself or other persons in so far as s 3(4) permits him to do so. Section 3(4) provides:

'Subject to any conditions or restrictions contained in the instrument, an attorney under an enduring power, whether general or limited, may (without obtaining any consent) act under the power so as to benefit himself or other persons than the donor to the following extent but no further, that is to say –

(a)   he may so act in relation to himself or in relation to any other person if the donor might be expected to provide for his or that person's needs respectively; and

(b)   he may do whatever the donor might be expected to do to meet those needs.'

Under s 1(1)(b) the court may direct or authorise the attorney to take action under the power.

Section 2(11) EPAA 1985 provides that an enduring power will be revoked on the exercise by the court of any of its powers under Pt VII Mental Health Act 1983 if, but only if, the court so directs.

The mental incapacity of the donee will revoke the power, and the court must cancel the registration of an enduring power if it is satisfied that it has been so revoked (s 8(4)(d) EPAA 1985).

The procedure for registering and cancelling the registration of an enduring power of attorney is discussed in CHAPTER 7.

Illegality

6.24   The EPAA 1985 does not specifically deal with this point; presumably the principles which apply to ordinary powers apply also to enduring powers. If the court is satisfied that, having regard to all the circumstances and in particular the attorney's relationship to or connection with the donor, the attorney is unsuitable to be the donor's attorney, it can cancel the registration (s 8(4)(g) EPAA 1985).

Summary

6.25

- The authority of the donee of a power will cease if the power is granted for a limited period and that period has elapsed, or the power is granted for a specific purpose and that purpose is fulfilled.

- A power may be revoked expressly or impliedly.

- The bankruptcy of the donor of a power will revoke the power; an ordinary power will not necessarily be revoked by the bankruptcy of the donee, but an enduring power will be.

- The winding up or dissolution of a company will usually revoke a power.

- Death of the donor or donee revokes a power.

- A power can be disclaimed, but if it is an enduring power, notice must be given to the donor, or to the court if (a) the attorney is under a duty to register the enduring power, or (b) it has already been registered.

- The mental incapacity of the donor or donee will revoke an ordinary power, but the mental incapacity of the donor will not revoke an enduring power.

- Illegality will revoke a power.

- Powers may be irrevocable.

- If it is an enduring power, notice of revocation may have to be given to the court.

Chapter 7

Registration of enduring powers of attorney

7.1 The Enduring Powers of Attorney Act 1985 ('EPAA 1985') contains safeguards to protect donors, donees and third parties. The donee of an enduring power is under an obligation to register the power and to give notice to the closest relatives. The provisions of the EPAA 1985 and the regulations dealing with registration and notification must now be examined in detail.

Previous regulations provided for a division of functions between the Public Trust Office and the Court of Protection. New regulations, which came into force on 1 April 2001, provide that all applications are to be made to the Court of Protection.

Subsections 11(2) and (3) provide that the EPAA 1985 applies to joint and to joint and several powers (with some modifications which are set out in the text).

Duty to register

7.2 An enduring power of attorney operates as an ordinary power until the attorney has reason to believe that the donor is or is becoming mentally incapable (s 4(1) EPAA 1985). The attorney is then under a duty to apply to the court as soon as practicable for the registration of the instrument creating the power (s 4(2)).

The duty arises only if the attorney has reason to believe that the donor *is or is becoming* mentally incapable. The donor does not have to be mentally incapable before the duty to register arises; the duty arises as soon as the attorney has reason to believe that the donor is becoming incapable. It is of course often difficult to decide when a donor has become mentally incapable, but the requirement to register as soon as the attorney has reason to believe that the donor is becoming incapable avoids this difficulty.

Section 13(1) provides that 'mentally incapable' or 'mental incapacity' means, in relation to any person, that he is incapable by reason of mental disorder of managing and administering his property and affairs.

What happens if the attorney considers that the donor is or is becoming incapable, but has doubts about the validity of the power, for example if the attorney thinks the donor may not have had capacity to grant the power originally? In an article in *The Law Society's Gazette* (29 April 1987) PD Lewis, Assistant Public Trustee, stated at page 1220 that the Master had decided that in this type of case the attorney would not be in breach of the duty imposed by s 4(2) if he made an application under s 4(5) to have the validity of the power determined (see 7.9 below).

Notice to relatives

Who is entitled to notice?

7.3   Section 4(3) and Sch 1 EPAA 1985 require the attorney to give notice to various relatives and the donor before making an application for the registration of an enduring power. Under Sch 1 Pt I para 2(1) EPAA 1985 the following persons are entitled to notice:

(a)   the donor's spouse;

(b)   the donor's children;

(c)   the donor's parents;

(d)   the donor's brothers and sisters, whether of the whole or half blood;

(e)   the widow or widower of a child of the donor;

(f)   the donor's grandchildren;

(g)   the children of the donor's brothers and sisters of the whole blood;

(h)   the children of the donor's brothers and sisters of the half blood;

(i)   the donor's uncles and aunts of the whole blood;

(j)   the children of the donor's uncles and aunts of the whole blood.

Paragraph 8(1) states that an illegitimate child is to be treated as if he were the legitimate child of his father or mother.

In *The Law Society's Gazette* (26 November 1986) PD Lewis at page 3568 raises the question of whether the widow or widower of a child should be notified if he or she has remarried. His view is that notification should be given.

This requirement to give notice could be impossible to satisfy. It is limited by paras 2(2), 2(3) and 2(4). Paragraph 2(2) provides that a person is not entitled to receive notice if:

(a)   his name or address is not known to the attorney and cannot be reasonably ascertained by him; or

(b)   the attorney has reason to believe that he has not attained eighteen years or is mentally incapable (for the definition of mental incapacity see s 13(1) EPAA 1985 and 7.2 above).

Paragraphs 2(3) and 2(4) provide that:

(a)   notice does not have to be given to more than three persons; but

(b)   if more than one person falls within classes (a) to (j) and at least one of those persons is entitled to notice, all the persons falling within that class are entitled to notice, unless they are not entitled to notice because the conditions of para 2(2) are satisfied;

(c)   in determining who is entitled to notice, persons within class (a) are to be preferred to those within class (b), persons falling within class (b) are to be preferred to those falling within class (c); and so on.

Thus if the donor has four children and appoints one child as his attorney, notice must be given to all the children. It is more than likely that the attorney will be within one of the classes of person entitled to notice, and to prevent the absurdity of the attorney having to give notice to himself, para 3(1) provides that an attorney is not required to give notice to himself or to any other attorney under the power who is joining in making the application, notwithstanding that he or, as the case may be, the other attorney is entitled to receive notice by virtue of para 2.

Although the attorney need not give himself notice, he need not give notice to a more distant person or class on the list in his place (PD Lewis, *The Law Society's Gazette* (26 November 1986) at page 3567). However, apart from this exception, the requirements of paras 2(3) and 2(4) must be satisfied.

Paragraph 3(2) authorises the court to dispense with the requirement to give notice if it is satisfied that:

(a)   it would be undesirable or impracticable for the attorney to give him notice; or

(b)   no useful purpose would be served by giving him notice.

Form of notice

7.4   Rule 6(1) Court of Protection (Enduring Powers of Attorney) Rules 2001 (SI 2001 No 825) ('CPR') provides that notice must be given in Form EP1 to those entitled to receive such notice and to any co-attorney. All such notices must be served within 14 days of each other. Form EP1 is reproduced in APPENDIX 3. PD Lewis in *The Law Society's Gazette* (26 November 1986) states at page 3567 that the form should not be sent out until the enduring power has been executed as the form is drafted on the basis that the power is already in existence.

Rule 6(2) CPR provides that an application to dispense with notice must be made in Form EP3 before any application for registration is made. The procedure on such an application is discussed at 7.18 below.

Section 12 EPAA 1985 empowers the Lord Chancellor to exempt attorneys of such descriptions as he thinks fit from the requirements of the EPAA 1985 to give notice to relatives before registration. No order has yet been made under this provision.

Notice to donor

7.5   Schedule 1 Pt I para 4(1) EPAA 1985 requires an attorney to give notice to the donor that he intends to apply for registration of the power, but under para 4(2) the court may dispense with this requirement if it is satisfied that:

(a)   it would be undesirable or impracticable for the attorney to give notice to the donor; or

(b)   no useful purpose is likely to be served by giving notice to the donor.

Form EP1 must be used to give notice to the donor, and the application to dispense with notice must be in Form EP3. Under r 15(1) CPR any document required to be given to the donor must be given to him personally, although an agent can be employed to do this (see PD Lewis, *The Law Society's Gazette* (26 November 1986) at page 3567). The procedure on such applications is discussed at 7.18 below.

PD Lewis in *The Law Society's Gazette* (26 November 1986) states at page 3568 that applications to dispense with service on the donor on the ground that he is incapable of understanding the registration procedure are unlikely to succeed, unless there is clear medical evidence that service would be detrimental to the donor's health. It is clearly right that the donor should be given notice of an application for registration. Although in some cases the donor may be mentally incapable and totally unable to understand what is happening, in other cases the donor may be more aware of the situation and wish to object to the registration of the power and *must* be given the opportunity to do so.

Notice to other attorneys

7.6   Before making an application for registration, Sch 1 Pt III para 7 EPAA 1985 requires an attorney under a joint and several power to give notice of his intention so to do to any other attorney under the power who is not joining in making the application. Note that if it is a joint power, all the attorneys must apply for registration.

As with the duty to give notice to relatives, an attorney is not entitled to receive notice if:

(a)   his address is not known to the applying attorney and cannot reasonably be ascertained by him; or

(b)   the applying attorney has reason to believe that he has not attained eighteen years or is mentally incapable (for definition of mental incapacity see s 13(1) EPAA 1985 and 7.2 above).

Under Sch 1 Pt I para 3(2) EPAA 1985, the court can dispense with the requirement to give notice if it is satisfied that:

(a)   it would be undesirable or impracticable for the attorney to give him notice; or

(b)   no useful purpose would be served by giving him notice.

Form EP1 should be used for the notice, and Form EP3 should be used for the application to dispense with the notice.

Form and service of notices

7.7   Schedule 1 Pt II EPAA 1985 and the Court of Protection (Enduring Powers of Attorney) Rules 2001 (SI 2001 No 825) ('CPR') prescribe the form of notice to be given to relatives, the donor, and co-attorneys. The Form, EP1, is reproduced in APPENDIX 3.

Under r 15(1) CPR, the notice must be given to the donor personally.

Schedule 1 Pt IV para 8(2) EPAA 1985 provides that for the purposes of the schedule a notice given by post will be regarded as given on the date on which it was posted. Rule 15(2) CPR provides that the notice will be served on any person other than the donor by sending it by first class post, or through a document exchange. Alternatively, it can be transmitted by fax or other electronic means.

Service on a solicitor is also permissible under r 16 CPR unless the solicitor is acting for the donor. The solicitor must endorse on the document or a copy of the statement that he or she accepts the document on behalf of that person, and the document will then be deemed to have been duly sent to that person, and to have been received on the date on which the endorsement was made.

Substituted service is also permissible. Rule 17 provides that where it appears to the court that it is impracticable for any document to be sent in accordance with r 15(2) CPR the court may give such directions for the purpose of bringing the document to the notice of the person to whom it is addressed as it thinks fit.

Grounds for objection to registration

7.8   A person who is served with notice of an application to apply for registration can object to the registration on various grounds specified in s 6(5) EPAA 1985. The grounds are as follows:

(a)   that the power purported to have been created by the instrument was not valid as an enduring power of attorney (for example, that it had not been signed by all or one of the parties);

(b)   that the power created by the instrument no longer exists (for example, that it had been revoked);

(c)   that the application is premature because the donor is not yet becoming mentally incapable;

(d)   that fraud or undue pressure was used to induce the donor to create the power;

(e)   that, having regard to all the circumstances and in particular the attorney's relationship to or connection with the donor, the attorney is unsuitable to be the donor's attorney. In the case of joint attorneys, this ground applies to any attorney (Sch 1 Pt I para 4 EPAA 1985).

In *Re W [2000] 1 All ER 175*, W appointed her daughter X as her attorney under an enduring power. There were two other children, Y and Z, and as a consequence of a dispute over a property, there was considerable hostility between X, Y and Z. It was held that this by itself did not mean that X was unsuitable within section 6(5)(e). Jules Sher QC, sitting as a Deputy Judge of the High Court, said at page 182:

'It seems to me that it is not right to say that (irrespective of the background) hostility of the kind we have seen in this case between the children renders any of them unsuitable to be Mrs. W's attorney. In this case the hostility will not impact adversely on the administration. It would, in my judgment, be quite wrong to frustrate Mrs. W's choice of attorney in this way. Whether it is or is not a good idea for a parent in Mrs. W's position, when such hostility exists, to appoint one child alone as attorney is another question.'

This decision has been confirmed by the Court of Appeal [2001] 4 All ER 88. Readers are also referred to *Re E, X v Y* (see 6.18).

If it is a joint and several power, objection may be taken to registration on a ground relating to any attorney, or to the power of any attorney whether or not the attorney is an applicant (s 11(5)(c) EPAA 1985).

Under r 9(1) CPR any objections to registrations must be in writing, and must contain:

(a)   the name and address of the objector;

(b)   the name and address of the donor, if the objector is not the donor;

(c)   any relationship of the objector to the donor;

(d)   the name and address of the attorney; and

(e)   the grounds for objecting to registration of the enduring power.

In *The Law Society's Gazette* (29 April 1987) PD Lewis states at page 1219 that if the objections to registration are not clearly expressed, the objector will be asked to give full particulars, and a copy will be sent to the applicant or his solicitors. A preliminary hearing for directions will be held, and directions may be given for the filing of particulars of the objection, and affidavit evidence, discovery and inspection of documents, allocation of a hearing date and costs. It may be that the issues can be resolved in correspondence without the need for a hearing (page 1220). PD Lewis also refers to one case where 'an objector (who had failed to give particulars of his objection after request) was ordered to do so, and to file affidavit evidence in support, with a condition that, in default, his objections should be dismissed. He failed to comply with the order, the objections were dismissed and taxed costs were awarded against him'.

Section 11(6) EPAA 1985 applies to joint and several powers, and provides that the court will not refuse an application for registration if a ground for objection is made out in respect of one attorney, but not as regards another attorney; the court will give effect to it by the prescribed qualification of the registration. If it is a joint power, and a ground for objection is made out in respect of one attorney, then the court will refuse the application for registration. The consequence of this is that the power is revoked.

Rule 9(2) CPR provides that any objection to registration received by the court on or after the date of registration will be treated as an application to cancel the registration.

Preliminary hearing as to validity of power

7.9   An attorney may consider that it is desirable for the court to rule on the validity of a power before applying for registration. Section 4(5) EPAA 1985 permits such an application, and provides that the attorney must comply with any direction given by the court.

Leave to bring an application

7.10   If a person who has not been served with notice of intention to register an enduring power wants to apply for relief, he must apply to the court for leave to do so (r 21 CPR).

The application for registration

7.11   Rule 7 CPR requires an application for registration of an enduring power to be made in Form EP2, which is reproduced in APPENDIX 3. (A new form must be used for all applications for registration submitted after 1 March 2003). The form must be lodged with the court office.

It is not necessary to file a Statement of Client's Assets and Income.

The enduring power of attorney must accompany the application; the fee for lodging the application is £220 (r 26 and Sch 2 CPR). Under r 26(3) this fee is payable out of the assets of the donor. Under r 26A(1) the court may remit or postpone the payment of the whole or any part of any fee where in its opinion hardship might otherwise be caused to the donor, or some such other person liable to pay the fee, or his dependants, or the circumstances are otherwise exceptional. Rule 26A(2) provides that the court may remit a payment of the whole or any part of any fee where the cost of calculation and collection would be disproportionate to the amount involved. The website of the Public Guardianship Office (www.publictrust.gov.uk) contains further details as to how these provisions will be operated.

Note that it is not possible to apply for a review of any decision under r 26A.

Rule 7 CPR also provides that Form EP2 must be lodged with the court office not later than ten days after the date on which, in relation to the donor and every relative entitled to receive notice and every co-attorney, either:

(a)   notice has been given; or

(b)   leave has been given to dispense with notice,

whichever may be the later.

Originally the time limit was three days. In *The Law Society's Gazette* (29 April 1987) PD Lewis reported at page 1220 that this time limit was frequently overlooked. Applications to extend the time limit are decided on their merits. He warned that 'it is very important to consider carefully the form of wording of the application to bring out the strength of the application'. Form EP3 should be used for the application for extension of time.

Rule 8(1) CPR provides that application to the court may be by letter unless the court directs that it should be made formally, when Form EP3 must be used; Form EP3 is reproduced in APPENDIX 3.

If the donor appoints two or more persons as joint attorneys, they must all apply for registration. If one joint attorney dies, the survivor(s) cannot exercise the power. If two or more persons are appointed joint and several attorneys, the survivor(s) can continue to exercise the power after the death of one. If the donor appoints successive attorneys, for example an appointment of A, but if he dies, then B, only one attorney should apply for registration. It will be necessary to file affidavit evidence as to which one is entitled to register (PD Lewis, *The Law Society's Gazette* (29 April 1987) at pages 1219 and 1220). It is doubtful if such an appointment is permissible.

Section 4(7) EPAA 1985 imposes criminal penalties for knowingly making false statements in an application for registration.

If the donor is blind, the attorney or his solicitors will have to inform the court how the donor was notified of the intention to apply for registration (see PD Lewis, *The Law Society's Gazette* (29 April 1987) at page 1220).

There is no need to send to the court copies of Form EP1 served on the donor and relatives (PD Lewis, *The Law Society's Gazette* (26 November 1986) at page 3567). In the same article, the author makes the following points about Form EP2:

- 'The age of the attorney may be shown as "over 18", although the exact age is more informative.'

- 'The date to be given in the third block (now part five) on the form (the application to register) is the date when the power was executed by the donor . . .'

- 'The relevant dates must be included in the fifth and sixth blocks (now parts 6 and 7) on the form.'

- 'If there are no relatives falling within the class entitled to be notified, it avoids an enquiry from the court if the block is completed to show that, rather than being left blank or crossed through.'

- 'If there is only one attorney, the reference in the sixth block (now part eight) (to notification of co-attorney) should be crossed out.

- 'The final block should be checked to see that it has been signed and dated and that the address where notices should be sent has been inserted.'

- 'Manuscript or typed amendments to the form should be initialled by the attorney(s). Amendments made by the use of correcting fluid are not acceptable; a fresh form should be used.'

- 'Any discrepancy between the spelling of the donor's or attorney's name in the enduring power and in the EP2 should be explained in a covering letter, as should any discrepancy between the donor's address on the EP2 and the address at which (s)he was served.'

Effect of application for registration

7.12   Section 1(1)(b) EPAA 1985 provides that if the donor becomes mentally incapable, the donee of the power may not do anything under the authority of the power, unless it is permitted under s 1(2), or it is authorised or directed by the court under s 5.

Section 1(2) provides that where an application for registration of a power has been made, the attorney may take action under the power:

(a)   'to maintain the donor or prevent loss to his estate; or

(b)   to maintain himself or other persons in so far as section 3(4) permits him to do so'.

Section 11(5)(a) provides that in the case of a joint and several power, an attorney who has not applied for registration may act under s 1(2) as well as an attorney who has applied.

Section 3(4) provides that subject to anything contained in the power, the attorney may act under the power so as to benefit himself or persons other than the donor to the following extent but no further:

(a) he may so act in relation to himself or in relation to any other person if the donor might be expected to provide for his or that person's needs respectively; and

(b) he may do whatever the donor might be expected to do to meet those needs.

Simultaneous receipt of application for registration and application to appoint a receiver

7.13 PD Lewis in the *The Law Society's Gazette* (29 April 1987) states at page 1219 that if an application for registration of an enduring power of attorney appointing X as attorney is received at the same time as an application to appoint Y as receiver under the Mental Health Act 1983, the court will usually register the power of attorney. If it is not possible to register the power, the court will consider the appointment of a receiver. The reason for this course of action is that it is the course preferred by the donor of the power. The Master may give directions, and may try to resolve the matter through correspondence.

Functions of court before registration

7.14 Section 5 EPAA 1985 gives the court power to exercise the powers it would have under s 8(2) once the power is registered if the court has reason to believe that the donor may be, or may be becoming, mentally incapable. The power is exercisable whether or not the attorney has made an application for registration; presumably a relative could apply. For a discussion of s 8(2), see 7.22 .

In *The Law Society's Gazette* (29 April 1987) PD Lewis dealt at page 1220 with the situation where an attorney wishes to sell property belonging to the donor before the attorney has applied to register an enduring power, or where there is a pending application for registration. Application must be made under s 5 EPAA 1985, and 'the court must receive evidence giving it reason to believe that the donor may be, or be becoming, mentally incapable and must be satisfied of the need for interim directions. In particular, it will need to be satisfied that, if the house to be sold is the donor's home, there is no reasonable likelihood of the donor returning to live there. If the donor is not yet becoming mentally incapable, the attorney may be able to use the power as an ordinary power, of course without reference to the court'.

The article also suggests that use could be made of s 1(2) (see 7.12 above).

Under Sch 3 Pt I para 3 EPAA 1985, which applies to joint powers, references to 'the attorney' in s 5 are to be read as including references to any attorney under the power. Under s 11(5)(a), which applies to joint and several powers, an attorney who is not an applicant may act under s 5, as well as an attorney who is an applicant, pending the initial determination of the application.

Functions of court on application for registration

7.15   Section 6 EPAA 1985 provides that if an application for registration has been made in accordance with s 4(3) and (4), the court will register the application unless:

(a)   it appears to the court that there is in force under Pt VII Mental Health Act 1983 an order appointing a receiver for the donor but the power has also not been revoked (s 6(2) EPAA 1985); or

(b)   a valid notice of objection to the registration has been received by the court before the expiry of five weeks beginning with the date or, as the case may be, the latest date on which the attorneys gave notice to any person under Sch 1; or

(c)   it appears from the application that there is no one to whom notice has been given under Sch 1 para 1; or

(d)   the court has reason to believe that appropriate inquiries might bring to light evidence on which the court could be satisfied that one of the grounds of objection was established (s 6(4)).

Section 6(6) EPAA 1985 provides that in these circumstances if any of the grounds of objection in s 6(5) is established to the satisfaction of the court, the court will refuse the application, but if in such a case it is not so satisfied, the court will register the instrument to which the application relates.

If the court decides that fraud or undue pressure was used to induce the donor to create the power, or that, having regard to all the circumstances and in particular the attorney's relationship to or connection with the donor, the attorney is unsuitable to be the donor's attorney, the court must revoke the power created by the instrument (s 6(7) EPAA 1985).

Rule 12(1) CPR provides that if there is no objection to registration, or the objection is withdrawn or dismissed, the enduring power will be registered and sealed by the court. The original power stamped with the date of registration is returned to the applicant attorney, but the court retains a copy (r 12(2) and 12(5)). Any qualification to the registration imposed by reason of s 11(6) or 11(7) EPAA 1985 must be noted on the register and on the power (r 12(4)); s 11(6) and s 11(7) contain provisions dealing with joint and several attorneys (see 7.8). Under r 12(3) any alterations on the face of an instrument when an application for registration is made must be sealed.

Section 6(8) EPAA 1985 provides that when the court refuses an application the instrument must be delivered up to be cancelled, unless the court otherwise directs. This provision does not apply, however, if the court refuses an application on the ground that it is premature because the donor is not yet becoming mentally incapable.

Dispensing with notice of application at the hearing

7.16 As described at 7.3–7.6 above, before applying for registration of the power it is possible to apply to the court to dispense with service of notice on those people who are required to be served under Sch 1 EPAA 1985. If this is not done, the court is empowered under s 6(3) EPAA 1985, at the hearing of the application for registration of the power, to treat the application as if notices have been given if it is satisfied that as regards each such person not served:

(a)   it was undesirable or impracticable for the attorney to give him notice; or

(b)   no useful purpose is likely to be served by giving him notice.

Evidence

7.17 Rule 20 CPR authorises the issue of a witness summons in Form EP6.

Under r 18, evidence which has been used in any proceedings relating to the donor may be used at any subsequent stage in those proceedings or in any other proceedings before the court.

Hearings

7.18 It may be necessary to have a hearing, for example to deal with an objection. Rule 10 CPR applies to the following applications (under EPAA 1985) to the court:

- applications to the court for directions or authority under s 1(1)(b);

- applications under s 4(5), prior to an application for registration, for determination of any question as to the validity of the power;

- applications under s 5 for the exercise of any power with respect to the power of attorney or the attorney before registration of the power;

- applications under s 6(3) for directions that notice has been given in accordance with s 4(3);

- applications under s 6(4), which deals with objections and failure to give notice;

- applications under s 8(2) for various matters once the power has been registered;

- applications under s 8(3) for confirmation of the revocation of the power by the donor;

- applications under s 8(4) for cancellation of the registration of a power;

- applications under s 11(5)(c) which deals with objections to registration when more than one attorney is appointed, and not all the attorneys apply for registration;

- applications under Sch 1 para 2(1) which deals with the persons entitled to receive notice of an application for registration of an enduring power;

- applications under Sch 1 para 3(2) to dispense with notice;

- applications under Sch 1 para 4(2) to dispense with notice to donor;

- applications under Sch 1 para 7(1) to dispense with service of notice on other attorneys.

Rule 10 applies only if the application is not made simultaneously with the application for registration of an enduring power.

Rule 8(1) provides that an application may be by letter, unless the court directs that the application should be formal, in which case it must be made in Form EP3; this form is reproduced in APPENDIX 3.

Rule 8(2) provides that any application made by letter under r 8(1), other than an objection to registration or disclaimer of attorneyship, must include the name and address of the applicant, the name of the donor if the applicant is not the donor, the form of relief or determination required and the grounds for the application. Rule 10(2) provides that on receipt of an application, the court may decide that no hearing should be held, or it may fix an appointment for directions, or for the application to be heard. Under r 10(3) the court may, on application or of its own motion, give such directions as it thinks proper. Notification of an appointment for directions, or for a hearing must be given by the applicant to the attorney (if he is not the applicant), to any objector, and to any other person directed by the court to be notified (r 10(4)), and the applicant and any person given notice of the appointment or hearing may attend or be represented (r 10(5)). Under r 10(6) the court can of its own motion make such order or give such directions as it thinks fit.

Rule 22 CPR provides that all persons who receive notice under r 10(4) must be notified by the applicant of the court's decision, and must also be sent a copy of any order made or directions given.

Notice of hearings

7.19   Unless the court directs otherwise, r 14(1) provides that ten clear days' notice must be given in the case of:

- an application to dispense with notice to the donor;

- an application to dispose of the donor's property before registration; and

- an objection to registration of an enduring power,

to the attorney, the donor, every relative defined in Sch 1 EPAA 1985 (see 7.3 above), to any co-attorney and to such other persons who appear to the court to be interested as the court may specify.

Seven clear days' notice must be given of any other application and to any other person interested in the proceedings (r 14(1)(b)).

The court may extend or abridge these time limits (r 14(3)), and r 14(4) provides that notice of hearing is given if the applicant sends a copy of the application to the person concerned, endorsed by the court with the hearing date.

Consolidation of proceedings

7.20   Rule 11 permits the court to consolidate any applications for registration or relief or any objections to registration if it considers that the proceedings relating to them can more conveniently be dealt with together.

Effect of registration

7.21   Section 7(1) EPAA 1985 provides that the effect of registration of an enduring power is that:

(a)   no revocation of the power by the donor will be valid unless and until the court confirms the registration under s 8(3);

(b)   no disclaimer of the power will be valid unless and until the attorney gives notice to the court or the Public Trustee;

(c)   the donor may not extend or restrict the scope of the authority conferred by the instrument;

(d)   no instruction or consent given by the donor after registration will, in the case of consent, confer any right and, in the case of an instruction, impose or confer any obligation or right on, or create any liability of, the attorney or other persons having notice of the instruction or consent. In effect, once the power is registered, the donor cannot give any consent or instructions.

Section 7(2) provides that s 7(1) applies for so long as a power is registered, even though the donor is mentally capable. For a further discussion of s 7, see 8.18 below.

Functions of court with regard to registered powers

7.22   Section 8 EPAA 1985 gives the court wide powers once a power has been registered. Under subs (2) the court may:

(a)   determine any question as to the meaning or effect of the instrument;

(b)   give directions with respect to:

    (i)   the management or disposal by the attorney of the property and affairs of the donor;

(ii) the rendering of accounts by the attorney and the production of records kept by him for the purpose;

(iii) the remuneration or expenses of the attorney, whether or not in default of or in accordance with any provision made by the instrument, including directions for the repayment of excessive, or the payment of additional remuneration;

(c) require the attorney to furnish information or produce documents or things in his possession as attorney;

(d) give any consent or authorisation to act which the attorney would have to obtain from a mentally capable donor;

(e) authorise the attorney to act so as to benefit himself or other persons than the donor otherwise than in accordance with s 3(4) and (5) (but subject to any conditions or restrictions contained in the instrument);

(f) relieve the attorney wholly or partly from any liability which he has or may have incurred on account of a breach of his duties as attorney.

Under Sch 3 Pt I para 5, which applies to joint attorneys, reference to 'the attorney' under s 8(2) includes references to any attorney under the power.

For a discussion of s 3(4) and (5), see 8.14–8.17 below.

The rights of an attorney to indemnity and remuneration are discussed in CHAPTER 10.

The question of the extent of the powers of the court under s 8(2)(b)(i) was discussed in *Re R [1990] 2 WLR 1219*. In that case R appointed her nephew as her attorney under an enduring power of attorney which was registered under the EPAA 1985. The applicant had been employed by R as a cook and housekeeper, but she alleged that she had become a companion, and that R had led her to believe that R would provide for her for the rest of her life. R went into a nursing home, and the applicant remained in R's flat. The attorney gave her notice terminating her employment, and wanted possession of the flat. The applicant asked the court to make provision for her under s 8(2)(b)(i) EPAA 1985. The application was refused. Vinelott J held that the section was concerned with administrative matters, and did not give the court power to dispose of the whole of R's property.

However, the Court of Protection will sanction gifts and settlements – see Practice Note 9.

Assumption of full mental capacity

7.23 Section 13(2) EPAA 1985 provides that any question arising under or for the purposes of the EPAA 1985 as to what the donor of the power might at any time be expected to do will be determined by assuming that he had full mental capacity at the time but otherwise by reference to the circumstances existing at that time.

Effect of failure to register

7.24   The EPAA 1985 does not provide for any penalties for non-registration. However, a donor who acts under an enduring power which should have been registered may be liable to a third party.

Cancellation of registration

7.25   Section 8(4) EPAA 1985 provides that the court will cancel the registration of an enduring power in the following circumstances:

(a)   on confirming the revocation of the power under s 8(3), or on receiving notice of disclaimer under s 7(1)(b);

(b)   on giving a direction revoking the power on exercising any of its powers under Pt VII Mental Health Act 1983;

(c)   on being satisfied that the donor is and is likely to remain mentally capable;

(d)   on being satisfied that the power has expired or has been revoked by the death or bankruptcy of the donor, or the death, mental incapacity or bankruptcy of the attorney or, if the attorney is a body corporate, its winding up or dissolution;

(e)   on being satisfied that the power was not a valid or subsisting enduring power when registration was effected;

(f)   on being satisfied that fraud or undue pressure was used to induce the donor to create the power; or

(g)   on being satisfied that, having regard to all the circumstances and in particular the attorney's relationship to or connection with the donor, the attorney is unsuitable to be the donor's attorney.

In *The Law Society's Gazette* (29 April 1987) PD Lewis states at page 1220 that if 'an application is made to cancel a registration on the ground that the donor has recovered, the court will expect to see written confirmation from the donor that he agrees, together with confirmation that he is not seeking to revoke the EPA. The original of any medical report or certificate will also need to be shown'.

If it is a joint power, Sch 3 Pt I para 6 EPAA 1985 provides that references to 'the attorney' include references to any attorney under the power, so that if, for example, one joint attorney becomes bankrupt, the registration must be cancelled completely so that the power ceases to have any effect.

Under s 11(7), which applies to joint and several powers, the court must not cancel any registration of an enduring power for any of the causes vitiating registration if there is one attorney who is not affected by those causes; instead the court must qualify the registration. So if one joint and several attorney becomes bankrupt, the registration will remain valid for the other attorney(s).

If the court is satisfied that grounds (f) or (g) exist, it must revoke the power created by the instrument (s 8(5) EPAA 1985); if the registration is cancelled on any ground other than (c), the instrument must be delivered up to be cancelled, unless the court otherwise directs (s 8(6)).

Rule 25(1) CPR provides that if the registration of an enduring power of attorney is cancelled, the court will send a notice to the attorney requiring him to deliver to the court the original instrument. Rule 25(2) provides that where the court is satisfied that the power has been revoked by the death or bankruptcy of the attorney, the notice must be given to the attorney's personal representative, or as the case may be the attorney's trustee in bankruptcy. If the attorney is a body corporate, and the court is satisfied that the power has been revoked by the winding up or the dissolution of the attorney, then notice must be given to the attorney's liquidator or as the case may be receiver;

If the instrument has been destroyed, the attorney served with notice under para 1 must give the court written details of the date on which the instrument was lost or destroyed and the circumstances in which that occurred (r 25(3)). Under r 25(4) CPR where registration is cancelled on any ground other than (c), the court will mark the power of attorney as cancelled. Rule 25(4A) provides that where registration has been cancelled because the court is satisfied that the donor is and is likely to remain mentally capable, the court shall mark on the power of attorney an endorsement that registration has been cancelled. This means that the power can continue as an ordinary power.

Rule 25(5) provides that any notices issued by the court under this rule may contain a warning that failure to comply with the notice may lead to punishment for contempt of court.

Reviews and appeals

7.26   Rule 23(1) enables a person who is aggrieved by a decision of the court not made on a hearing, within fourteen days of the date on which the decision was given, to have the decision reviewed by the court.

On reviewing a decision, the court may confirm or revoke the decision or may make or give any other order or decision.

Rule 23(3) provides that any person aggrieved by any order or decision of the court made on considering an application for review may apply to the court for an attended hearing within fourteen days of the date on which the order was made or decision given.

Rule 24(1) permits any person aggrieved by any order or decision of the court on an attended hearing to appeal to a judge within fourteen days from the date of entry of the order or, as the case may be, from the date of the decision. Under r 24(2), the appellant must serve notice of appeal in Form EP7 on:

- every person who is directly affected by the decision; and

- any other person whom the court may direct, and

the appellant must lodge a copy at the court office.

The court fixes the time and place at which the appeal is to be heard, and notifies the appellant who must then notify every person who has been served with notice of appeal (r 24(3)). Further evidence can be filed only with leave of the court (r 24(4)).

Time

7.27   Rule 5 contains provisions for the computation of time. Rule 5(1) provides that where the time so fixed for doing an act in the court office expires on a day on which the office is closed, and for that reason the act cannot be done on that day, the act will be in time if it is done on the next day on which the office is open.

Rule 5(2) provides that where the act is required to be done within a specified period after or from a specified date, the period starts immediately after that date.

Rule 5(3) provides that where the period in question consists of three days or less and which includes a day on which the court office is closed, that day will be excluded.

Privacy of documents filed in court

7.28   Rule 19(1) provides that any person who has filed an affidavit or other document is entitled on request, unless the court otherwise directs, to be supplied by the court with a copy of it.

Rule 19(2) permits an attorney or his solicitor to have a search made for, and may inspect and request a copy of, any document filed in proceedings relating to the enduring power of attorney under which the attorney has been appointed.

Apart from these exceptions, no documents filed in the court are open to inspection without the leave of the court, and no copy of any such document or extract can be taken by or issued to any person without such leave (r 19(3)).

Searches and copies

7.29   Rule 13(1) authorises any person to request the court to search the register, and to say whether an enduring power of attorney has been registered. Form EP4 must be used for the search, and the appropriate fee must be paid.

Under r 13(2) the court may supply any person with an office copy of a registered enduring power if it is satisfied that he has good reason for requesting a copy and that it is not reasonably practicable to obtain a copy from the attorney.

Rule 13(3) provides that an 'office copy' is a photocopy or facsimile of an enduring power of attorney, marked as an office copy and sealed. However, the office copy need not contain the explanatory information endorsed on the original power (r 13(4)).

Summary

7.30

- As soon as the attorney has reason to believe that the donor is or is becoming mentally incapable, the attorney must apply for registration of the power.

- Before application is made, notice must be given to various relatives.

- Notice must also be given to the donor.

- In certain circumstances the court can dispense with the requirements of notice.

- A person served with notice of application can object to registration on various specified grounds.

- The effect of an application for registration is that the attorney cannot do anything under the power, although there are some limited exceptions to this rule.

- Once the power is registered, the attorney can continue to act.

- The registration can be cancelled on various grounds.

Chapter 8

Extent of the authority

8.1 An attorney is under no duty to exercise the power, unless there is some contractual obligation to do so. For example, if a solicitor or accountant in private practice is appointed by a client to be his attorney, there may be a binding contract under which the solicitor or accountant is under a duty to exercise the power; if there is no such contractual relationship, the attorney need not exercise the power, although usually he or she will want to do so because, for example, the donor is a relative.

If the donor is prepared to exercise the power, the extent of the authority will depend on the express terms of the power, but in some situations the law imposes limitations on this power. There is considerable overlap between the powers of an attorney under an ordinary and an enduring power, but because there are differences it is necessary to consider each power separately.

I. Ordinary powers of attorney

Actual authority

8.2 An attorney can do anything within the actual authority conferred by the power. This authority may permit the attorney to do anything which the donor of the power could have lawfully done, or it may be limited to a particular transaction, for example the sale of a particular house. The interpretation of a limited power of attorney is discussed at 8.3–8.7 below.

If a general power is to be granted, use should be made of the general power of attorney form set out in Sch 1 Powers of Attorney Act 1971 (the form is reproduced in APPENDIX 1). Section 10(1) Powers of Attorney Act 1971 provides that a general power of attorney in that form, or in a form to the like effect but expressed to be made under the Act, operates to confer:

(a) on the donee of the power; or

(b) if there is more than one donee, on the donees acting jointly or acting jointly and severally, as the case may be,

authority to do on behalf of the donor anything which he can lawfully do by an attorney.

This is a very wide power which, for example, permits the attorney to operate the donor's bank or building society account, sell the donor's house or flat, buy a house or flat, sell and buy stocks and shares and even run a business.

However, subs (2) provides that subject to s 1 of Trustee Delegation Act 1999 the attorney cannot exercise functions which a donor has as a trustee or personal representative or as a tenant for life or statutory owner within the meaning of the Settled Land Act 1925. Trustees wishing to delegate may make use of other statutory provisions. Under s 25 Trustee Act 1925, a trustee can delegate by power of attorney, and for a maximum period of twelve months, the trusts, powers and discretions vested in him; and under s 9 Trusts of Land and Appointment of Trustees Act 1996 a trustee of land may delegate his functions by power of attorney to any beneficiary.

Section 1 of the Trustee Delegation Act 1999 provides that the donee of a power of attorney can exercise trustee functions in respect of:

(a)   land;

(b)   capital proceeds of a conveyance of land; and

(c)   income from land,

provided the donor has a beneficial interest in the land, proceeds or income (these sections are discussed further in CHAPTER 9).

A further limitation on the power in s 10(1) is illustrated by *Clauss v Pir [1987] 2 All ER 752*. In that case, the defendant was required by a court order to file an affidavit verifying a list of documents. The affidavit was sworn by his wife to whom he had granted a power of attorney. It was held 'that a party cannot do by an attorney some act the competency to do which arises by virtue of some duty of a personal nature requiring skill or discretion for its exercise' (page 755). The argument that s 7, which deals with the execution of instruments by the donee of a power of attorney, permitted this was rejected on the ground that the section was merely procedural, and did not enlarge the authority of the donee (page 756). For a discussion of s 7, see 11.2 below.

If the attorney is authorised to begin court proceedings, they should be in the name of the donor (*Jones and Saldhana v Gurney [1913] WN 72*).

Interpretation of a limited power

Limited powers

8.3   If a limited power is to be granted, great care must be exercised in drafting the power to ensure that the attorney is authorised to carry out the contemplated transaction, as the courts construe powers of attorney very strictly. In *Bryant, Powis and Bryant Ltd v La Banque du Peuple [1893] AC 170* Lord Macnaghten said at page 177:

'Nor was it disputed that powers of attorney are to be construed strictly – that is to say, that where an act purporting to be done under a power of attorney is challenged as being in excess of the authority conferred by the power, it is necessary to show that on a fair construction of the whole instrument the authority in question is to be found within the four corners of the instrument, either in express terms or by necessary implication.'

In *Re Dowson and Jenkins's Contract [1904] 2 Ch 219* a transferee of a mortgage had entered into possession of the mortgaged property, and executed a power of attorney. This power authorised the attorney 'to sell any real or personal property now or hereafter belonging to me by public auction or by private contract, and subject to any condition as to title or otherwise'. The attorney sold the property, but it was held that the power of attorney did not authorise him to do this. The power did not authorise the sale of property mortgaged to the donor.

However, in *Hawksley v Outram [1892] 3 Ch 359* a partner granted another partner a power of attorney authorising the attorney 'to sell, or concur in selling, any of my real, leasehold, or personal property to any person or persons, company or companies whatsoever, and either by public auction or privately, upon such terms, subject to such special or other conditions, and in such manner as the attorney shall approve . . .'. The attorney joined in a sale of the partnership business, and agreed that the vendors would not carry on business within fifty miles of a certain place. The Court of Appeal was of the opinion that the restraint of trade was authorised by the power of attorney.

Limited power followed by a general power

8.4   If there is a limited power followed by a general power, the general power will be construed as restricted to the purposes permitted by the limited power. In *Perry v Holl (1860) 2 De G F & J 38, 45 ER 536* Lord Campbell LC at page 48, 540 said:

> 'I fully agree with the cases cited by Mr Craig to show that, if there is a power of attorney to do a particular act followed by general words, these general words are not to be extended beyond what is necessary for doing that particular act for which the power of attorney is given.'

An example of the application of this rule is *Lewis v Ramsdale (1886) 55 LT 179*. According to the headnote to the case, A gave a power of attorney to B to manage real estate, recover debts, settle actions, also to 'sell and convert into money' personal property and to execute and perform any contract, agreement, deed, writing or thing that might in B's opinion be necessary or proper for effectuating the purpose aforesaid, or any of them, and 'for all or any of these purposes' of those presents to use A's name and generally to do any other act whatsoever which in B's opinion ought to be done in or about A's concerns as fully as if A were present and did the same, his desire being that all matters respecting the same should be under the full management of B. It was held that the general words were limited by the special purpose of the power of attorney, and did not authorise a mortgage of personal property.

Effect of recitals

8.5   Care must also be taken if the power contains recitals, for example a statement of the reasons for the granting of power. In *Rooke v Lord Kensington (1856) 2 K & J 753, 69 ER 986* Sir W Page Wood V-C at page 769, 992 stated:

> 'It is true that the courts have held ... that you cannot control clear words of a conveyance by words of recital. ... But the expression "clear words of conveyance" is subject to interpretation ... general words are not within that description of clear words of conveyance which cannot be controlled by that recital.'

If the power is limited, the recital will not control it, but if it is a general power, the recital will control it. An example of the operation of this rule is *Danby v Coutts & Co (1885) 29 Ch D 500* where a wide power of attorney recited that the donor was going abroad, and that he was desirous of appointing attorneys to act for him whilst he was absent from England. It was held that the recital controlled the operative part of the deed, and that the attorney could act only when the donor was abroad.

Wide powers

8.6   Even a wide power may not permit some transactions. In *Reckitt v Barnett, Pembroke and Slater Ltd [1929] AC 176* Sir Harold Reckitt appointed a solicitor as his attorney. The power authorised the solicitor 'to manage his affairs while he was abroad and for the purposes of his affairs to sign and execute all documents which might be necessary or such as the solicitor might think fit'. Later, Sir Harold signed a letter stating that he wished the power to cover the drawing of cheques upon a bank without any restriction. The solicitor issued a cheque in settlement of a private debt in favour of Barrett, Pembroke and Slater Ltd. It was held that the company had to refund the money.

Position in relation to land

8.7   Section 10 of the Trustee Delegation Act 1999 has clarified the extent of an attorney's authority in relation to land. Section 10(1) provides that where the donee of a power of attorney is authorised by the power to do an act of any description in relation to any land, his authority to do so at any time includes authority to do it with respect to any estate or interest in land which is held at that time by the donor (whether alone or jointly with any other person or persons). This makes it clear that a donee of a power of attorney has authority to deal with both the legal estate and the equitable interest of the donor in the land. It is subject to any contrary intention shown in the instrument creating the power of attorney and has effect subject to the terms of that instrument (s 10(2)). Section 10(3) provides that this only applies to powers of attorney created after the commencement of the Act.

Incidental or implied powers

8.8   The courts will imply into a power of attorney whatever powers are necessary to carry out the main purpose or purposes of the power. In *Ex parte Wallace; In re Wallace (1884) 14 QBD 22* a power of attorney authorised the donee 'to commence and carry on, or to defend at law or in equity, all actions, suits, or other proceedings touching anything in which I or my ships or other personal estate may be in anywise concerned'. It was held that the attorney had power to sign a bankruptcy petition on behalf of the donor. At page 24 Bagallay LJ said:

> 'No doubt we shall be going a step further in holding that the power authorises the signature of a document on behalf of the principal, but the signature is essential to the doing of the act – the commencement of proceedings in bankruptcy – which is authorised.'

In *Henley v Soper (1828) 8 B & C 16, 108 ER 949*, a partner gave his son a power of attorney 'to act on his behalf in dissolving a partnership, with authority to appoint any other person as he might see fit'. The son submitted the accounts to arbitration, and it was held that he had power to do so.

In *Ex parte Frampton; In the Matter of Frampton (1859) 1 De G & F & J 263* the appellant left the country, but appointed his uncle Edward Frampton his general agent for settling such of his affairs as remained to be settled. He was adjudicated bankrupt, and Edward Frampton instructed solicitors to dispute the adjudication. It was held that Edward had power to instruct solicitors to do this.

However it is very unwise for an attorney to rely on incidental or implied powers except in clear cases as the courts will not carry this idea too far. In *Harper v Godsell (1870) LR 5 QB 422* Porro, a partner in B Williams & Co, gave Newton, one of his partners, a power of attorney in the following terms:

> 'for the purposes hereinafter expressed, that is to say, for the purposes of exercising for me, all or any of the powers and privileges conferred by a certain indenture of partnership constituting the firm B Williams & Co . . . and to receive and give receipts for all sums of money payable to me by virtue of the said indenture and all other debts or sums of money or securities for money which may be at any time due or payable to me in the United Kingdom and generally to do, execute, and perform any other act, deed, matter or thing whatsoever which ought to be done, executed, or performed, in or about my concerns, engagements, and business of every nature and kind to all intents and purposes as I myself could do if I were present and did the same in my own proper person, it being my intent and desire that all matters and things respecting the same shall be under the full management and direction of my said attorney'.

Newton executed deeds dissolving the partnership, and assigning Porro's share. It was held that these actions were not authorised by the power. Mellor J said at page 429:

'. . . I think it is clear that the power of attorney refers only to things done in furtherance of partnership purposes, and that it does not extend to give a power to dissolve the partnership.'

It was also held that the general words of the power did not have an unrestricted effect because they were cut down by the special terms of the first part of the power.

In *Jacobs v Morris [1902] 1 Ch 816* the plaintiff was a tobacco merchant, and appointed an agent under a power of attorney. The agent was authorised 'to purchase and to make and enter into, sign and execute any contract or agreement with any persons, firm, company or companies for the purchase of any goods or merchandise in connection with the business carried on by me . . .'. The attorney purported to act under the power of attorney, and obtained a loan from a firm of cigar merchants. The merchants did not read the power. It was held that the power of attorney did not confer any implied authority to borrow.

Great care must thus be taken when drafting a limited power to ensure that the attorney is given the powers that he or she will need. A power to sell a property might not authorise the mortgaging or leasing of the property, and it is possible that it might not permit the attorney to take proceedings against a purchaser for breach of contract.

Gifts and wills

8.9   Unless specifically authorised, an attorney under an ordinary power has no power to make gifts (*Re Bowles (1874) 31 LT 365*).

An attorney cannot make a will for the donor. This topic is examined in more detail in CHAPTER 15.

Ratification

8.10   An unauthorised act by the donee of a power can be ratified subsequently by the donor of the power. According to Wright J in *Firth v Staines [1897] 2 QB 70* at page 75, to constitute a valid ratification three conditions must be satisfied:

- the agent whose act is sought to be ratified must have purported to act for the principal;

- at the time the act was done the agent must have had a competent principal;

- at the time of ratification the principal must be legally capable of doing the act himself.

Thus there will be no ratification if the donee purports to act for himself, or if at the time when the act was done, or the time of ratification, the principal was mentally incapacitated.

In *Imperial Bank of Canada v Begley [1936] 2 All ER 367*, a Privy Council case, the respondent executed a power of attorney which conferred a very wide power on the donee. The donee transferred money from the respondent's account to his own account at the appellant bank. Subsequently the respondent took a promissory note from the donee for the amount transferred. It was held that the respondent had not ratified the transfer as the donee was not acting as agent for the respondent but for himself. At page 374 it was said:

> 'The first essential to the doctrine of ratification, with its necessary consequence of relating back, is that the agent shall not be acting for himself, but shall be intending to bind a named or ascertainable principal.'

An attorney may be appointed by a company which has not been formed. Section 36C Companies Act 1985, which came into force on 31 July 1990, provides that a contract which purports to be made by or on behalf of the company at a time when the company has not been formed has effect as one made with the person purporting to act for the company or as agent for it, and he is personally liable on the contract accordingly.

Execution of documents

8.11   Section 7(1) Powers of Attorney Act 1971, as amended by the Law of Property (Miscellaneous Provisions) Act 1989, provides that the donee of a power of attorney may, if he thinks fit:

(a)   execute any instrument with his own signature; and

(b)   do any other thing in his own name,

by the authority of the donor of the power; and any document executed or thing done in this manner is as effective as if executed or done by the donee with the signature and seal, or, as the case may be, in the name, of the donor of the power.

Thus an attorney can execute a document either in the name of the donor or in his own name.

If a company has appointed a person as attorney to convey any interest in property in the name or on behalf of the company, the attorney may execute the conveyance by signing the name of the corporation in the presence of at least one witness (s 74(3) Law of Property Act 1925). Section 7(2) Powers of Attorney Act 1971, as amended by the Law of Property (Miscellaneous Provisions) Act 1989, provides that for the avoidance of doubt an instrument to which s 74(3) Law of Property Act 1925 applies may be executed either as provided in that subsection or as provided in s 7 Powers of Attorney Act 1971.

If a company is appointed an attorney, s 74(4) Law of Property Act 1925 provides that an officer appointed for that purpose by the board of directors may execute the deed or other instrument in the name of such other person.

Delegation

8.12   The basic rule is that an agent has no right to delegate – *delegatus non potest delegare*. But having decided on a course of action authorised by the power, an attorney has authority to employ, if necessary, solicitors, estate agents, accountants, builders, plumbers and so on to implement that decision (*Ex parte Frampton; In the Matter of Frampton (1859) 1 De G & F & J 263, CA*). For example, an attorney authorised to sell a property cannot delegate the decision as to whether to sell, or as to whether a particular offer should be accepted. But having decided to sell, the attorney can instruct an estate agent to find a buyer, and a solicitor to deal with the conveyancing.

Section 25(8) of Trustee Act 1925 as amended permits an attorney to whom a trustee has delegated his powers to delegate the power to transfer inscribed stock – see 9.5 below. It is common for brokers to be given a discretion as to the management of stocks and shares. In addition, the introduction of CREST means that shares may be held by a nominee. If the donor has shareholdings, it may be desirable to give the donee of any power the power to entrust a broker with management of shares, and to hold them in the names of nominees.

An attorney who wishes to delegate decisions about investment must have specific authority to do so.

II. Enduring powers of attorney

8.13   It will be recalled that the donee of an enduring power is under a duty to apply for registration of the power if he has reason to believe that the donor is, or is becoming, mentally incapable. Registration does not alter the extent of the attorney's authority, and so third parties dealing with an attorney under an enduring power which has been registered should still have a look at the power to ensure that the transaction is authorised by it. For a discussion of the donee's powers between the application for registration and registration, see 7.12 above.

Actual authority

8.14   As with ordinary powers, an enduring power may confer a general or limited authority on the donee. Section 3(1) EPAA 1985 provides that an enduring power may confer general authority on the attorney to act on the donor's behalf in relation to all or a specified part of the property and affairs of the donor and may confer on him authority to do specified things on the donor's behalf, and the authority may, in either case, be conferred subject to conditions and restrictions. The prescribed form has provision for a general or limited power.

Although s 3(1) permits limited powers, or powers subject to restrictions or conditions, it may be undesirable to grant a limited power. A limited power may not authorise all the transactions which might be desirable, and it might be necessary to apply to the Court of Protection for the appointment of a receiver to deal with the assets not included in the enduring power of attorney (see the Law Commission's Report on *The Incapacitated Principal* (Law Com No 122 Cmnd 8977 at page 30).

If a general power is granted, s 3(2) EPAA 1985 provides that where an instrument is expressed to confer general authority on the attorney, it operates to confer, subject to restrictions on gifts and to any conditions or restrictions contained in the instrument, authority to do on behalf of the donor anything which the donor can lawfully do by an attorney. Thus a donee under a general power can, for example, sell or mortgage the donor's house, operate bank and building society accounts, and buy and sell shares.

Section 3(4) permits an attorney under a general or limited enduring power to benefit himself or persons other than the donor, but there are limits to this power. The donee can benefit himself or any other person only if the donor of the power might be expected to provide for the donee's or that other person's needs, and he can only do whatever the donor might be expected to do to meet those needs. Thus, if the donor appoints his or her spouse as attorney, the spouse can exercise the power so as to benefit himself or herself, but only if the donor would have done so, and only to the extent to which the donor might be expected to meet those needs. Presumably this power would permit the purchase of expensive luxury items if the conditions in the subsection are satisfied.

In *Re Cameron (deceased) [1999] 2 All ER 924* the testatrix executed an enduring power of attorney, which was registered. She also executed a will leaving her residuary estate to her four sons. The attorneys paid a total of £62,596 to trustees to pay for the education of a son of one of her children, Donald. It was held that this was a valid exercise of the enduring power, and it was also held that the gift adeemed the share of Donald in the residuary estate up to the amount of the gift.

Section 7(1)(c) EPAA 1985 provides that if an enduring power is registered, the donor may not extend or restrict the scope of the authority conferred by the instrument and no instruction or consent given by him after registration will, in the case of an instruction, impose or confer any obligation or right on, or create any liability of, the attorney or other persons having notice of the instruction or consent. Section 7 is discussed at 7.21 above.

In *Gregory v Turner (on the application of Morris) v North Somerset District Council [2003] EWCA Civ 183* it was held that a lay attorney acting under an enduring power could not conduct litigation or exercise rights of audience on behalf of the donor.

Interpretation of a limited enduring power

8.15 The rules for the interpretation of limited enduring powers are the same as for ordinary powers, and they will be construed strictly.

Incidental or implied powers

8.16   The rules are the same for enduring powers; however, s 3(4) EPAA 1985 (see above) gives the attorney under an enduring power the power to benefit himself and other persons, subject to any conditions and restrictions contained in the instrument. Thus an enduring power limited to the sale of a house does not authorise gifts.

Gifts

8.17   An attorney under an ordinary power has no power to make gifts, but s 3(5) EPAA 1985 authorises an attorney to make gifts in certain circumstances. It provides that, subject to any conditions or restrictions contained in the instrument, an attorney under an enduring power, whether general or limited, may (without obtaining any consent) dispose of the property of the donor by way of gift to the following extent but no further:

(a)   he may make gifts of a seasonal nature or at a time, or on an anniversary, of a birth or marriage, to persons (including himself) who are related or connected with the donor; and

(b)   he may make gifts to any charity to whom the donor made or might be expected to make gifts,

provided that the value of each such gift is not unreasonable having regard to all the circumstances and in particular the size of the donor's estate. This power is without prejudice to the power conferred by s 3(4).

There is no definition of 'related' or 'connected' in the EPAA 1985. In many cases, it will be clear that the person to be benefitted is related or connected, but there could be problems in deciding if an acquaintance is connected with the donor. Note also that the gift must be of a seasonal nature, or made on an anniversary of a birth or marriage. With charities, the attorney can clearly benefit a charity which the donor has supported in the past, but it might be difficult to justify a gift to a charity which the donor has never supported. However, it would probably be in order to benefit, say, a charity for the relief of cancer if a relative or friend of the donor had died from that disease, even though the donor had not contributed to such a charity in the past.

The value of any gift must not be unreasonable having regard to the circumstances and the size of the estate. Gifts of £5, £10, or £20 are probably in order, unless the estate is very small. A gift of £1,000 out of an estate in excess of £500,000 is clearly permissible, but if the estate is under £10,000, it is probably unreasonable. A gift to a close relative with whom the donor has had no contact for many years is also probably unreasonable.

The court has no power to order the attorney to make gifts. Reference has already been made (7.22 above) to *Re R [1990] 2 WLR 1219*, where the applicant was employed by R as a cook and housekeeper and lived in R's flat.

R gave her nephew an enduring power of attorney, and shortly afterwards she moved to a nursing home. The enduring power of attorney was registered, and the nephew terminated the employment of the applicant, and required her to give up possession of the flat. The applicant alleged that R had promised to provide for her for the rest of her life, and that she had worked for less than the market rate for her services. She applied for provision from R's estate. The application was unsuccessful. Vinelott J said at pages 1222 and 1223:

> 'It is quite plain, and it is not in dispute, that the only authority that the Court of Protection could have to give directions to the attorney, requiring him to make provision for the applicant, would have to be found, if at all, in s 8(2)(b)(i). The case put by the applicant's counsel is that that subparagraph does give the court unrestricted power to direct an attorney to dispose of any part of the property of the donor by way of gift or in recognition of some moral obligation, unaccompanied by any legal obligation.

> I find that an impossible view. Of course the word "disposal" is, in some contexts, capable of being given a very wide meaning, and could include a disposition by way of gift. But it seems to me that in the context of section 8 it cannot have been intended that it should bear that wide meaning. It is in a paragraph, (b), which is plainly concerned with administrative matters: the management of the donor's property; the rendering of accounts and the determination of the remuneration of the attorney. These are all part of the jurisdiction which the court is given to supervise the conduct of the attorney and to see that he is exercising his powers of management and administration properly. It would be remarkable, in a paragraph directed to matters of that sort, to find an unrestricted power given to the court to dispose of the whole of the donor's property by way of gift . . .'.

If an attorney wishes to make a gift, which would be outside those permitted by section 5(3), then the attorney will have to apply to the Public Guardianship Office or the Court of Protection. The procedure is described on Practice Note 9. If the application is to make gifts not exceeding £15,000 per year, then application should be made to the Public Guardianship Office by letter, provided the gifts can be satisfied from capital or income which is surplus to requirements.

If it is desired to make a larger gift, or to create a settlement, then a formal application must be made to the Court of Protection. Form CP9 must be used for the application, and it must be supported by an affidavit containing details of the client's family, assets etc.

An attorney cannot make a will on behalf of the donor of the power; this topic is examined in more detail in CHAPTER 15.

Ratification

8.18   The rules are the same as for ordinary powers until the power has been registered, but if the power is registered, and the donee enters into a transaction not permitted by the enduring power, the donor cannot ratify that transaction. This is because s 7(1)(c) EPAA 1985 provides that no consent given after registration can confer any right. However, where a power is registered s 8(2)(d) EPAA 1985 authorises the court to give any consent or authorisation to act which the attorney would have to obtain from a mentally capable donor. On the face of it, this is wide enough to permit the court to ratify an act outside the authority conferred by an enduring power, but in the light of *Re R* it seems that the court might not adopt such a construction.

Section 8(2)(f) permits the court to relieve the attorney wholly or partly from any liability which he has or may have incurred on account of a breach of his duties as attorney. Perhaps this subsection could be used to ratify an act outside the authority of the attorney.

Execution of documents

8.19   There is nothing in the EPAA 1985 dealing with the execution of documents, and so the same rules apply to both ordinary and enduring powers.

Delegation

8.20   There is no specific provision dealing with delegation in the EPAA 1985, and so the rule is the same as for ordinary powers; delegation of managerial decisions is not permissible, although the attorney may employ others to carry out his or her decisions.

Power to appoint new trustees

8.21   Section 20 of the Trusts of Land and Appointment of Trustees Act 1996 applies where –

(a)   a trustee is incapable by reason of mental disorder of exercising his functions as a trustee;

(b)   there is no person who is both entitled and willing and able to appoint a trustee in place of him under s 36(1) of the Trustee Act 1925; and

(c)   the beneficiaries under the trust are of full age and capacity and (taken together) are absolutely entitled to the property subject to the trust.

If these conditions are satisfied, and they will usually only apply if there is a sole trustee who has become mentally incapable, or two trustees both of whom have become mentally incapable, the beneficiaries may give a written direction to appoint by writing the person(s) specified in the direction to be trustee(s) in place of the incapable trustee. This written direction may be given *inter alia* to an attorney acting for the trustee under the authority of a power of attorney created by an instrument which is registered under s 6 EPAA 1985.

Section 8 of the Trustee Delegation Act 1999 inserts a new sub-section into s 36 of the Trustee Act 1925. Section 36(6A) confers on the donee of an enduring power a limited power to appoint a new trustee. The subsection applies to a person who is either –

(a)   both a trustee and attorney for the other trustee (if one other), or for both of the other trustees (if two others), under a registered power; or

(b)   attorney under a registered power for the trustee (if one) or for both or each of the trustees (if two or three) (s 36(6A)).

Thus a trustee who is one of two trustees, and is appointed attorney by the other trustee, can appoint another trustee. Similarly a trustee who is one of three trustees and is appointed attorney by the other two trustees can appoint a fourth. An attorney who is not a trustee can also exercise this power, but must have been appointed by all the trustees. Note that all the powers must be registered.

The attorney must as attorney under the power intend –

(a)   to exercise any function of the trustee or trustees by virtue of s 1(1) Trustee Delegation Act 1999; or

(b)   to exercise any function of the trustee or trustees in relation to any land, capital proceeds of a conveyance of land or income from land by virtue of its delegation to him under s 25 Trustee Delegation Act 1999 or the instrument (if any) creating the trust (s 36(6B) Trustee Act).

Thus the attorney must intend to exercise any trustee function, but it is immaterial whether the power is granted under s 1 Trustee Delegation Act 1999, or s 25 of the Trustee Act as substituted.

Section 36(6D) states that s 36(6A) is subject to any contrary intention expressed in the instrument creating the power of attorney (or, where more than one, any of them) or the instrument (if any) creating the trust, and has effect subject to the terms of those instruments.

III. Powers with a foreign element

8.22   If a power is entered into abroad, and it is intended that it should be used in England and Wales, it will be governed by English law. In *Sinfra Atkiengesellschaft v Sinfra Ltd [1939] 2 All ER 675* Lewis J said at page 682:

'It is a one-sided instrument . . ., and, although it was argued that a different law should be applied to the document depending upon whether the court was considering the formation, the extent, the operation or the termination of the power, I am satisfied that the proper law for an English court to apply is the law of the country in which the power is to operate – that is to say, English law.'

The Contracts (Applicable Law) Act 1990 gives the force of law to various conventions concerning which law governs a contract where there is a choice. The Act applies if there is a contract between the donor and the donee, but the question of whether an agent is able to bind a principal is specifically excluded (Sch 1 Article 1 part 2(f)).

Summary

8.23

- An attorney can do anything which he is permitted to do under the power, provided the action is permitted under the general law.

- A limited power will be construed strictly.

- The courts will imply into a limited power whatever incidental powers are necessary to carry out the main purpose of the power.

- An attorney under an enduring power can make gifts; an attorney under an ordinary power cannot do so unless specifically authorised to make them.

- A donor may be able to ratify an unauthorised act, except in the case of an enduring power which has been registered.

- An attorney can execute a document with his own signature, or in the name of the donor.

- An attorney cannot usually delegate, but he may be able to employ others to carry out the decisions made by the attorney.

Chapter 9

Capacity of donor and donee

9.1   This chapter deals with the capacity of the donor or donee to grant a power of attorney and to accept it, and with other related matters which might affect the validity of a power of attorney; it is not concerned with what happens if the donor and donee had capacity to grant and accept the power, but one or both subsequently become incapable. The effect of subsequent incapacity was dealt with in CHAPTER 6.

The rules for determining whether a donor has capacity at the time when the power is granted are in some cases the same for both ordinary and enduring powers, but there are differences, and so they will be treated separately.

I. Capacity of donor to grant an ordinary power

9.2   The rules for determining whether a donor has the capacity to grant a power of attorney are similar to those for determining whether a person has capacity to enter into a contract.

Minors

9.3   There is some doubt about whether an infant can grant a power of attorney (see page 35 of *Law of Agency* (Sweet & Maxwell, 17th edition, 2001) by Bowstead and Reynolds).

It is submitted that there is no reason why an infant should not confer a revocable authority on an agent, and that the contracts entered into by the agent should bind the infant if they would have done so if the infant had entered into them personally. This was the view of the Law Commission in its Report on *The Incapacitated Principal* (Law Com No 122 Cmnd 8977 at page 3). However, there is a risk that the agent might be personally liable for breach of warranty of authority if the contract does not bind the infant.

Mentally disordered persons

9.4   A person suffering from mental disorder may not be able to grant a power of attorney. What type of disorder will prevent a person granting a power of attorney? In *Elliot v Ince (1857) 7 De GM & G 475, 44 ER 186*, Lord Cranworth, when dealing with the validity of powers of attorney, said at pages 489, 191:

'... whether at the time when they were executed and acted on respectively [the donor] was of sound mind, so as to be sufficient for the government of herself, her lands and possessions.'

It follows from this quotation that a person suffering from mental disorder can grant a power of attorney in a lucid interval; otherwise the power will be void (see 9.30 below). However, in *Law of Agency* by Bowstead and Reynolds it is suggested at page 36 that a person suffering from mental disorder, whose affairs are under the supervision of the Court of Protection under the Mental Health Act 1983, cannot grant a valid power of attorney during a lucid interval. The authority for this assertion is the case of *Re Walker [1905] 1 Ch 160*, where the illegitimate daughter of Benjamin Walker was found to be a lunatic. She suffered from delusions but, at the time she executed a deed poll, she fully understood what was happening and was not suffering from any insane delusions. Vaughan Williams LJ said at page 173:

'I do not think I need say much more with respect to the present application than we ought not to recognise this deed in any way. The Court ought to treat this deed as entirely void, on the plain and simple ground that its execution is inconsistent with the control which the Crown has the right and duty of exercising over the property of a lunatic, and that is a sufficient reason for the conclusion at which we have arrived.'

If there is any doubt about the capacity of a person to grant a power of attorney, his or her doctor should be asked to confirm that the person is capable of managing his or her own affairs. However, there is no mandatory requirement that this should be done.

Even though a power may have been validly granted, an ordinary power will be revoked by the subsequent mental incapacity of the donor. An enduring power will not be so revoked, but the donee of the power is under a duty to register it as soon as he has reason to believe that the donor is or is becoming mentally incapable (s 4(1) EPAA 1985; see CHAPTER 7).

Trustees and ordinary powers of attorney

9.5   The Trustee Delegation Act 1999, which came into force on 1 March 2000, has substantially amended the law. Most of the provisions of the Act only apply to powers created after the commencement of the Act and, where relevant, these have been noted in the text.

Section 10(1) Powers of Attorney Act 1971 provides for a general power of attorney in a specified form, but a trustee cannot use this general power to delegate his powers and discretions as s 10(2) specifically states that the section does not apply to functions which the donor has as a trustee or personal representative or as tenant for life or statutory owner within the meaning of the Settled Land Act 1925. This is still the position, but not in relation to powers within s 1 Trustee Delegation Act 2000 (see below).

Section 82(1) Charities Act 1993 permits charity trustees to confer on not less than two of their body a general or limited authority to execute in the names and on behalf of the trustees assurances or other deeds and/or instruments for giving effect to transactions to which the trustees are a party. Under s 82(2) the authority can be conferred in writing or by resolution of a meeting of the trustees.

Section 9 Trusts of Land and Appointment of Trustees Act 1996 extended the powers of trustees to delegate, although it is a limited power.

Section 9(1) provides that trustees of land can delegate any of their functions by power of attorney. The attorney must be a beneficiary of full age, and must also be entitled to an interest in possession in land subject to the trust. The power must be given by all the trustees jointly, and may be revoked by one or more of them, unless expressed to be irrevocable and to be given by way of security. If another person is appointed trustee, the power is revoked, although the death of any of the original appointors will not cause a revocation. Similarly, if an appointor ceases to be a trustee for any reason, the power will not be revoked (s 9(3)).

The delegation can be for any period or can be indefinite (s 9(5)), but an enduring power cannot be used (s 9(6)) for the purposes of delegation of their functions under s 9(1).

Section 9(4) provides that if the attorney ceases to be a person beneficially entitled to an interest in possession in land, and is the sole attorney, the power is revoked. If there is more than one attorney, the power is still exercisable by the other beneficiaries, provided that the functions delegated to them are specified to be exercised by them jointly and not separately, and they continue to be beneficially entitled to an interest in possession in the land in question.

Section 9(7) provides that the beneficiaries to whom functions have been delegated under s 9(1) are in the same position as trustees with the same duties and liabilities. However, they are not regarded as trustees for any other purpose, including in particular any enactment permitting the delegation of functions by trustees or imposing requirements relating to the payment of capital money. This means that the life tenant cannot give a valid receipt for capital; instead it must be paid to at least two trustees or a trust corporation.

Section 9(8) deals with the liability of the trustees for the acts and defaults of the attorneys. The trustees are only liable if they did not exercise reasonable care in deciding to delegate the function to the beneficiary or beneficiaries.

Section 9(2) provides protection for persons dealing with the attorney. It provides that if a person deals with the attorney in good faith, the attorney shall be presumed to have been a person to whom the functions could be delegated unless that other person has knowledge at the time of the transaction that he was not such a person.

Subsequent purchasers of land are also protected if the person dealing with the attorney makes a statutory declaration before or within three months after completion of the purchase that he dealt in good faith and did not know that the attorney was a person to whom the functions could not be delegated.

The section applies to trusts where a beneficiary has a life interest, and also to co-ownership where the trustees and beneficiaries are different persons. It is believed that little use is made of this provision – the author has never used it himself, and has never met a solicitor who is aware of the section, let alone used it!

Section 1(1) of the Trustee Delegation Act 1999 ('TDA') provides that the donee of an ordinary and an enduring power of attorney can exercise the trustee functions of the donor in relation to:

(a)   land;

(b)   capital proceeds of a conveyance of land; or

(c)   income from land.

It is immaterial whether or not the donor is a sole trustee, or is a joint trustee (s 1(2)(b)). However, the donor must have a beneficial interest in the land, its proceeds or income when the act is done.

Thus if spouses hold land on trust for themselves as joint tenants, and one executes an ordinary power of attorney in favour of a child, that child will be able to exercise the trustee functions of the parent and will be able to give a valid receipt for capital money if the land is sold. Note that s 7 preserves the two trustee rule so that two people must sign any transfer of real property in order to give a valid receipt for capital money. Spouses who are co-owners of the matrimonial home can appoint each other, but one cannot sign a transfer of the home as attorney and in their personal capacity. Whilst it is relatively easy to appoint another trustee, it may be desirable to appoint different children or persons as attorneys in order to comply with s 7. The same rules apply to co-owners who are not spouses. These issues are considered at para 9.22 in connection with enduring powers of attorney.

Section 1(1) can be excluded by the instrument, and has effect subject to the terms of that instrument (s 1(3)).

What is the position if the donee of the power does an act which would be a breach of trust if committed by the donor? Section 1(4) provides that the donor will be liable in this situation. However, the donor is not liable by reason only that the function is exercised by the donee. Section 1(4) is subject to any contrary intention expressed in the trust instrument and has effect subject to the terms of such an instrument (s 1(5)).

Section 1(6) provides that the fact it appears that in dealing with any shares or stock the donee of a power of attorney is exercising a function by virtue of s 1(1) does not affect with any notice of any trust a person in whose books the shares are, or stock is, registered or inscribed. Thus registrars of companies do not need to take any account of the fact that it is clear the attorney is exercising trustee powers.

If the donee of a power of attorney is acting under a statutory provision or a provision in the instrument (if any) creating the trust, under which the donor of the power is expressly authorised to delegate the exercise of all or any of his trustee functions by power of attorney, he is acting under a trustee delegation power and is not to be regarded as exercising a trustee function by virtue of s 1(1).

Section 1 only applies if the donor of the power has a beneficial interest in the land. How can a purchaser from the attorney be certain that this is the case? Section 2 provides that an appropriate statement is, in favour of a purchaser, conclusive evidence that the donor of the power had a beneficial interest in the property at the time of the doing of the act. An 'appropriate statement' means a signed statement made by the donee –

(a) when doing the act in question, or

(b) at any other time within the period of three months beginning with the day on which the act is done,

that the donor has a beneficial interest in the property at the time of the donee doing the act (s 2(3)). If the appropriate statement is false, the donee is liable in the same way as he would be if the statement were contained in a statutory declaration.

Section 10(2) of the Powers of Attorney Act 1971 provides that a general power of attorney in the form set out in Schedule 1 to that Act, or a similar form, does not confer on the donee of the power any authority to exercise functions of the donor as trustee. Section 3 TDA provides that s 10 is now subject to s 1 TDA. Thus the donee of a general power can exercise the trustee powers of the donor if that donor has a beneficial interest in the land, proceeds or income.

Section 5 TDA has substituted a new s 25 in the Trustee Act 1925. The two main changes are that, where there are two trustees, the other trustee can be appointed attorney, and the introduction of a new prescribed form. Section 25(1) provides that notwithstanding any rule of law to the contrary a trustee may, by power of attorney, delegate the execution or exercise of all or any of the trusts, powers and discretions vested in him as trustee either alone or jointly with another person or persons. A trust corporation may be an attorney, and an enduring power can be used.

A delegation under this section commences with the date of execution of the power if the instrument makes no provision as to the commencement of the delegation, and lasts for twelve months or any shorter period specified by the instrument creating the power (s 25(2)).

Section 25(6) sets out a form which can be used (see APPENDIX 1). If a single donor uses this form, or a form to the like effect but expressed to be made under s 25(5), it operates to delegate the person identified in the form as the single donee of the power the execution and exercise of all the trusts, powers and discretions vested in the donor as trustee under the single trust so identified. The form is also effective where the donor is a joint trustee.

The donor must give written notice of the giving of the power to –

(a)   each person (other than himself), if any, who under any instrument creating the trust has power (whether alone or jointly) to appoint a new trustee; and

(b)   each of the other trustees, if any.

The written notice must specify:

(a)   the date on which the power comes into operation;

(b)   its duration;

(c)   the donee of the power;

(d)   the reason why the power is given; and

(e)   where only some are delegated, the trusts, powers, and discretions that are.

The notice must be given within seven days of the giving of the power.

Failure to comply with subs (4) does not invalidate any act done or instrument executed by the donee in favour of a person dealing with the donee of the power.

What happens if the donee of the power commits a breach of trust? Section 25(7) provides that the donor of the power is liable for the acts or defaults of the donee in the same manner as if they were the acts or defaults of the donor.

Section 25(8) provides that for the purpose of executing or exercising the trusts or powers delegated to him, the donee may exercise any of the powers conferred on the donor as trustee by statute or by the instrument creating the trust, including power, for the purpose of the transfer of any inscribed stock, himself to delegate to an attorney power to transfer, but not including the power of delegation conferred by this section. In effect, the donee stands in the shoes of the donor, and can delegate the power to do the administrative act of transfer to another attorney but, not the decision whether or not to sell.

Section 25(9) provides that the fact it appears from any power of attorney given under that section, or from any evidence required for the purposes of any such power of attorney or otherwise, that in dealing with any stock the donee of the power is acting in the execution of a trust, that shall not be deemed for any purpose to affect any person in whose books the stock is inscribed or registered with any notice of the trust. Thus the registrar of a company need not take any notice of a trust even if it is clear from the power of attorney that the donor is a trustee.

Section 25(10) provides that the section applies as much to a personal representative, tenant for life and statutory owner as it applies to a trustee. However, the written notice as required by s 25(4) has to be given –

(a)   in the case of a personal representative to each of the other personal representatives, if any, except any executor who has renounced probate;

(b)   in the case of a tenant for life, to the trustees of the settlement and to each person, if any, who together with the person giving the notice constitutes the tenant for life; and

(c)   in the case of a statutory owner, to each of the persons, if any, who together with the person giving the notice constitute the statutory owner and, in the case of a statutory owner by virtue of s 23(1)(a) of the Settled Land Act 1925, to the trustees of the settlement.

Section 7 TDA preserves the two trustees rule so that if land is to be sold, delegation to a sole co-trustee does not mean that the sole co-trustee can give a valid receipt for capital money (see 9.6 below). Thus if spouses are holding the legal estate on trust for themselves and one grants a power of attorney under s 25 to the other, the donee of the power cannot give a valid receipt for capital money.

The Trustee Act 2000 contains wide powers enabling trustees collectively to employ agents, delegate their asset management functions and appoint nominees and custodians. These powers can be exercised without granting powers of attorney, and so strictly are outside the remit of this book. However, APPENDIX 4 contains details of the powers.

Joint tenants or tenants in common/co-owners and ordinary powers of attorney

9.6   Frequently spouses or partners hold the legal estate in their home as trustees for themselves in equity as joint tenants or tenants in common.

Section 1 TDA, which applies only to powers created after the commencement of the TDA, provides that the donee of a power of attorney can exercise trustee functions in relation to land, capital proceeds of a conveyance of land, or income from land, provided the donor has a beneficial interest in land at the time when the act is done. Section 25 of the Trustee Act 1925 as substituted by TDA s 5 permits delegation, where there are two trustees, by one trustee to the other. However, s 7 preserves the two trustees rule. Section 7(1) provides that a requirement imposed by an enactment:

(a)   that capital money be paid to, or dealt with as directed by, at least two trustees or that a valid receipt for capital money be given otherwise than by a sole trustee; or

(b)   that, in order for an interest or power to be overreached, a conveyance or deed be executed by at least two trustees,

is not satisfied by money being paid to or dealt with as directed by, or a receipt for money being given by, a relevant attorney or by a conveyance or deed being executed by such an attorney. 'Relevant attorney' means a person (other than a trust corporation within the meaning of the Trustee Act 1925) who is acting either –

(a)   both as a trustee and as attorney for one or more other trustees, or

(b)   as attorney for two or more trustees,

and who is not acting together with any other person or persons.

The effect of these provisions is that spouses or partners should be wary of delegating to each other or the same person as it may then be difficult to comply with s 7.

Section 7(3) provides that the section applies whether a relevant attorney is acting under a power created before the commencement of the TDA.

Whilst in theory spouses and cohabitees who are co-owners could delegate their powers as trustees by means of an ordinary power, in practice they will not do so as such a power will be revoked by the subsequent mental incapacity of the donor. They are far more likely to delegate their powers by means of an enduring power of attorney, which will not be revoked by the subsequent mental incapacity of the donor. These are considered in 9.22 below.

Personal representatives, tenants for life and statutory owners and ordinary powers of attorney

9.7   Tenants for life and statutory owners occur when land is subject to a settlement within the Settled Land Act 1925; these are not very common, and it is no longer possible to create one since the Trusts of Land and Appointment of Trustees Act 1996 came into force on 1 January 1997.

Section 25(8) Trustee Act 1925 permits personal representatives, tenants for life and statutory owners to delegate in the same manner as trustees, but the requirements as to notice are different. They are as follows:

* *Personal representatives:* notice must be given to each of the other personal representatives, if any, except any executor who has renounced probate.

* *Tenants for life:* notice must be given to the trustees of the settlement and to each person, if any, who – together with the person giving the notice – constitutes the tenant for life.

- *Statutory owners:* notice must be given to each person, if any, who – together with the person giving the notice – constitutes the statutory owner. If there is no tenant for life, any person of full age on whom such powers are by the settlement expressed to be conferred has the powers of the tenant for life (s 23(1)(a) Settled Land Act 1925). In this situation, notice must also be given to the trustees of the settlement.

Companies

9.8   Companies can grant powers of attorney. Section 38(1) Companies Act 1985 provides that a company may, by writing under its common seal, empower any person, either generally or in respect of any specified matters, as its attorney, to execute deeds on its behalf in any place elsewhere than in the United Kingdom. Subsection (2) provides that a deed signed by such an attorney on behalf of the company and under his seal binds the company and has the same effect as if it were under the company's common seal.

Section 35 Companies Act 1985, as amended by the Companies Act 1989 which came into force on 1 July 1990, provides that the validity of an act done by a company will not be called into question on the ground of lack of capacity by reason of anything in the company's memorandum. Section 35A(1) provides that in favour of a person dealing with a company in good faith, the power of the board of directors to bind the company, or authorise others to do so, will be deemed to be free of any limitation under the company's constitution. Under s 35A(2)(b) a person will not be regarded as acting in bad faith by reason only of his knowing that an act is beyond the powers of the directors under the company's constitution. Section 35A(2)(c) provides that a person will be presumed to have acted in good faith unless the contrary is proved. Section 35B provides that a party to a transaction with a company is not bound to enquire (i) as to whether the transaction is permitted by the company's memorandum or (ii) as to any limitation on the powers of the board of directors to bind the company or authorise others to do so. Article 71 of Table A provides:

> 'The directors may, by power of attorney or otherwise, appoint any person to be the agent of the company for such purposes and on such conditions as they determine, including authority for the agent to delegate all or any of his powers.'

The effect of these provisions is that a third party can deal safely with an attorney appointed by a company, unless the third party is acting in bad faith; the mere knowledge that an act is beyond the powers of the directors does not mean that the third party is acting in bad faith.

(For a more detailed discussion of this section, readers are referred to more specialist works on the subject, such as *Tolley's Company Law*.)

Administrators, administrative receivers and liquidators

9.9 Schedule 1 para 11 Insolvency Act 1986 authorises an administrator or administrative receiver to appoint an agent to do any business which he is unable to do himself or which can more conveniently be done by an agent.

Schedule 4 Pt III para 12 authorises a liquidator to appoint an agent to do any business which the liquidator is unable to do himself.

Within the limits of these powers, administrators, administrative receivers, and liquidators can appoint attorneys.

Trustees in bankruptcy

9.10 A trustee in bankruptcy can execute a power of attorney (s 314(5) and Sch 5 para 14 Insolvency Act 1986).

Public authorities

9.11 These are statutory creations, and have only the powers conferred by the statute creating them. Section 101(1) Local Government Act 1972 provides:

'Subject to any express provision contained in this Act or any Act passed after this Act, a local authority may arrange for the discharge of any of their functions –

(a)by a committee, a sub-committee or an officer of the authority.'

Section 111(1) provides:

'. . . a local authority shall have power to do anything (whether or not involving the expenditure, borrowing or lending of money or the acquisition of or disposal of any property or rights) which is calculated to facilitate, or is conducive or incidental to, the discharge of any of their functions'.

A local authority can thus grant a power of attorney to an officer of the authority; possibly s 111(1) permits the grant of a power of attorney to an independent third party, provided the grant was calculated to facilitate, or was conducive or incidental to, the discharge of the functions of the local authority, although there may be limits on the powers which can be delegated. Readers are referred to more specialised works for a discussion on this topic.

Drunkards

9.12   If a donor, when granting a power of attorney, is so drunk as not to know what he is doing, the grant is at least voidable, and may be void. In *Gore v Gibson (1845) 13 M & W 623, 153 ER 260* at page 626, 262 Parke B said:

'But where the party, when he enters into the contract, is in such a state of drunkenness as not to know what he is doing, and particularly when it appears that this was known to the other party, the contract is void altogether, and he cannot be compelled to perform it.'

On sobering up, however, the donor can ratify the power. Ratification is discussed in CHAPTER 8.

Enemy aliens

9.13   A person who lives or carries on business in an enemy state cannot appoint an attorney to act for him in the United Kingdom (*O'Mealey v Wilson and Another (1808) 1 Camp 482, 170 ER 1029* and *M'Connell v Hector (1802) 3 Bos & P 113, 127 ER 61*). However, a citizen of an enemy country, who neither lives nor carries on business there, can appoint an attorney to act for him in the United Kingdom.

It may be that the donor of a power living in occupied territory can grant an enduring power of attorney. In *Hangkam Kwintong Woo v Lin Lan Fong [1951] 2 All ER 567* the donor of a power of attorney lived in Hong Kong, which at the time was in the occupation of the Japanese. After the donor of the power had left Hong Kong, the donee sold a house belonging to the donor. It was held that the power was still in existence at the date of the sale. In delivering the judgment of the Privy Council, Lord Simonds said at page 572:

'The result seems plainly to ensue that, whatever consequences may follow outside the occupied territory if one of its inhabitants, who has left it, seeks to maintain or to initiate relations with another who has stayed within it, yet the courts of that country cannot regard either him who has left or him who has stayed behind as enemies of the King or enemies of each other.'

Duress

9.14   If a person is compelled to sign a power of attorney by force or threat of force, it will be void so far as the donor and donee are concerned (*Alexander Baton v Alexander Ewan Armstrong and Others [1976] AC 104*). The positions of third parties dealing with an attorney acting under a power tainted with duress is unclear; if the third party is innocent of any wrongdoing, the transaction may bind the donor, although the attorney will be liable in damages to the donor (see CHAPTER 11).

Force or threat of force to a near relative may also be sufficient to invalidate a power, but duress to goods is probably not sufficient. In *Pao On v Lau Yiu Long [1979] 3 All ER 65* at page 79 Lord Scarman said:

'It is doubtful, however, whether at common law any duress other than duress to the person sufficed to render a contract voidable . . .'

Economic duress may also invalidate a power. In *Pao On v Lau Yiu Long* Lord Scarman stated at page 79:

'In their Lordships' view, there is nothing contrary to principle in recognising economic duress as a factor which may render a contract voidable, provided always that the basis of such recognition is that it must amount to a coercion of will, which vitiates consent. It must be shown that the payment made or the contract entered into was not a voluntary act.'

In *Atlas Express Ltd v Kafco (Importers and Distributors) Ltd [1989] 1 All ER 641* the plaintiffs were carriers, and they agreed to carry basketware for the defendants at a price of £1.10 per carton. They then demanded a minimum of £440 per load. The defendants were unable to find an alternative carrier, and had to agree to the minimum charge in order to save a contract with a retail chain. It was held that the consent was vitiated by economic duress.

If a creditor forces a debtor to give him a power of attorney by threatening to make the debtor bankrupt, it is probable that the power will be invalid.

Undue influence

9.15   Powers of attorney will frequently be granted in family situations, and it may be that the 'attorney' will use undue influence to procure the execution of a power in his favour. If the power is tainted with undue influence, it can be set aside, and any transaction in favour of the attorney is also liable to be set aside.

What constitutes undue influence? In *Allcard v Skinner (1887) 36 Ch D 145* at page 171, Cotton LJ said:

'The question is – Does the case fall within the principles laid down by the decisions of the Court of Chancery in setting aside voluntary gifts executed by the parties who at the time were under such influence as, in the opinion of the court, enabled the donor afterwards to set the gift aside? These decisions may be divided into two classes – First, where the court has been satisfied that the gift was the result of influence expressly used by the donee for the purpose; second, where the relations between the donor and donee have at or shortly before the execution of the gift been such as to raise a presumption that the donee had influence over the donor. In such a case the court sets aside the voluntary gift, unless it is proved that in fact the gift was the spontaneous act of the donor acting under circumstances which enabled him to exercise an independent will and which justifies the court in holding that the gift was the result of a free exercise of the donor's will. The first class of case may be considered as depending on the principle that no one shall be allowed to retain any benefit arising from his fraud or wrongful act. In the second class of cases the court interferes, not on the ground that any wrongful act has been committed by the donee, but on the ground of public policy, and to prevent the relations which existed between the parties and the influence arising therefrom being abused.'

In *Bank of Credit and Commerce International SA v Aboody [1992] 4 All ER 955* at 964 the Court of Appeal adopted the following classification:

Class 1:   actual undue influence.

Class 2:   presumed undue influence, which can be subdivided into:

Class 2a: relationships where there is a presumption of undue influence, for example solicitor and client.

Class 2b: relationships not within class 2a, but where the complainant proves the *de facto* existence of a relationship under which the complainant generally reposed trust and confidence in the wrongdoer, the existence of such a relationship raises the presumption of undue influence.

In *Royal Bank of Scotland plc v Etridge (No 2)* [2001] 3 WLR 1021 Lord Nicholls at pages 1032–1033 stressed that even if there was a presumption of undue influence, more was required to reverse the burden of proof. He said at page 1033:

'So something more is needed before the law reverses the burden of proof, something which calls for an explanation. When that something more is present the greater the disadvantage to the vulnerable person, the more urgent must be the explanation before the presumption will be regarded as rebutted.'

In the House of Lords case, *Barclays Bank plc v O'Brien [1993] 4 All ER 417*, Lord Browne-Wilkinson discussed the effect of undue influence on third parties. If the third party had actual or constructive notice of the undue influence, then any transaction affecting the third party could be set aside. Presumably if undue influence is used to persuade a donor to grant a power, any transaction with a third party will be voidable if the third party is aware or should have been aware of the undue influence.

Fraud

9.16   If a donor is fraudulently induced to execute a power of attorney, for example, by a misrepresentation that the power is another document, or by a misrepresentation as to its effect, any transactions benefiting the donee can be set aside. Transactions between innocent third parties and a donee acting under a power tainted with fraud may not be set aside, although the attorney will be liable in damages to the donor.

II. Capacity of donor to grant an enduring power

Minors

9.17　　The rules appear to be the same as for ordinary powers. The Law Commission, in its report on *The Incapacitated Principal* (Law Com No 122 Cmnd 8977) stated at page 22 that infants could grant enduring powers.

Mentally disordered persons

9.18　　It may be that different tests apply to ordinary powers and enduring powers of attorney. In *Re K; Re F [1988] 1 All ER 358* donors executed enduring powers. At the time when they executed the powers, both donors were verging on mental incapacity to manage their own affairs, but they understood the nature and effect of the enduring power. Hoffmann J held that both powers were valid. He pointed out that the EPAA 1985 did not specify the mental capacity needed to execute a power of attorney. A power of attorney is normally revoked by the subsequent mental incapacity of the donor (see CHAPTERS 6 AND 7), but Hoffmann J rejected the view that a person suffering from mental incapacity which would have revoked a power could not validly create one. He said at pages 362, 363:

> 'In practice it is likely that many enduring powers will be executed when symptoms of mental incapacity have begun to manifest themselves. These symptoms may result in the donor being mentally incapable in the statutory sense that she is unable on a regular basis to manage her property and affairs. But, as in the case of Mrs. F, she may execute the power with full understanding and with the intention of taking advantage of the Act to have her affairs managed by an attorney of her choice rather than having them put in the hands of the Court of Protection. I can think of no reason of policy why this intention should be frustrated.'

He then went on to define what degree of understanding is involved. He said:

> 'Plainly one cannot expect that the donor should have been able to pass an examination on the provisions of the 1985 Act. At the other extreme, I do not think that it would be sufficient if he realised only that it gave [the donee of the power] power to look after his property. Counsel as *amicus curiae* helpfully summarised the matters which the donor should have understood in order that he can be said to have understood the nature and effect of the power: first, if such be the terms of the power, that the attorney will be able to assume complete authority over the donor's affairs; second, if such be the terms of the power, that the attorney will in general be able to do anything with the donor's property which the donor could have done; third, that the authority will continue if the donor should be or become mentally incapable; fourth, that if he should be or become mentally incapable, the power will be irrevocable without confirmation by the court.'

It is uncertain whether a similar test is applicable to ordinary powers; they are of course different in that there are considerable safeguards in the EPAA 1985 which do not apply to ordinary powers.

In *Re W [2000] 1 All ER 175*, which has already been referred to at 7.8 above, an enduring power of attorney was challenged on the ground that the donor did not have capacity to grant it. The judge held that as he was not satisfied that the donor did not have capacity, the power should be registered.

Trustees and enduring powers of attorney

Position before the Trustee Delegation Act 1999 came into force

9.19   Section 2(8) EPAA 1985 provided that a power of attorney under s 25 Trustee Act 1925 could not be an enduring power. However, s 3(3) EPAA 1985 authorised an attorney under a general or limited enduring power to execute or exercise, without obtaining any consent, all or any of the trusts, powers or discretions vested in the donor as trustee. The attorney could also give a valid receipt for capital or other money paid without the concurrence of any other person. These powers were subject to any conditions and restrictions contained in the instrument creating the power of attorney. RT Oerton in an article in the *Solicitors' Journal* (10 January 1986) points out at page 23 that this provision did not form part of the original proposals of the Law Commission, and that its effect was very wide.

Position since the Trustee Delegation Act 1999 came into force

9.20   Both s 1 TDA and s 25 Trustee Act 1925 apply to enduring powers as well as ordinary powers (s 6 TDA); for a fuller discussion of these provisions, see 9.5 above. Section 3(3) was inserted at a late stage in the EPAA, and was perhaps much wider in its effect than was intended or desirable. The TDA recognises this, and s 4 provides that s 3(3) EPAA is not to apply to enduring powers created after the commencement of the Act. It also provides that s 3(3) ceases to apply to enduring powers created before the commencement of the Act –

(a)   where an application for the registration of the instrument creating such an enduring power is made before the commencement of the Act, or during the period of one year from that commencement, and the instrument is registered pursuant to that application (whether before commencement or during or after that period), when the registration of that instrument is cancelled, and

(b)   if the application is finally refused during or after that period, when the application is finally refused.

In all other cases, it ceases to apply at the end of the period of one year from the commencement (s 4(2) and s 4(3)).

The TDA came into force on 1 March 2000.

Section 4(5) provides that an application is finally refused –

(a)   if the application is withdrawn or any appeal is abandoned, when the application is withdrawn or the appeal is abandoned, and

(b)   otherwise, when the proceedings on the application (including any proceedings on, or in consequence of an appeal) have been determined and any time for appealing or further appealing has expired.

Thus s 3(3) EPAA ceased to apply to enduring powers created before the commencement of the TDA at the end of the period of one year from the commencement of the TDA if no application for registration was made. If the power is registered, s 3(3) ceases to apply when the registration is cancelled. Solicitors may wish to notify clients who are trustees but not beneficiaries and who have granted enduring powers prior to the commencement of the TDA of the effect of the repeal of s 3(3).

Note that s 1 TDA 1999 will apply to pre-TDA powers if the donor has a beneficial interest in the land, proceeds or income when s 3(3) EPAA ceases to apply. In this situation, the power will be effective to delegate the trustee powers vested in the donor.

Before dealing with the legal estate vested in a trustee who is incapable by reason of mental disorder, section 22 of the Law of Property Act 1925 imposes a requirement to appoint a new trustee or discharge an incapable trustee. Section 9 TDA has added a subsection to s 22 of the Law of Property Act 1925 to make it clear that where the donee of an enduring power is entitled to act for the incapable trustee, there is no need to appoint a new trustee or discharge the incapable trustee.

Joint tenants or tenants in common/co-owners and enduring powers of attorney

Position before the Trustee Delegation Act 1999 came into force

9.21   If an enduring power had been granted, s 3(3) EPAA 1985 authorised the donee *inter alia* to execute any of the trusts vested in the donor. A trustee who held land on trust for joint tenants or tenants in common, and who granted an enduring power, conferred authority on the attorney to exercise his powers as trustee. A co-trustee could be appointed, and that co-trustee could give a valid receipt for capital money. It is believed that enduring powers were frequently granted in this situation, but RT Oerton argued that an enduring power of attorney granted solely for the purpose of exercising trustee powers vested in the donor might be invalid (see *Butterworth's Wills, Probate and Administration Service*). However, it had become common practice for spouses or cohabitees who were co-owners to grant each other enduring powers of attorney. If one became mentally incapable, then the other would sign any transfer as attorney and in their personal capacity.

Position after the Trustee Delegation Act 1999 came into force

9.22   Section 3(3) EPAA does not apply to enduring powers created after the commencement of the TDA. However, there are various other statutory provisions enabling trustees to delegate their powers.

Section 1 TDA enables a trustee to delegate his powers to an attorney as long as the trustee has a beneficial interest in the land, proceeds or income.

Section 25 Trustee Act 1925 as amended permits a trustee to delegate for a period not exceeding one year.

Section 9 does permit trustees to delegate, but an enduring power cannot be used.

The most appropriate provision for co-owners to use is s 1 TDA. However, s 7 preserves the two trustee rule, so that trustees should be wary about delegating to themselves, or the same person.

Co-owners now have the following options:

(a)   Co-owners can delegate their powers by means of an enduring power to the children of the donor, or the other co-owner and a child of the donor.

(b)   Section 7 does not apply to personalty, and so co-owners can grant each other enduring powers limited to the personal estate. A separate power – limited to the real estate – could then be granted to each other and a child. If one co-owner then becomes mentally incapable, the power can be registered, but there will be at least two people to sign any transfer so as to comply with s 7.

(c)   Another possibility is for both co-owners to appoint each other attorneys under enduring powers. If one becomes mentally incapable, the other can make use of s 8 TDA to appoint another trustee.

The section inserts a new section into s 36 Trustee Act 1925. Section 36(6A) confers on the donee of an enduring power a limited power to appoint a new trustee. The subsection applies to a person who is either:

(a)   both a trustee and attorney for the other trustee (if one other), or for both of the other trustees (if two others), under a registered power; or

(b)   attorney under a registered power for the trustee (if one) or for both or each of the trustees (if two or three) (s 36(6A)).

Thus a trustee who is one of two trustees, and is appointed attorney by the other trustee, can appoint another trustee. Similarly a trustee who is one of three trustees and is appointed attorney by the other two trustees can appoint a fourth.

An attorney who is not a trustee can also exercise this power, but must have been appointed by all the trustees. Note that all the powers must be registered.

The attorney must as attorney under the power intend:

(a)   to exercise any function of the trustee or trustees by virtue of s 1(1) Trustee Delegation Act 1999; or

(b)   to exercise any function of the trustee or trustees in relation to any land, capital proceeds of a conveyance of land or income from land by virtue of its delegation to him under s 25 Trustee Delegation Act 1999 or the instrument (if any) creating the trust (s 36(6B) Trustee Act).

Thus the attorney must intend to exercise any trustee function, but it is immaterial whether the power is granted under s 1 Trustee Delegation Act 1999, or s 25 Trustee Act as substituted.

Section 36(6D) states that s 36(6A) is subject to any contrary intention expressed in the instrument creating the power of attorney (or, where more than one, any of them) or the instrument (if any) creating the trust, and has effect subject to the terms of those instruments.

Spouses or cohabitees could make use of this power to appoint each other as attorneys. If one becomes mentally incapable, the one retaining capacity can appoint another trustee. If the co-owned house is then sold, the transfer can be executed by the spouse retaining capacity in his or her personal capacity, as attorney for the spouse lacking capacity and the additional trustee, thereby satisfying the requirements of s 7.

Pre-TDA powers

9.23   It should be noted that s 7 applies to enduring powers of attorney whenever created so that at least two persons are required to give a receipt for capital money. However, this is without prejudice to the continuing application of s 3(3) EPAA. Section 3(3) EPAA will continue to apply to enduring powers where registered before the TDA came into force, or if application for registration was made within twelve months of the TDA coming into force and the power is duly registered (see 9.19–9.20). In these situations, it seems that the co-owner retaining capacity can execute any transfer as attorney and in his personal capacity.

If the enduring power was not registered before the date when the TDA came into force, and no application for registration was made before 28 February 2001, s 3(3) no longer applies. In the case of co-owners, s 1 TDA may apply, so that the enduring power is still effective to delegate trustee powers. However, this may not be of much use to co-owners who have granted enduring powers of attorney to each other as s 7 requires that at least two persons should sign any transfer, conveyance or mortgage. If both parties are still mentally capable, there is of course no problem. They can execute and transfer in their personal capacities. If, however, one or both has become mentally incapable, the one retaining mental capacity cannot sign the transfer both as attorney and in his personal capacity. In this situation, the co-owner lacking mental capacity can be removed as a trustee with the consent of the Court of Protection and another trustee appointed.

Personal representatives, tenants for life and statutory owners and enduring powers of attorney

Position before the Trustee Delegation Act 1999 came into force

9.24   There is nothing in the EPAA 1985 dealing specifically with the question of whether the donee of an enduring power can exercise the powers of a donor in his capacity as a personal representative.

If a donor was a tenant for life or statutory owner, he or she was a trustee (ss 107(1) and 16(1) Settled Land Act 1925). Section 3(3) EPAA 1985 was probably wide enough to permit the donee to exercise the powers enjoyed by the donor as tenant for life or statutory owner.

Position after the Trustee Delegation Act 1999 came into force

9.25   Section 3(3) does not apply to enduring powers created after the commencement of TDA, and its application to powers created before the commencement of the Act is restricted. Section 25 permits personal representatives, tenants for life and statutory owners to delegate (see 9.7 above). Section 1 permits the donee of a power of attorney to exercise trustee functions if the donor has a beneficial interest in the land, proceeds and income (see 9.5 above).

Companies

9.26   A company cannot create an enduring power of attorney – it is only individuals who can do so (s 1(1) EPAA 1985).

Administrators, administrative receivers, liquidators and trustees in bankruptcy

9.27   It is arguable that s 3(3) EPAA 1985 permitted the donee to exercise any powers vested in the donor as an administrator, administrative receiver, liquidator or trustee in bankruptcy. However, as already mentioned s 3(3) has been repealed.

Public authorities

9.28   A public authority cannot grant an enduring power.

Drunkards, enemy aliens, duress, undue influence and fraud

9.29   The rules are the same as for ordinary powers. Under s 8(4)(e) and (f) EPAA 1985 the court must cancel a registration on being satisfied that the power was not a valid and subsisting power when registration was effected, or on being satisfied that fraud or undue pressure was used to induce the donor to create the power.

III. Void powers of attorney – third party rights

Ordinary powers

9.30   If the power of attorney is void, for example because of mental incapacity, or because the donor is an enemy alien, any transaction entered into by the attorney will also be void. In *Daily Telegraph Newspaper Company Ltd v McLaughlin [1904] AC 777,* P executed a power of attorney whilst of unsound mind. Acting under the authority, the donee executed a transfer of shares. The High Court of Australia held that the power was void, and the transfer a nullity. The Privy Council declined to grant leave to appeal. Lord Macnaghten said at page 779:

> 'After careful review of the facts the High Court, differing from the judge of first instance, came to the conclusion that when the plaintiff executed the power of attorney in question he had no knowledge of what he was doing, except that he knew that he was signing his name, which under the circumstances was as described by Dr. Lamrock, who was his medical attendant, "a mere mechanical act". Having come to this conclusion on the facts of the case, the High Court held that the power of attorney was void, and the deed of transfer a nullity. Now the petitioners, as their Lordships understand, do not propose to contest the finding of the High Court on the question of fact, nor indeed would their Lordships be disposed to advise His Majesty to admit an appeal on such a question.'

At page 780 it was stated:

> 'Now, if the power of attorney is mere waste paper, it is difficult to see how anything which rests on it as the foundation and groundwork of the whole superstructure can be of any validity, whether the transaction is beneficial to the lunatic or not. The risk to a company acting on a power of attorney is, no doubt, considerable, but the directors can protect themselves to some extent by making inquiries – a precaution not apparently taken in this case.'

This quotation highlights the point that there is very little protection for a person dealing with an attorney under a void power. This topic is discussed in more detail in CHAPTER 12.

Enduring powers

9.31 The basic rule is the same as for ordinary powers, but if the power is registered, s 9 EPAA 1985 may protect a third party. Section 9 is discussed in detail in CHAPTER 12.

IV. Capacity of donee

9.32 Donees of ordinary powers of attorney do not need to have capacity themselves (see *Re D'Angibou; Andrews v Andrews (1880) 15 Ch D 228 CA*), but clearly it is very unwise to appoint an infant or mentally disordered person or drunkard or bankrupt as an attorney.

However, an agent lacking capacity will be liable to the principal or the third party only in so far as the agent would have been liable if the contract had been made in his personal capacity (*Smally v Smally (1700) 1 Eq Ca Abr 6, 21 ER 831,* and see *Law of Agency* (Sweet & Maxwell, 17th edition, 2001) by Bowstead and Reynolds at page 37). For example, a person suffering from mental disorder cannot enter into a valid contract, and will not therefore be liable either to the third party or to his principal. At common law, contracts entered into by infants are voidable at the option of the infant, although they bind the other party. A similar rule applies to contracts entered into by agents who are infants.

If it is intended to grant an enduring power of attorney, s 2(7) EPAA 1985 provides that a power of attorney cannot be an enduring power unless, when he executes the instrument creating it, the attorney is:

(a)   an individual who has attained eighteen years and is not bankrupt; or

(b)   a trust corporation.

Section 13(1) EPAA 1985 defines 'trust corporation' as meaning the Public Trustee or a corporation either appointed by the High Court or the county court (according to their respective jurisdictions) in any particular case to be a trustee or entitled by rules under s 4(3) Public Trustee Act 1906 to act as custodian trustee (the role of the Public Trustee has now passed to the Chief Executive of the Public Guardianship Office).

If joint attorneys are appointed, the reference to the time when the attorney executes the instrument is to be read as a reference to the time when the second or last attorney executes the instrument (Sch 3 Pt I para 1).

Summary

9.33

- Infants can grant powers of attorney, but will be bound by contracts entered into by the donee only if the infant would have been liable if he or she had entered into them personally.

- Mentally disordered persons, drunkards, and enemy aliens cannot grant powers of attorney.

- Trustees, personal representatives, companies, administrators, administrative receivers, liquidators, trustees in bankruptcy, and public authorities can all grant powers of attorney, although there may be limitations on their power to do so. Only individuals can grant enduring powers of attorney.

- Duress, undue influence, and fraud may invalidate a power.

- Donees of a power need not have capacity themselves, but an infant and a bankrupt cannot be an attorney under an enduring power.

- Co-owners can grant enduring powers of attorney to each other, but if one becomes mentally incapable, the other will not be able to give a valid receipt for capital by signing the transfer in his or her personal capacity and as attorney for the other trustee. Another trustee can be appointed under s 8 TDA.

Chapter 10

Duties and rights of donees

10.1   Frequently, the grant of a power of attorney is a family affair where the donor does not expect to remunerate the donee, the donee does not expect to be remunerated by the donor, and neither party intends to enter into a contractual arrangement. This will usually be the case when a parent grants a power of attorney to his or her child, or a spouse grants a power to the other spouse. However, if a client asks a professional person like a solicitor or accountant to act as attorney, there will almost invariably be a contract between the donor and the donee of the power.

Both paid and unpaid attorneys owe similar duties to the donor of the power, although the duties do differ in certain minor respects, and in one major respect.

It should be stressed that if there is a contract between parties, the duties of the parties will depend on the express or implied terms of that contract. The courts are reluctant to imply terms into a contract; in *Lazarus v Cairn Line of Steamships Ltd (1912) 106 LT 378* Scrutton J at page 380 stated:

> 'I read them (the earlier authorities) as deciding (1) that the first thing to consider is the express words the parties have used; (2) that a term they have not expressed is not to be implied because the court thinks it is a reasonable term, but only if the court thinks it is necessarily implied in the nature of the contract the parties have made.'

Despite this reluctance to imply terms into a contract, it is more than likely that terms will have to be implied. If a solicitor or accountant is appointed to act as attorney by a client, it is possible that the parties will not agree any express terms.

I. Duties of donees of ordinary powers

To act

10.2   It is this aspect where there is a major difference between a donee under a contract, and a donee who is not acting pursuant to any contract.

A donee who is not acting under any contract does not have to act under the power of attorney. Of course, the donor and donee will often be related in this situation, and the donee will usually want to exercise the power.

However, a donee who is acting under a contract may be under a contractual duty to act. Whether the donee is or is not under such a duty depends on the express or implied terms of the contract between the donor and donee. If a client gives a solicitor or an accountant a power of attorney, there will usually be a duty on the solicitor or accountant to act.

The question of termination of powers of attorney is discussed in CHAPTER 6, but if the donee is under a contractual obligation to act, the donee may have to continue acting until the contractual obligation has been discharged.

Utmost good faith to the donor

10.3   In *Rothschild v Brookman (1831) 2 Dow & Cl 188, 6 ER 699*, at page 198, 703, Lord Wynford said:

> '. . . and I think it fit that your Lordships should say, in language which cannot be misunderstood, that in these transactions of trust and confidence there must be, on the part of the person trusted, that most marked integrity, that *uberrimae fides*, which cannot leave a doubt as to the fairness of the transaction'.

Many of the duties discussed in this chapter are illustrations of this rule, but for convenience they are dealt with separately.

To keep accounts

10.4   It is essential that the attorney keeps accurate accounts and records. In *Gray v Haig (1855) 20 Beav 219, 52 ER 587,* Sir John Romilly MR said at pages 238 and 239, 594 and 595:

> 'It cannot, however, be too generally known or understood, amongst all persons dealing with each other, in the character of principal and agent, how severely the court deals with any irregularities on the part of the agent, how strictly it requires that he who is the person trusted shall act, in all matters relating to such agency, for the benefit of his principal, and how imperative it is upon him to preserve correct accounts of all his dealings and transactions in that respect, and that the loss and still more destruction of such evidence, by the agent, falls most heavily upon himself.'

An attorney who is a solicitor will of course be bound by the Solicitors' Accounts Rules, and will in any event have to keep accurate records. However, a lay attorney should also keep accurate records. Relatives who are appointed attorneys are under a similar duty (*Dadswell v Jacobs (1887) 34 Ch D 278*).

If the attorney combines the property of the donor with his own so that it is not possible to determine what belongs to the donor, the whole will be taken to belong to the donor (*Lupton v White (1808) 15 Ves 432, 33 ER 817*). Thus it is undesirable for an attorney to combine his own money with the donor's in one bank or building society account; ideally, there should be a separate account for the money belonging to the donor.

To disclose all relevant facts in certain transactions

10.5   The donee of a power of attorney is not prohibited from purchasing the property of the donor of the power, or selling his own property to the donor, provided that he makes full disclosure of all material facts (*Dunne v English (1874) LR 18 Eq 524* and *Armstrong v Jackson [1917] 2 KB 822*). In *Dunne v English,* Sir George Jessel MR said at page 533:

> 'It is not enough for an agent to tell the principal that he is going to have an interest in the purchase, or to have a part in the purchase. He must tell him all the material facts. He must make full disclosure.'

In *McPherson v Watt (1877) 3 App Cas 254 HL*, a Scottish advocate purchased property belonging to two ladies for whom he was agent in the name of his brother. Lord O'Hagan listed at page 266 the requirements for such a transaction to be upheld; the agent must be able to show that:

(a)   he has acted with the most complete faithfulness and fairness;

(b)   his advice has been free from all taint of self-interest;

(c)   he has not misrepresented or concealed anything;

(d)   he has given an adequate price;

(e)   his client has had the advantage of the best professional assistance which, if he had been engaged in a transaction with a third party, he could possibly have afforded;

(f)   if the purchase is to be made in the name of another, this fact has been disclosed.

Similar principles govern the following transactions between the donor and donee of a power of attorney:

- loan of money by donor to donee;

- loan of money by donee to donor;

- the grant of a mortgage by the donor to the donee;

- the grant of a mortgage by the donee to the donor;

- the grant of a lease by the donor to the donee;

- the grant of a lease by the donee to the donor.

This is not an exclusive list, and there may be other transactions which are governed by the same principles.

Even after the power of attorney has terminated, the donee may still be under a duty to disclose all relevant facts. In *Alison v Clayhills (1907) 97 LT 709* Parker J at page 711 said:

'It appears to me to be quite clear that a solicitor is not wholly incapacitated from purchasing or taking a lease from his client, but, where the relationship of solicitor and client exists, the onus of upholding the vitality of such a transaction will rest upon the solicitor. It is, I think, equally clear that although the relationship of solicitor and client in its strict sense has been discontinued, the same principle applies as long as the confidence naturally arising from such a relationship is proved or may be presumed to continue.'

Not to make secret profits

10.6   In *Turnbull v Garden (1869) 38 LJ Ch 331* at page 334 James V-C said:

'What appears in this case shows the danger of allowing even the smallest departure from the rule that a person who is dealing with another man's money ought to give the truest account of what he has done, and ought not to receive anything in the nature of a present or allowance without the full knowledge of the principal that he is so acting.'

An attorney must therefore disclose to the donee of the power any profits or commissions which he receives as a consequence of the agency, or as a consequence of the use of trust property, or as a consequence of the use of confidential information acquired as agent. For example, if the attorney insures the property of the donor, and receives commission from the insurance company, he would have to disclose this commission to the donor of the power. Even if full disclosure is made, the attorney may still have to account for the commission unless the donor agrees that the attorney can retain it. However, if the donor delays taking action to recover secret profits, the agent will be allowed to keep them. In *Great Western Insurance Co v Cunliffe (1874) LR 9 Ch App 525* an insurance company in New York appointed a firm of merchants in London as its agents. The agents arranged reinsurance, and were paid a commission of 5 per cent, and in addition 12 per cent of certain profits. The insurance company discovered what was happening in 1866, but did not object until 1868. It was held that it could not recover the commissions.

Not to exceed the authority conferred by the power

10.7   If the donor has conferred a general power on the attorney, the donee can do anything which the donor could have lawfully done (see s 10(1) Powers of Attorney Act 1971). If the donor has conferred only a limited power on the donee, for example to sell a particular property for not less than a fixed price, the donee must ensure that he acts within the limitations of the power, and sells the property for not less than the fixed price. The donee must not rely on the courts giving a liberal interpretation as limited powers of attorney are construed strictly (see CHAPTER 8).

To take care and be skilful

10.8   Whether or not the grant of a power of attorney has created a contractual relationship, the donee of the power is under a duty to discharge his duties with reasonable care. The standard of care required depends on the qualifications of the donee. In *Harmer v Cornelius (1858) 5 CBNS 236, 141 ER 94*, Willes J at pages 246, 98 said:

> 'When a skilled labourer, artisan, or artist is employed, there is on his own part an implied warranty that he is of skill reasonably competent to the task he undertakes ... Thus, if an apothecary, a watchmaker, or an attorney be employed for reward, they each impliedly undertake to possess and exercise reasonable skill in their several arts. The public profession of an art is a representation and undertaking to all the world that the professor possesses the requisite ability and skill.'

In *Hart & Hodge v John Frame, Son, & Co (1839) 6 C & F 193, 7 ER 670* at pages 209, 676, the Lord Chancellor stated:

> 'Professional men, possessed of a reasonable portion of information and skill, according to the duties they undertake to perform and exercising what they so possess with reasonable care and diligence in the affairs of their employers, certainly ought not to be held liable for errors in judgement, whether in matters of law or discretion. Every case, therefore, ought to depend on its own peculiar circumstances; and when an injury has been sustained which could not have arisen except from the want of such reasonable skill and diligence, or the absence of the employment of either on the part of the attorney, the law holds him liable.'

Thus a far higher standard of care will be expected from a solicitor or accountant than an unqualified person.

It may be that there is a different test for gratuitous donees. In *Beal v South Devon Railway Company (1864) 3 H & C 337, 159 ER 560* Crompton J said at pages 341, 562:

> 'What is reasonable varies in the case of a gratuitous bailee and that of a bailee for hire. From the former is reasonably expected such care and diligence as persons ordinarily use in their own affairs, and such skill as he has. From the latter is reasonably expected care and diligence, such as are exercised in the ordinary and proper course of similar business and such skill as he ought to have, namely the skill usual and requisite in the business for which he receives payment.'

A solicitor who is the donee of a power of attorney, and who is paid, must exercise the skill of a reasonably competent solicitor, but if he is unpaid and is usually incompetent as a solicitor, he need exercise only the skill he applies to his own affairs and the skill he exercises as an incompetent solicitor.

If the donee has a discretion, for example to choose an insurance company with which to insure the donor's property, or an auctioneer to sell it, he will not be liable provided he acts in a *bona fide* manner (*Moore v Mourge (1776) 2 Cowp 479, 98 ER 1197*).

II. Duties of donees of enduring powers

10.9   The duties of donees of enduring powers of attorney are by and large the same as the duties imposed on donees of ordinary powers. However, there is one additional duty imposed on the donees of enduring powers, which is to register the power. If an attorney under an enduring power of attorney has reason to believe that the donor is or is becoming mentally incapable, the attorney must, as soon as practicable, make an application to the court for the registration of the instrument creating the power (s 4(1) and (2) EPAA 1985). This requirement of registration is discussed in CHAPTER 7.

The EPAA 1985 sometimes imposes extra requirements, and these will now be considered.

To act

10.10   Unless there is a contractual obligation to do so, there is no obligation on the donee of an enduring power to act. However, if the donee is under a duty to apply for registration of the power, no disclaimer of the power is valid unless and until the attorney gives notice of it to the court (s 4(6)); similarly, once the power is registered, no disclaimer of the power is valid unless and until the attorney gives notice of it to the court.

The procedural requirements are discussed in CHAPTER 7.

Utmost good faith to the donor

10.11   The same duty applies to the donee of an enduring power and the donee of an ordinary power.

To keep accounts

10.12   The same duty applies to the donee of an enduring power and the donee of an ordinary power.

Once a power is registered, under s 8(2)(b)(ii) EPAA 1985 the court may give directions with respect to the rendering of accounts by the attorney and the production of records kept by him for the purpose, and under s 8(2)(c) the court may require the attorney to furnish information or produce documents or things in his possession as attorney.

Rule 25A(1) CPR provides that where the court directs that the attorney render accounts, that direction shall include directions as to –

(a)   whether the accounts are to be delivered annually or, if not, the intervals at which the accounts are to be delivered; and

(b)   the time and manner in which accounts are to be delivered.

Rule 25A(2) provides that the attorney shall answer such requisitions on his accounts as the court shall raise and in such manner and in such time as the court shall direct.

To disclose all relevant facts in certain transactions

10.13   The donee of an enduring power is under the same duty as the donee of an ordinary power.

Once an enduring power has been registered, the court in effect stands in the shoes of the donor, and under s 8(2)(b)(i) EPAA 1985 the court may give directions with respect to the management or disposal by the attorney of the property and affairs of the donor. Under s 8(2)(d) the court may give any consent or authorisation to act which the attorney would have to obtain from a mentally capable donor, and under s 8(2)(e) the court may authorise the attorney to act so as to benefit himself or other persons than the donor (but subject to any conditions and restrictions contained in the instrument).

Thus if the donee of an enduring power, which has been registered, wants to enter into some transaction concerning the property of the donor, for example, purchasing or leasing property belonging to the donor, he must obtain the consent of the court.

It should be noted that if the power is not registered, the donee need not obtain the consent of the court.

Not to make secret profits

10.14   The same duty applies to the donee of an enduring power as to the donee of an ordinary power. Once the power is registered, s 8 EPAA 1985 applies. Section 8(2)(d) provides that the court may give any consent or authorisation to act which the attorney would have to obtain from a mentally capable donor, and s 8(2)(e) permits the court to authorise the attorney to act so as to benefit himself or persons other than the donor.

Thus if the donee of a registered enduring power wants to receive any profit or commission as a consequence of the agency, he must obtain the consent of the court. There is no such need, however, if the power is not registered.

Not to exceed the authority conferred by the power

10.15   If an enduring power confers a general authority on the attorney, under s 3(2) EPAA 1985 it confers on the attorney authority to do on behalf of the donor anything which the donor can lawfully do by attorney. This is subject to the restriction imposed in subs (5) with regard to gifts.

If a limited power is conferred, the donee must not exceed the authority conferred, and it is unwise to rely upon the courts giving the power a liberal interpretation.

Once the power is registered, s 7(1)(c) EPAA 1985 provides that the donor may not extend or restrict the scope of the authority, and any instruction or consent given by the donor is ineffective. However, under s 8(2)(d) the court can given any consent or authorisation to act which the attorney would have to obtain from a mentally capable donor, and under s 8(2)(f) the court can relieve the attorney wholly or partly from any liability which he has or may have on account of a breach of his duties as attorney. In the light of the restricted interpretation placed upon s 8 in *Re R [1990] 2 WLR 1219*, it may be that the court will give these subsections a limited interpretation. A court might be unwilling to authorise an act completely outside the power originally conferred on the donee.

To take care and be skilful

10.16   The same duty applies to donees under both ordinary and enduring powers.

Section 8(1)(f) enables the court to relieve the attorney wholly or partly from any liability which he has or may have incurred on account of a breach of his duties as attorney.

III. Duties with regard to investment

10.17   An attorney is in very similar position to a trustee. Many attorneys will only be dealing with relatively small estates, which will be rapidly diminishing if the donor is in a home. However, some will be dealing with relatively large estates. In these cases, the attorneys, whether acting under an ordinary or an enduring power, would be well advised to comply with the requirements of the Trustee Act 2000 with regard to investment.

The Trustee Act 2000 substantially amended the law with regard to investment. It repealed most of the Trustee Investment Act 1961, which most practitioners considered too restrictive. However, in view of what has happened to the Stock Market recently, it may be that the approach adopted by the 1961 Act of requiring trust funds to be split into two, and a proportion invested in narrower range securities had much to commend it.

Whilst the Act refers to trustees, attorneys are probably under similar duties.

Section 3(1) of the 2000 Act provides that subject to the provisions of Part II of the Act, a trustee may make any kind of investment that he could make if he were absolutely entitled to the assets of the trust. Subsection (2) provides that the power under subs (1) is called 'the general power of investment'. Section 3(3) provides that the general power of investment does not permit a trustee to make investments in land other than in loans secured on land. However, s 8 does contain a power to invest in land. Section 8 is discussed below. Section 3(4) provides that a person invests in a loan secured on land if he has rights under any contract under which:

(a)   one person provides another with credits, and

(b)   the obligation of the borrower to repay is secured on land.

'Credit' is given a wide meaning in s 3(5), where it is defined as including any cash loan or other financial accommodation. Section 3(6) provides that cash includes money in any form.

It should be noted that whilst the Act has provisions dealing with loans secured on land, there is nothing in the Act dealing with unsecured loans. Presumably these are permissible if they can be classed as an investment. In any event, it may be a breach of the duty of care for a trustee to make an unsecured loan if it proves to be irrecoverable.

The general power of investment is subject to various restrictions. Section 4 lays down the standard investment criteria. Section 4(1) provides that in exercising any power of investment, a trustee must have regard to the standard investment criteria. This duty applies whether or not the powers under the Act are being exercised, and so it applies to trustees who invest under an express investment clause in a will or settlement. Section 4(2) provides that a trustee must from time to time review the investments of the trust and consider whether, having regard to the standard investment criteria, they should be varied. Section 4(3) provides that the standard investment criteria, in relation to a trust, are –

(a)   the suitability to the trust of investments of the same kind as any particular investment proposed to be made or retained and of that particular investment as an investment of that kind, and

(b)   the need for diversification of investments of the trust in so far as is appropriate to the circumstances of the trust.

It should be noted that these standard investment criteria apply to trustees exercising express powers of investment just as they apply to trustees exercising the powers conferred by the Act.

(a) means that trustees must first consider in what areas they wish to invest. Having decided that they wish to invest in a particular area, they must then decide in which companies they are going to invest in that area.

With regard to (b) it would clearly be wrong to invest a large sum of money in one company. A prudent trustee will invest in different types of assets. However, the need for diversification may be difficilt or impossible to satisfy if there is only one asset comprised in the trust, the matrimonial home, or the family farm, or shares in the family company. In this situation, the trustees may be justified in not diversifying on the basis that it is not appropriate to the circumstances of the trust.

A trustee is also under a duty to obtain advice, whether investing under the Act, or an express power of investment. Section 5(1) provides that before exercising any power of investment, a trustee must obtain and consider proper advice about the way in which, having regard to the standard investment criteria, the power should be exercised. The duty to obtain and consider advice also applies when trustees are reviewing the investments of the trust. Section 5(2) provides that a trustee must obtain and consider proper advice about whether, having regard to the standard investment criteria, the investments should be varied. The Act is silent about how frequently the investments should be reviewed or advice sought. Presumably the interval should not be longer than a year, and there might be circumstances in which the interval should be much shorter for example, if there is a large trust fund.

Section 5(3) provides that a trustee need not obtain such advice if he reasonably concludes that in all the circumstances it is unnecessary or inappropriate do so. If the trust fund is large, trustees cannot reasonably claim it is inappropriate. On the other hand, if the trust fund were under £100 it would be reasonable for a trustee to conclude that it was unnecessary and inappropriate. 'Proper advice' is defined in s 5(4) as the advice of a person who is reasonably believed by the trustee to be qualified to give it by his ability and practical experience of financial and other matters relating to the proposed investment.

Anyone advising trustees must be authorised under the Financial Services and Markets Act 2000. Trustees can choose between various types of advisers; usually the choice will be between brokers or independent financial advisers.

The general power of investment is in addition to powers conferred on trustees otherwise than by the Act, but it is subject to any restriction or exclusion imposed by the trust instrument or by any enactment or any provision of subordinate legislation (s 6(1)). Section 6(2) provides that for the purposes of the Act, an enactment or a provision of subordinate legislation is not to be regarded as being, or as being part of, a trust instrument.

Acquisition of land

10.18   Part III of the Act contains default powers for trustees to acquire freehold and leasehold land.

Section 8(1) provides that a trustee may acquire freehold or leasehold land in the United Kingdom –

(a)   as an investment,

(b)   for occupation by a beneficiary, or

(c)   for any other reason.

Section 8(2) provides that 'freehold or leasehold land' means–

(a)   in relation to England and Wales, a legal estate in land,

(b)   in relation to Scotland–

>   (i)   the estate or interest of the proprietor of the *dominium utile* or, in the case of land not held on feudal tenure, the estate or interest of the owner, or

>   (ii)   a tenancy, and

(c)   in relation to Northern Ireland, a legal estate in land, including land held under a fee farm grant.

Thus there is power to aquire a leasehold interest. The Act does not impose any requirement as to the length of lease which must remain unexpired, although a lease which has little time left to run will not be a good buy.

Note that there is no power to acquire land situated abroad, or equitable interests in land. If either of these situations is likely, then the trustees should include express powers in the will or settlement authorising them to hold land abroad or equitable interests.

General duties with regard to investment

10.19   The duty of care applies to a trustee:

(a)   when exercising the general power of investment conferred on him by the trust instrument;

(b)   when carrying out a duty to which he is subject under ss 4 or 5 (duties relating to the exercise of a power of investment or to the review of investments) (Sch 1 para 1).

Section 1 defines the duty of care. A trustee must exercise such care and skill as is reasonable in the circumstances, having regard in particular –

(a) to any special knowledge or experience that he has or holds himself out as having, and

(b) if he acts as trustee in the course of a business or profession, to any special knowledge or experience that it is reasonable to expect of a person acting in the course of that kind of business or occupation.

Pre-Trustee Act 2000 cases may still be relevant in deciding whether or not there has been a breach of this duty. Lindley MR in *Re Whiteley (1886) Ch D 347* at page 355 said:

'The duty of a trustee is not to take such care only as a prudent man would take if he had only himself to consider; the duty rather is to take such care as an ordinary prudent man would take if he were minded to make an investment for the benefit of other people for whom he felt morally bound to provide.'

A prudent man might be prepared to take a chance on an investment if he was only acting for himself, but if he was aiming to provide for his children, he might think twice before making a hazardous investment. The duty is thus higher than merely acting prudently.

More recently the duty of trustees with regard to investment was considered in *Nestle v National Westminster Bank plc [1993] 1 WLR 1260* where the action against the bank failed. Leggatt LJ said at page 1282:

'The essence of the bank's duty was to take such steps as a prudent businessman would have taken to maintain and increase the value of the trust fund. Unless it failed to do so, it was not in breach of trust. A breach of duty will not be actionable, and therefore will be immaterial, if it does not cause loss. I would endorse the concession by Mr Nugee for the bank that "loss" will be incurred by a trust fund when it makes a gain less than would have been made by a prudent businessman. A claimant will therefore fail who cannot prove a loss in this sense caused by breach of duty. So here in order to make a case for an inquiry, the plaintiff must show that loss was caused by breach of duty on the part of the bank.'

It was held that the plaintiff had not proved that she had suffered loss as a result of the breaches of trust by the bank.

In *Cowan v Scargill [1985] Ch 270* there was a dispute about the investment policies of the mineworkers' pension fund. Megarry V-C said at pages 287–288:

'The assertion that trustees could not be criticised for failing to make a particular investment for social or political reasons is one that I would not accept in its full width. If the investment in fact made is equally beneficial to the beneficiaries, then criticism would be difficult to sustain in practice, whatever the position in theory . . . .

In considering what investments to make trustees must put on one side their own personal interest and views . . . .

. . . if the only actual or potential beneficiaries of a trust are all adults with very strict views on moral and social matters, condemning all forms of alcohol, tobacco and popular entertainment, as well as armaments, I can well understand that it might not be for the "benefit" of such beneficiaries to know that they are obtaining rather larger financial returns under the trust by reason of investments in those activities than they would have received if the trustees had invested the trust funds in other investments.'

Attorneys whether acting under an ordinary power of attorney or an enduring power would be well advised to comply with the provisions of the Trustee Act 2000. In particular, even relatively small estates:

(a)   should take advice from a person qualified to give advice before making an investment;

(b)   should review investments periodically (at least once a year) and take advice.

It is difficult to be precise as to the level beneath which advice is unnecessary; attorneys who are not relatives should always take advice. If the attorney is a relative of the deceased, it may be that they can safely ignore these duties, for example, if the attorney is an only child, and the sole beneficiary under the will of the donor.

IV. Rights of donees of ordinary powers

Indemnity

10.20   The donee may incur expenses in exercising the powers conferred by a power of attorney. If the donor and donee of the power are related, the donee may be prepared to meet these expenses himself. If he is not prepared to do so, there will usually be an implied right to an indemnity if one is not expressly given by the power. In *Adamson v Jarvis (1827) 4 Bing 66, 130 ER 693*, Best CJ at pages 72, 695 said:

'. . . every man who employs another to do an act which the employer appears to have a right to authorise to do undertakes to indemnify him for all such acts as would be lawful if the employer had the authority he pretends to have'.

If there is an express right of indemnity, it may extend to payments which the agent is liable to make, but for which the principal is not liable. In *Adams v Morgan and Company Ltd [1924] 1 KB 751*, P sold a business to D, a company. It was agreed that P would carry on the business as D's agent, but that he would be entitled to an indemnity. P incurred a liability for supertax in respect of the period during which he carried on the business as D's agent. It was held that P was entitled to be indemnified against this supertax even though companies were not liable for supertax.

There is no right to an indemnity, however, if the agent exceeds his authority (*Barron v Fitzgerald (1840) 6 Bing NS 201, 133 ER 79*). Similarly, there will be no right to an indemnity if neither the agent nor the principal is under any legal liability (*Owen v Tate [1976] 1 QB 402*). In addition, the expense must be reasonable.

Remuneration

10.21   Whether an agent is entitled to remuneration depends on whether there is any express or implied term in a contract to the effect that the attorney should be paid. Most powers of attorney do not contain any express term about payment; therefore most donees will have to rely upon an implied term if they want payment. In what circumstances will the courts imply a term so as to give an attorney a right to remuneration? In *Way v Latilla [1937] 3 All ER 759* Lord Atkin said at page 763:

> 'But, while there is, therefore, no concluded contract as to the remuneration, it is plain that there existed between the parties a contract of employment under which Mr. Way was engaged to do work for Mr. Latilla in circumstances which clearly indicated the work was not to be gratuitous.'

If a donor appoints a solicitor or accountant as his attorney, there will usually be an implied agreement that the donee should be remunerated. On the other hand, if a relative of the donor is appointed as attorney, the courts will probably say that the circumstances are not such as would entitle the attorney to be paid, unless of course the relative was in practice as a solicitor or accountant.

Even if there is no contract, the court may be prepared to order remuneration on a *quantum meruit* basis. In *Craven-Ellis v Canons Ltd [1936] 2 KB 403* the contract between P and a company was void. It was held that P was entitled to recover on a *quantum meruit* basis. Greer LJ said at page 409:

> 'The contract, having been made by directors who had no authority to make it with one of themselves who had notice of their want of authority, was not binding on either party. It was, in fact, a nullity, and presents no obstacle to the implied promise to pay on a quantum meruit basis which arises from the performance of the services and the implied acceptance of the same by the company.'

Before the court will order payment on a *quantum meruit* basis, there must thus be a performance of services and an acceptance of those services.

What guidelines will the court use in fixing the amount of remuneration? The court will award a reasonable amount as remuneration, and will have regard to any trade usage (*Way v Latilla*). Solicitors will therefore be entitled to charge on their usual basis, provided of course that that is reasonable.

If the donee exceeds his authority, or is guilty of a breach of duty, he will not be entitled to any remuneration (*Marsh v Jelf (1862) 3 F & F 234, 176 ER 105*).

V. Rights of donees of enduring powers

Indemnity and remuneration

10.22   In an article in the *Solicitors' Journal* (20 June 1986) RT Oerton argues at page 458 that s 3 EPAA 1985, which deals with the scope of the authority of an attorney under an enduring power, does not specifically authorise an attorney to charge. However, the author considers that s 8(2)(b)(iii) of the Act may resolve the problem.

Section 8(2)(b)(iii) EPAA 1985 empowers the court to give directions with respect to the remuneration or expenses of the attorney, whether or not in default of or in accordance with any provision made by the instrument, including directions for the repayment of excessive remuneration, or the payment of additional remuneration. This clearly contemplates that an attorney under an enduring power can be paid.

On the assumption that an attorney under an enduring power is entitled to be paid, it seems that the law which is applicable to ordinary powers as regards indemnity and remuneration applies also to enduring powers.

In *Enduring Powers of Attorney: Guidelines for Solicitors* (September 1999) (see APPENDIX 5) it is suggested that a professional charging clause should be included in an enduring power, which could include a provision that the costs should be approved by a third party if the donor becomes mentally incapable.

VI. Liens

10.23   A lien is the right to retain property belonging to another person who owes money to the person in possession of the property. It may be that the donee of both an ordinary power of attorney and an enduring power will have a lien on property which belongs to the donor and which is in the possession of the donee. This lien must either be given by the general law or by contract (*Gladstone v Birley (1817) 2 Mer 401, 35 ER 993*).

At common law solicitors have a lien on property, funds, documents and papers belonging to a client which are in their possession for moneys due to the solicitor. See Halsbury's *Laws of England* (4th edition) volume 44 paragraph 226 onwards.

Other donees are entitled to particular but not general liens. This means that if the donee spends money maintaining a car on behalf of the donor, the donee would be entitled to a lien on the car. However, if the donee spends money maintaining a house on behalf of the same donor, he cannot claim a lien on the car for that expenditure (*Bock v Gorrissen (1860) 2 De GF & J 434, 45 ER 689*).

VII. Solicitors and powers of attorney

10.24   The issues discussed here are also discussed in CHAPTER 4, but are again considered here for the convenience of readers.

Conflict of interests

10.25   Solicitors are frequently appointed attorneys by clients. Their relationship is governed by the general law, and in addition by the rules and principles governing the professional conduct of solicitors. The donee under a general power of attorney is in a very powerful position as regards the assets of the donor; all the assets of the donor can be sold, and different assets bought with the proceeds. Can a solicitor acting under a general power sell property to the donor, or buy property from the donor? Can such a solicitor lend money to the donor, or borrow money from the donor? Can the solicitor acting under the power of attorney invest the money of the donor in a company in which he is a majority shareholder? There is clearly a conflict of interest between the donor and the donee in these situations. In all these cases, the donor must have independent legal advice; if the donor does not obtain independent advice, the solicitor must not go on with the sale, purchase, loan or investment. Advice is not limited to legal advice; it may include the advice of a valuer as to the value of property. If an enduring power has been registered it may be necessary to obtain the consent of the court under s 8(2)(d) of the EPAA.

A solicitor can charge the donor for the work done on behalf of the donor, provided that the solicitor would have advised the client to pay if another solicitor had rendered the bill; in other words the charges must be reasonable (see The Law Society's *Guide to the Professional Conduct of Solicitors 1999* at page 318).

It may be desirable to include an express charging clause in an enduring power of attorney.

Financial services

10.26   The Financial Services Authority became the regulator for solicitors' firms on 1 December 2001. A small minority of firms will be regulated directly by the new authority, but the great majority will not. These firms may carry on certain regulated activities without being regulated by the Financial Services Authority. However, they must comply with the Solicitors' Financial Services (Scope) Rules 2001. Rule 3 prescribes certain prohibited activities, and rule 4 states that a firm which carries on any regulated activities must ensure that:

(a)   the activities arise out of, or are complementary to, the provision of a particular professional service to a client;

(b)   the manner of the provision by the firm of any service in the course of carrying on the activities is incidental to the provision by the firm of professional services;

(c)   the firm accounts to the client for any pecuniary reward or other advantage which the firm receives from a third party;

(d)   the activities are not of a description, nor do they relate to an investment of a description, specified in any order made by the Treasury under s 327(6) of the Financial Services and Markets Act 2001;

(e)   the firm does not carry on, or hold itself out as carrying on, a regulated activity other than one which is allowed by these rules or one in relation to which the firm is an exempt person;

(f)   there is not in force any order or direction of the Financial Services Authority under s 328 or s 329 of the Act which prevents the firm from carrying on the activities; and

(g)   the activities are not otherwise prohibited by these rules.

Rule 5 prescribes other restrictions. A firm must not manage assets belonging to another person in circumstances which involve the exercise of discretion except where the firm or a partner, officer or employee of the firm is a trustee, personal representative, donee of a power of attorney or receiver appointed by the Court of Protection, and either:

(a)   all routine or day-to-day decisions, so far as relating to that activity, are taken by an authorised person with permission to carry on that activity or an exempt person; or

(b)   any decision to enter into a transaction, which involves buying or subscribing for an investment, is undertaken with the advice of an authorised person with permission to give advice in relation to such an activity or an exempt person.

Rule 8 defines 'authorised person' by reference to the definition in s 31 of the Act. It also defines 'exempt person'.

Readers are also referred to article 38 of the Financial Services and Markets Act 2000 (Regulated Activities) Order 2001, and the Law Society guidance on Financial Services and Solicitors dated August 2001.

Summary

10.27

- A gratuitous attorney is under no duty to act, but an attorney may be under a contractual obligation to do so.

- An attorney owes a duty of utmost good faith to the donor.

- An attorney must keep accounts.

- An attorney may be under a duty to disclose all relevant facts.

- An attorney must not make secret profits.

- An attorney must not exceed the authority conferred by the power.

- An attorney must take care and be skilful; the degree of care and skill required depends on various factors.

- The donee under an enduring power is under similar duties, but they may be modified by the EPAA.

- The donee of an enduring power must apply for registration of the power if he has reason to believe that the donor is or is becoming mentally incapable.

- An attorney is entitled to be indemnified against all expenses properly incurred in the performance of his duties.

- An attorney may be entitled to remuneration.

- An attorney may be entitled to a lien.

- Solicitors who are attorneys can have dealings with the donee, but the donee may have to be independently advised.

- Solicitors who are attorneys must comply with the Financial Services and Markets Act 2000 and regulations made thereunder.

Chapter 11

Rights and liabilities of donor, donee and third parties

11.1 Although many of the cases referred to relate to contracts entered into by agents not authorised under a power of attorney, the same principles usually apply to contracts entered into by the donee of a power of attorney.

I. Ordinary powers of attorney

Acts within the express authority of the donee

Rights and liabilities of the donor

11.2 The donor of a power is bound by all acts within the express authority of the donee. The extent of the express authority conferred on the attorney must be ascertained by looking at the power, which may confer a general or limited power on the attorney.

If the act is within the express authority of the donee, the donor will be liable, even though the donee has committed some breach of duty owed to the donor. In *Hambro v Burnand [1904] 2 KB 10, CA* at page 20 Collins MR said:

> 'It would be impossible as it seems to me, for the business of a mercantile community to be carried on, if a person dealing with an agent was bound to go behind the authority of the agent in each case, and inquire whether his motive did or did not involve the application of the authority for his own private purposes.'

Although a person dealing with an attorney need not make inquiries to confirm that the attorney is acting properly, he should always check the power of attorney to make sure that it authorises the proposed transaction(s). As the courts are reluctant to imply powers, a person dealing with the attorney should ensure that there is an express power authorising the transaction.

There is some doubt as to whether a donor of a power of attorney can sue and be sued on a deed entered into by the donee. The rule at common law is that the donor can sue and be sued on the deed only if the deed states that he is a party, and the donee has executed the deed in the name of the donor (*In re International Contract Company; Pickering's claim (1871) LR 6 Ch 525* and *Berkeley v Hardy (1826) 5 B & C 355*). Equity will in appropriate circumstances hold that the donee is a trustee for the principal, and therefore the donor can enforce the trust (*Harmer v Armstrong [1934] 1 Ch 65*).

It may be that the Powers of Attorney Act 1971 has amended these rules. Section 7(1), as amended by the Law of Property (Miscellaneous Provisions) Act 1989, provides that if the donee of a power of attorney is an individual, he may, if he thinks fit:

'(a)   execute any instrument with his own signature, and,

'(b)   do any other thing in his own name,

by the authority of the donor of the power; and any document executed or thing done in that manner shall be as effective as if executed by the donee with the signature and seal, or, as the case may be, in the name, of the donor of the power.'

In *Law of Agency* (17th edition) by Bowstead and Reynolds, it is stated at page 358 that there are two problems with this subsection:

(i)   Should the donee have specific authority to act in his own name?

(ii)   Must the principal be named in the deed?

Bowstead is of the opinion that the donee need not have specific authority to act in his name, but that the principal must be named. The authority for this second proposition is *Harmer v Armstrong*, where Lawrence LJ said at page 86:

'It is well settled and not disputed by the plaintiffs that at common law no one can sue on a contract under seal except the contracting parties.'

Bowstead concludes that:

'The effect of the section is therefore to allow execution by an attorney in his own name: but the principal should be mentioned in the body of the deed, and though it may not be strictly necessary, it is highly desirable that the attorney should express that he executes as attorney or on behalf of the principal . . .' (page 428).

Section 56(1) Law of Property Act 1925 provides that a person may take an immediate or other interest in land or other property, or the benefit of any condition, right of entry, covenant or agreement over or respecting land or other property, although he may not be named as a party to the conveyance or other instrument. The interpretation of this section is uncertain (see *Chitty on Contracts* (26th edition, Sweet & Maxwell, 1989) paragraph 1362), and it is unwise to rely on it.

Rights and liabilities of the donee

11.3   If the donee discloses that he is an agent, and reveals the name of the donor, there is a contract between the donor and the third party, and the basic rule is that the donee cannot sue the third party, and cannot be sued by the third party. In *Montgomerie v UK Mutual SS Assn Ltd [1891] 1 QB 370* at page 371 Wright J said:

'There is no doubt whatever as to the general rule as regards an agent, that where a person contracts as agent for a principal the contract is the contract of the principal, and not that of the agent; and prima facie, at common law the only person who may sue is the principal, and the only person who can be sued is the principal.'

However, the agent will not always escape liability. In *Montgomerie*, Wright J said at page 371:

'To that rule there are of course many exceptions: first, the agent may be added as the party to the contract if he has so contracted, and is appointed as the party to be sued.'

At page 372 he continued:

'Also, and this is very important, in all cases the parties can by their express contract provide that the agent shall be the person liable either concurrently with or to the exclusion of the principal, or that the agent shall be the party to sue either concurrently with or to the exclusion of the principal.'

The donee of a power of attorney should therefore take care not to become a party to the contract, or to become liable jointly with the donor.

In *Bridges & Salmon v The Swan (Owner) [1968] 1 Lloyd's Rep 5* Brandon J stated:

'Where A contracts with B on behalf of a disclosed principal C, the question whether both A and C are liable on the contract or only C depends on the intention of the parties. That intention is to be gathered from (1) the nature of the contract, (2) its terms and (3) the surrounding circumstances . . . The intention for which the court looks is not the subjective intention of A or of B. Their subjective intentions may differ. The intention for which the court looks is an objective intention of both parties, based on what two reasonable businessmen making a contract of that nature, in those terms and in those surrounding circumstances, must be taken to have intended.

Where a contract is wholly in writing, the intention depends on the true construction, having regard to the nature of the contract and the surrounding circumstances, of the document or documents in which the contract is contained. Where . . . the contract is partly oral and partly in writing, the intention depends on the true effect, having regard again to the nature of the contract and the surrounding circumstances, of the oral and written terms taken together.

Many of the decided cases on questions of this kind relate to contracts wholly in writing. But it seems to me that, in principle, there can be no difference in the approach to the problem whether the contract concerned is wholly in writing or partly in writing and partly oral. In either case the terms of the contract must be looked at and their true effect ascertained.'

A donee may thus become personally liable on a contract entered into on behalf of the donor if it would appear to a reasonable businessman that it was the intention of the donee to be personally liable. However, it is possible to avoid this consequence if the donee makes it '"as agent for", or "on account of", or "on behalf of", or simply "for" a principal' (Brandon J in *The Swan* at page 13). Similarly, signing as 'attorney for' will enable the donee to escape personal liability on the contract.

If the donee is personally liable, he can sue to enforce the contract (*Joseph v Knox (1813) 3 Camp 320, 170 ER 1397*).

A donee can sue on a deed if he has executed the deed using his own name, and is a party to the deed (*Appleton v Binks (1804) 5 East 148, 102 ER 1025*). It is not clear whether the donee is liable under s 7 Powers of Attorney Act 1971 (see *Law of Agency* (17th edition) by Bowstead and Reynolds at pages 358 and 491).

Acts within the implied or usual authority of an agent

11.4   The courts will imply into a power of attorney whatever powers are necessary to carry out the main purpose of the power; this topic was discussed in CHAPTER 8.

An agent may also have the authority which an agent in that position would normally have. This is known as usual authority, and in *Watteau v Fenwick [1893] 1 QB 346* Willes J said at page 348:

'. . . the principal is liable for all the acts of the agent which are within the authority usually confided to an agent of that character . . .'

A power of attorney may specifically authorise the donee to run a business, and a general power will include authority to do so. The donee running a business under a power of attorney will have the authority which one would expect a person running that type of business to have. Any restriction on the power in the power of attorney will not be effective unless the third party is aware of it. However, the donor will not be liable if the person dealing with the donee knew or ought to have known that the donee was exceeding his authority.

In *Reckitt v Barnett, Pembroke and Slater Ltd [1929] AC 176 HL*, a solicitor was appointed an attorney, and drew a cheque in favour of the respondents in settlement of a private debt. Viscount Dunedin said at page 184:

'. . . on the face of the cheque they received they saw two things (1) that it was Reckitt's account which was being drawn on, not Lord Terrington's; (2) that Lord Terrington ascribed his power to draw on that account to his position as Reckitt's attorney. The respondents made no further enquiry. They took the cheque for what it was worth ... The respondents not having made any enquiry cannot be in a better position than if they had made enquiry'.

The best procedure is for anyone who knows he is dealing with an attorney to confirm that the attorney has power to enter into the proposed transaction; if he does not, and the transaction is outside the power, the donor of the power may not be liable.

If an act is within the implied or usual authority of the donee, the rights and liabilities of the donor and donee are the same as when the act is expressly authorised.

Acts within the ostensible authority of an attorney

11.5   The donor of a power is liable for the acts of the attorney within the ostensible authority of the attorney (*Uxbridge Permanent Benefit Building Society v Pickard [1939] 2 KB 248*). Ostensible authority is the authority which an attorney appears to have, because the donor has held the agent out as having that authority. In *Freeman & Lockyer (A firm) v Buckhurst Park Properties (Mangal) Ltd [1964] 2 QB 480* Diplock LJ said at page 503:

'An "apparent" or "ostensible" authority, on the other hand, is a legal relationship between the principal and the contractor created by a representation, made by the principal to the contractor, intended to be and in fact acted upon by the contractor, that the agent has authority to enter on behalf of the principal into a contract of a kind within the scope of the "apparent" authority, so as to render the principal liable to perform any obligations imposed upon him by such a contract. To the relationships so created the agent is a stranger. He need not be (although he generally is) aware of the existence of the representation, but he must not purport to make the agreement as principal for himself. The representation, when acted upon by the contractor by entering into a contract with the agent, operates as an estoppel, preventing the principal from asserting that he is not bound by the contract. It is irrelevant whether the agent had actual authority to enter into the contract.'

A person dealing with the donee of a power of attorney may not be aware that that person is acting under a power. If the donee buys goods from that person, and the donor pays for them, future purchases of those goods will be within the ostensible authority of the donee, even though they may not be expressly authorised by the power.

If an act is within the ostensible authority of the donee, the rights and liabilities of the donor and donee are identical to the rights and liabilities when the act is expressly authorised.

Acts outside the actual or ostensible authority of the donee

11.6   The donor of a power of attorney is not liable for acts outside the actual or ostensible authority of the donee, unless he ratifies them expressly, or accepts the benefit of the transaction (*Jacobs v Morris [1902] 1 Ch 816*). For example, if the donee buys food for the donor, which the donor eats, the donor will not be allowed to claim that the purchase is outside the authority of the donee. Ratification is discussed at 8.10 above.

If the donee of a power of attorney borrows money without authority, and uses it to pay off debts of the donor, the lender will be able to recover the money from the donor to the extent that it was applied in paying off the debts of the donor (*Jacobs v Morris [1902] 1 Ch 816* and *Bannatyne v D & C Maciver [1906] 1 KB 103 CA*).

If the donee has no authority, any person dealing with the donee will be able to sue the donee for breach of warranty of authority. In *Starkey v Bank of England [1903] AC 114 HL* a broker relied upon a power of attorney to arrange a transfer of stock; the broker did not know that the power of attorney was forged. It was held that the broker had impliedly warranted that he had authority, and he was liable to indemnify the Bank of England which had had to indemnify the original stockholder.

However, if the person dealing with the attorney knew that the attorney was acting without authority, the attorney will not be liable. In *Halbot v Lens [1901] 1 Ch 344* the defendant signed a memorandum concerning an arrangement between his creditors in the following manner:

> 'for self and wife and Dr. Clarke'.

The plaintiff also signed the memorandum. Under it, Dr Clarke was to release all claims against the plaintiff. The defendant had no authority to sign for his wife or Dr Clarke, and before signing he had made it clear that he had no authority to sign for Dr Clarke. It was held that he was not liable in damages for failing to obtain the release from Dr Clarke.

Failure by the donee to disclose the name of the principal, or the fact of agency

11.7   If the donee of a power of attorney fails to disclose that he is acting as an attorney within his actual or implied authority, the donor can still sue and be sued on the contract. In *Teheran-Europe Co Ltd v ST Belton (Tractors) Ltd [1968] 2 QB 545* at pages 552 and 553 Lord Denning said:

> 'It is a well established rule of English law that an undisclosed principal can sue and be sued upon a contract, even though his name and even his existence is undisclosed, save in those cases when the terms of the contract expressly or impliedly confine it to the parties to it. The rule is an anomaly,

but is justified by business convenience. It has been held so for many years. The only question in the case is whether this rule (that an undisclosed principal can sue and be sued) extends to a case where the principal is a foreigner. In my opinion, the rule applies to a foreign principal, just as to an English principal.'

There is some doubt about the liability of an undisclosed principal if the agent is acting within the scope of his *usual* or *apparent* authority. In *Watteau v Fenwick [1893] 1 QB 346* the defendants were brewers, and they held out their manager as being the owner of the business. The manager was forbidden to purchase certain items other than from the defendants, but in breach of this prohibition the defendant bought items from the plaintiffs. The plaintiffs discovered who was the real owner of the business, and sued for the cost of these items. It was held that the plaintiffs could sue. Willes J said at page 348:

'... once it is established that the defendant was the real principal, the ordinary doctrine of principal and agent applies – that the principal is liable for all acts of the agent which are within the authority usually confided to an agent of that character, notwithstanding limitations, as between the principal and agent put upon that authority'.

This seems to suggest that in all cases of agency, the undisclosed principal can sue and be sued, including the case where the agent is acting within the scope of his usual or apparent authority. It is uncertain whether this case is correct; for a fuller discussion, readers are referred to *Law of Agency* (7th edition, Butterworths, 1996) by Fridman at page 71 onwards and pages 265 and 266.

Unauthorised property transactions

11.8   The donor of a power will clearly be bound by any disposal of property within the actual, implied, usual, and ostensible authority of the donor. He will also be bound by any such disposal, even though the disposal may not have been in the manner originally contemplated, provided that the third party is not aware of this fact (*Lloyds and Scottish Finance Ltd v Williamson [1965] 1 All ER 641*).

The donor of a power will not be bound by a disposition of his property which is outside the actual, implied, usual or ostensible authority of the donee, even if the donor has been negligent (*Farquharson Brothers & Co v King & Co [1902] AC 325* at page 336).

However, the donor may be estopped from denying that the donee had authority to sell the asset. If the donor has held the donee out as owning an asset, or as having power to sell the asset, the donor will not be allowed later on to deny that the donee could transfer a good title to the third party.

To what extent can a donee who is entrusted with property of the donor deal with it for his own benefit? For example, can a donee who is entrusted with the title deeds of a house deposit them with a bank as security for the repayment of a loan made to the donee personally? In *Brocklesby v Temperance Building Society [1895] AC 173* the appellant was a solicitor in partnership with his son. He authorised the son to borrow money from a certain bank, and entrusted him with certain deeds relating to a mortgage and leasehold house. The son used the deeds to borrow more money from another bank. It was held that the appellant was bound by the transaction. Lord Watson said at page 183:

'. . . it appears to me to be just and reasonable that, the agent having the control of the securities for the purpose of borrowing, with the consent of the principal, a lender, who has no notice to the contrary, should be entitled to deal with him on the footing that he had authority to pledge the securities to the full amount of their value'.

Thus if a donor of a power of attorney permits the donee to have possession of property or evidence of ownership, and the donee sells that property to an innocent third party, the third party may be able to defeat any claim by the donor. Similarly, if the donee uses the property to obtain a loan, the donor will have to repay the loan before the property can be recovered.

If the person dealing with the donee knows or ought to know of the lack of authority, that person may become a trustee of the property (*Reckitt v Barnett, Pembroke and Slater Ltd [1929] AC 176 HL*).

Effect of payment to the attorney

11.9   A third party owes money to the donor, and pays it to the donee of a power. Is the third party discharged from liability? If the donee had authority to receive the money, the third party will be discharged. Similarly, even if the donee had no authority to accept payment, if the donee pays the money received from the third party to the donor, the third party will be discharged (see *Law of Agency* (7th edition) by Fridman at pages 224–225).

If a third party, not knowing that a donee is in fact acting under a power of attorney, pays the donee, that will operate as a discharge for the third party, and the donor will not be able to sue the third party, even if the donee has not accounted to the donor for the money (*Coates and Another v Lewes and Another (1808) 1 Camp 444, 170 ER 1015*).

Election

11.10   A third party may have to elect whether to sue the donor or donee, as it would be clearly unjust to permit a third party to recover twice. In *Priestly v Fernie (1865) 3 H & C 977, 159 ER 820,* it was held that a third party could not sue the owner of a ship on a bill of lading having obtained judgment against the master of the ship who had signed the bill. Bramwell B at pages 983 and 984, 823 said:

'If this were an ordinary case of principal and agent, where the agent, having made a contract in his own name, has been sued on it to judgment, there can be no doubt that no second action would be maintainable against the principal.'

However, the mere issue of proceeding will not usually amount to an election to sue that particular defendant, although the issue of proceeding against either the donee or donor is a rebuttable presumption of an election (*Clarkson, Booker Ltd v Andjel [1964] 3 All ER 260* at page 265). Therefore, a third party must elect whether to sue the donee or the donor, if both are liable, and having obtained judgment against one, an action cannot be brought against the other.

II. Enduring powers of attorney

Before the duty to register arises

11.11   A donee is under a duty to apply for registration of an enduring power in the event of the actual or impending mental incapacity of the donor (s 4 EPAA 1985; see CHAPTER 7). Until the duty to register arises, the power operates as an ordinary power, and the rights and liabilities of the donor and donee and third parties are the same whether the donee is acting under an ordinary power or an enduring power.

Between the duty to register arising and registration

11.12   During the period between the occurrence of the duty to register and registration, with some limited exceptions the donee may not do anything under the power (s 1(1)(b) EPAA 1985; see CHAPTER 7). It is submitted that transactions occurring during this period – and not subject to any of the exceptions – can be effective legally. Section 1(1)(c) EPAA 1985 applies s 5 Powers of Attorney Act 1971 to this situation. Section 5 is discussed in CHAPTER 12 in detail, but s 5(2) in effect provides that if a person deals with the donee of a power without knowledge of the mental incapacity, the transaction between them shall, in favour of that person, be as valid as if the power had then been in existence. It would thus seem that acts within the actual, implied, usual or ostensible authority of the donee of an enduring power between the duty to register arising and registration will have the same consequences as for ordinary powers, provided the third party is ignorant of the mental incapacity.

After registration

11.13   Section 7(1)(c) EPAA 1985 provides that the donor may not extend or restrict the scope of the authority conferred by the instrument, and no instruction or consent given by him after registration will, in the case of a consent, confer any right and, in the case of an instruction, impose or confer any obligation or right on or create any liability of the attorney or other person having notice of the instruction or consent. The effect of this provision is that the authority of the donee is limited to the acts permitted by the power or the EPAA 1985; presumably this includes acts within the implied and usual authority of the donee, but not acts within the ostensible authority of the donee. However, it can be argued that any ostensible authority acquired by the donee before registration survives registration as s 7(1)(c) applies only to instructions or consents given after registration. Any act outside the authority of the attorney will not bind the donor, although the donee might be liable for breach of warranty of authority.

It should be noted that s 8(2)(f) EPAA 1985 authorises the court to relieve the attorney wholly or partly from any liability he has, or may have, incurred on account of a breach of his duties as an attorney.

Summary

11.14

- A donor is bound by all acts within the express authority of the donee.

- If the donee discloses the fact that he is an agent, the primary liability is that of the donor.

- There is some doubt as to whether a donor of a power of attorney can sue and be sued on a deed entered into by the donee.

- The donor will be bound by acts within the implied or usual authority of the donee.

- The donor will be bound by acts within the ostensible authority of the donee.

- The donor will be liable even if the donee fails to disclose the fact of agency.

- A third party may have to elect whether to sue the donor or donee if both are liable.

- If the donee is acting under an enduring power, rights and liabilities vary according to whether there is a duty to register, whether application has been made for registration, and whether the power has been registered.

Chapter 12

Protection of third parties and subsequent purchasers

12.1 Various events such as the death of the donor, cause the revocation of a power of attorney. Revocation is discussed fully in CHAPTER 6. If the power has been revoked, any transactions entered into by the donee will be void. This could cause serious injustice to a third party dealing with an attorney, who might have no means of finding out whether it had been revoked. To deal with this problem, both the Powers of Attorney Act 1971 and the Enduring Powers of Attorney Act 1985 ('EPAA 1985') contain provisions protecting third parties.

It is necessary to consider separately the protection afforded to persons dealing with the donee of an ordinary power and persons dealing with the donee of an enduring power.

I. Ordinary powers of attorney

Protection of persons dealing with the donee

12.2 Section 5(2) Powers of Attorney Act 1971 provides that where 'a power of attorney has been revoked and a person, without knowledge of the revocation, deals with the donee of the power, the transaction between them shall, in favour of that person, be as valid as if the power had then been in existence'.

If the attorney is acting within his *actual* authority, the person dealing with the attorney is clearly protected. It is submitted that this subsection also protects a person dealing with the attorney if the attorney is acting within his implied, usual or ostensible authority – these acts would have bound the donor if the power had then been in existence.

Thus a person dealing with an attorney without knowledge that the power had been revoked will be protected under s 5(2) Powers of Attorney Act 1971. What is meant by knowledge? Section 5(5) provides that knowledge of the revocation of a power of attorney includes knowledge of any event (such as the death of the donor) which has the effect of revoking the power. A person dealing with an attorney cannot argue that, although he knew about the death, he did not appreciate that that event revoked the power.

Section 1 of the Trustee Delegation Act 1999 only applies if the donor of the power has a beneficial interest in the land. How can a purchaser from the attorney be certain that this is the case? Section 2 provides that an appropriate statement is, in favour of a purchaser, conclusive evidence that the donor of the power had a beneficial interest in the property at the time of the doing the act. An 'appropriate statement' means a signed statement made by the donee –

(a)   when doing the act in question, or

(b)   at any other time within the period of three months beginning with the day on which the act is done,

that the donor has a beneficial interest in the property at the time of the donee doing the act (s 2(3)). If the appropriate statement is false, the donee is liable in the same way as he would be if the statement were contained in a statutory declaration.

Protection of subsequent purchasers

12.3   Section 5(2) Powers of Attorney Act 1971 protects the person dealing with the donee of the power, and is not of much help to subsequent purchasers of the property as they may have difficulty in proving that the person dealing with the donee of a power of attorney did not have any knowledge of the revocation of the power (see 12.2). To assist subsequent purchasers, s 5(4) provides that where the interest of a purchaser depends on whether a transaction between the donee of a power of attorney and another person was valid by virtue of s 5(2), it will be conclusively presumed that the person dealing with the donee of the power did not at the material time know of the revocation of the power if:

(a)   the transaction between that person and the donee was completed within twelve months of the date on which the power came into operation; or

(b)   that person makes a statutory declaration, before or within three months after the completion of the purchase, that he did not at the material time know of the revocation of the power.

Example

A appoints B to be his attorney utilising the general power of attorney contained in Sch 1 Powers of Attorney Act 1971.

Two years later B sells A's house to C.

One year later C sells the house to D.

C is protected by s 5(2). D is not protected by s 5(4)(a) as the transaction between B and C was completed more than twelve months after the power came into operation. However, D is protected by s 5(4)(b) if C makes a statutory declaration before or within three months after the completion of the purchase by himself that at the material time he did not know of the revocation of the power.

Section 5(5) should be borne in mind; this provides that knowledge of the revocation of a power of attorney includes knowledge of the occurrence of any event (such as the death of the donor) which has the effect of revoking the power.

Section 5(6) provides that 'purchaser' and 'purchase' have the meanings specified in s 205(1) Law of Property Act 1925. There 'purchaser' is defined as a purchaser in good faith for valuable consideration, and includes a lessee, mortgagee, or other person who for valuable consideration acquires an interest in property. So a purchaser from a person who dealt with an attorney (D in the example above) is not protected by s 5(4) if he was aware that the power had been revoked, but subsequent purchasers in good faith are protected.

Transferees under stock exchange transactions

12.4   Section 6(1) Powers of Attorney Act 1971 provides additional protection for transferees under stock exchange transactions. It provides that, without prejudice to s 5 of the Act, where:

(a)   the donee of a power of attorney executes, as transferor, an instrument transferring registered securities; and

(b)   the instrument is executed for the purpose of a stock exchange transaction,

it will be conclusively presumed in favour of the transferee that the power had not been revoked at the date of the instrument if a statutory declaration to that effect is made by the donee of the power on or within three months after that date.

Irrevocable powers

12.5   Section 4 Powers of Attorney Act 1971 deals with irrevocable powers given as security for a proprietary interest of the donee of the power, or for the performance of an obligation owed to the donee. The section provides that so long as the donee has that interest or the obligation remains undischarged, the power cannot be revoked by the donor without the consent of the donee; nor can it be revoked by the death, incapacity or bankruptcy of the donor or, if the donor is a body corporate, by its winding up or dissolution.

Where, in the instrument creating it, a power is expressed to be irrevocable and to be given by way of security then, unless the person dealing with the donee knows that it was not in fact given by way of security, s 5(3) provides that he will be entitled to assume that the power is incapable of revocation except by the donor acting with the consent of the donee; he will accordingly be treated for the purposes of s 5(2) as having knowledge of the revocation only if he knows that it has been revoked in that manner. Thus a person dealing with the donee of an irrevocable power will be protected unless he knows it has been revoked by the donor with the consent of the donee, or he knows the power was not given by way of security. Subsequent purchasers will be able to take advantage of the protection afforded by s 5(4) (see para 12.3).

Situations where a power can be made irrevocable:

(a)   A mortgagee may be given a power of attorney by the mortgagor to enable the mortgagee to sell the mortgaged property. Such a power is given both to secure a proprietary interest of the mortgagee or donee, and the performance of an obligation owed to the mortgagee or donee.

(b)   A partner may give his other partners a power of attorney limited to the affairs of the partnership. Such a power may secure a proprietary interest of the donee or partner; alternatively, or in addition, it may secure the obligations or duties owed by the donee of the power to the other partners.

(c)   In conveyancing transactions, builders sometimes take the existing house of a purchaser in part exchange for a new house. Rather than take a conveyance of the existing house, and incur liability for stamp duty, the builder is granted a power of attorney by the purchaser authorising the builder to transfer the purchaser's existing house to the purchaser from the builder. Such a power clearly secures a proprietary interest of the builder. Home relocation companies also take powers of attorney rather than a transfer of the house concerned.

Third party protection when power is void from the outset

12.6   It may be that a power is granted by someone who did not have the capacity to do so. A person dealing with the 'donee' of the power may have no means of ascertaining if this is the case, but any transaction under the power will be void (*Daily Telegraph Newspaper Co Ltd v McLaughlin [1904] AC 777* and CHAPTER 9). The Powers of Attorney Act 1971 does not contain any provision protecting the attorney in this situation. However, an attorney lacking authority will be liable for breach of warranty of authority (see CHAPTER 11), and provided the attorney has enough money to satisfy any judgment, the third party will not suffer any loss. Accordingly, the risk in dealing with professionally qualified attorneys is slight. However, if a person dealing with an attorney suspects that all is not in order, further enquiries should be made as to the validity of the power.

II. Enduring powers of attorney

12.7   Section 5 Powers of Attorney Act 1971 and s 2 of the Trustee Delega-tion Act 1999 protect persons dealing with the donee and subsequent purchas-ers. However, the EPAA 1985 has some additional provisions.

Protection of persons dealing with the donee

12.8   Section 1(2) EPAA 1985 applies to the period between application for registration of an enduring power, and the initial determination of that application. It permits the attorney to take action under the power to maintain the donor or prevent loss to his estate, or to maintain himself or other persons in so far as s 3(4) permits him to do so. Section 1(3) protects a person who deals with an attorney without knowledge that the attorney is acting outside s 1(2).

Section 9 EPAA 1985 deals with the situation where an instrument which did not create a valid power has been registered (whether or not the registration has been cancelled at the time of the act or transaction in question). For example, it applies to a power which was invalid because the donor lacked capacity at the time of the grant, but which had still been registered. It is quite common for an enduring power of attorney to be granted when the donor is exhibiting at the very least signs of mental incapacity, and so some protection is necessary for persons dealing with the attorney in this situation.

Section 9(3) EPAA 1985 provides that any transaction between the attorney and another person shall, in favour of that person, be as valid as if the power had then been in existence, unless at the time of the transaction that person knows that:

(a)   the instrument did not create a valid enduring power; or

(b)   an event has occurred which, if the instrument had created a valid enduring power, would have had the effect of revoking the power; or

(c)   if the instrument had created a valid enduring power, the power would have expired before that time.

Schedule 2 EPAA 1985 provides further protection for a third person dealing with the donee of an invalid enduring power. It applies where an instrument framed in the prescribed form creates a power which is not a valid enduring power, and is revoked by the mental incapacity of the donor. Under Sch 2 para 3 any transaction between the attorney and another person shall, in favour of that person, be as valid as if the power had been in existence, unless at the time of the transaction that person knows that:

(a)   the instrument did not create a valid power; and

(b)   the donor has become mentally incapable.

Protection of subsequent purchasers

12.9   Section 9(3) and Sch 2 para 3 EPAA 1985 protect persons dealing with the attorney. Subsequent purchasers are protected by s 9(4) and Sch 2 para 4; these measures provide that where the interest of a purchaser depends on whether a transaction between the attorney and another person was valid by virtue of s 9(3) or Sch 2 para 3, it will be conclusively presumed in favour of the purchaser that the transaction was valid if:

(a)   the transaction between that person and the attorney was completed within twelve months of the date on which the instrument was registered; or

(b)   that person makes a statutory declaration, before or within three months after the completion of the purchase, that he had no reason at the time of the transaction to doubt that the attorney had authority to dispose of the property which was the subject of the transaction.

It will be recalled that s 9 applies to the situation where an instrument which did not create a valid power has been registered (whether or not the registration has been cancelled at the time of the act or transaction in question), and that Sch 2 applies to an instrument in the prescribed form which is not a valid enduring power, and which has been revoked by the mental incapacity of the donor.

Section 9(7) EPAA 1985 provides that 'purchaser' and 'purchase' have the meanings specified in s 205(1) Law of Property Act 1925. These are discussed above; if a purchaser is not acting in good faith, he will not be able to take advantage of s 9.

Section 9(5) EPAA 1985 states that if the donor revokes the power, and such revocation is invalid unless and until confirmed by the court, knowledge of the confirmation of the revocation is knowledge of the revocation. However, knowledge of the unconfirmed revocation does not amount to knowledge of the revocation of the power. Thus the donee of the power and any other person are not concerned with any revocation of the power until it has been confirmed by the court.

Applications of s 5 Powers of Attorney Act to enduring powers

12.10   Section 9(2) and (4) EPAA 1985 are of limited application – they apply only where an instrument which did not create a valid power has been registered. Schedule 2 applies where the instrument failed to create a valid enduring power, and the power has been revoked by the donor's mental incapacity (s 9(6)). In other situations, s 5 Powers of Attorney Act 1971 applies.

Although there are some limited exceptions, s 1(1)(b) EPAA 1985 provides that if the donor of an enduring power becomes mentally incapable, the donee of the power may not do anything under the authority of the power until it is registered. Section 1(1)(c) provides that s 5 Powers of Attorney Act 1971 applies to enduring powers for so long as the donor's authority is suspended under s 1(1)(b); this provision is necessary because s 5 applies only when the power has been revoked, and not merely suspended.

Third party protection when power is invalid

12.11   Section 9 and Sch 2 EPAA 1985 may be wide enough to protect the person dealing with the attorney under an invalid power. These are discussed above. A person who deals with a donee, or a purchaser from a donee, under a registered power which was invalid, or which is in the prescribed form but does not create a valid enduring power and is revoked by the mental incapacity of the donor, is in a much stronger position than a person who deals with a donee, or a purchaser from a donee, of an invalid ordinary power, whose only remedy may be to sue the attorney for breach of warranty of authority.

Summary

12.12

- Section 5(2) Powers of Attorney Act 1971 protects a person dealing with an attorney without knowledge of the revocation of the power of attorney.

- Section 5(4) protects subsequent purchasers.

- Section 4 protects persons dealing with the donee of an irrevocable power.

- Section 9 and Sch 2 EPAA 1985 provides additional protection for persons dealing with the donees of invalid enduring powers which have been registered, and donees of powers in the prescribed form which are invalid and have been revoked by the mental incapacity of the donor.

- There is no protection for a person dealing with a 'donee' under an invalid ordinary power, but if it is an enduring power, such a person may be able to take advantage of s 9 EPAA 1985.

Chapter 13

Execution of documents, conveyancing and grants of representation

I. Execution of documents

By an individual

13.1 Section 7(1) Powers of Attorney Act 1971, as amended by the Law of Property (Miscellaneous Provisions) Act 1989, provides that the donee of a power of attorney may, if he thinks fit:

(a)   execute any instrument with his own signature, and

(b)   do any thing in his own name,

by the authority of the donor of the power; and any document executed or thing done in that manner is as effective as if executed or done by the donee with the signature and seal, or, as the case may be, in the name, of the donor of the power.

An attorney can thus execute a document using his own name or the name of the donor.

Section 74(3) Law of Property Act 1925 provides that where a person is authorised under a power of attorney to convey any interest in property in the name or on behalf of a company, he may as attorney execute the conveyance by signing the name of the company in the presence of at least one witness, and such execution takes effect and is valid as if the corporation had executed the conveyance.

Section 7(2) Powers of Attorney Act 1971 states that an instrument to which s 74(3) Law of Property Act 1925 applies may be executed either as provided in s 74(3) of the 1925 Act or as provided in s 7 of the 1971 Act.

By a company

13.2   If a company has been appointed an attorney, s 74(4) Law of Property Act 1925 provides that an officer appointed for that purpose by the board of directors by resolution, or otherwise, may execute the deed or other instrument in the name of such other person; and where an instrument appears to be so executed by an officer so appointed, then in favour of a purchaser the instrument will be deemed to have been executed by an officer duly authorised. Section 205(1)(xxi) defines a purchaser as meaning a purchaser in good faith for valuable consideration.

II. Conveyancing

Protection of purchasers

13.3   Section 5 Powers of Attorney Act 1971 and s 9 and Sch 2 EPAA 1985 protect purchasers dealing with the donee of both an ordinary and an enduring power. This topic is discussed in CHAPTER 12.

Registered conveyancing and powers of attorney

Proof of powers of attorney

13.4   The Land Registration Rules 2003 come into force on 13 October 2003. Rule 61(1) provides that if a document executed by an attorney is delivered at the Registry, the registrar must be furnished with:

(i)   the instrument creating the power; or

(ii)   a copy by means of which its contents may be proved under either s 3 Powers of Attorney Act 1971 or s 7(3) EPAA 1985 or a document which complies with s 4 Evidence and Powers of Attorney Act 1940; or

(iii)   a certificate by a conveyancer in Form 1 (this is reproduced in APPENDIX 1).

Section 3(1) Powers of Attorney Act 1971 provides that the contents of an instrument creating a power of attorney may be proved by a copy which:

'(a)   is a reproduction of the original made with a photographic or other device for reproducing documents in facsimile; and

(b)   contains the following certificate or certificates signed by the donor of the power or by a solicitor or stockbroker, that is to say –

(i)   a certificate at the end to the effect that the copy is a true and complete copy of the original; and

(ii)   if the original consists of two or more pages, a certificate at the end of each page of the copy to the effect that it is a true and complete copy of the corresponding page of the original.'

Under s 3(2) the contents of an instrument creating a power of attorney may also be proved by a copy of a copy complying with s 3(1) if the further copy complies with s 3(1).

Section 3 applies to both ordinary powers and enduring powers. Section 7(3) EPAA 1985, which applies only to enduring powers, provides that a document purporting to be an office copy of an instrument registered under the EPAA 1985 will be evidence of the contents of the instrument and of the fact that it has been so registered. Section 7(4) EPAA 1985 provides that subs (3) is without prejudice to s 3 Powers of Attorney Act 1971 and to any other method of proof authorised by law.

Section 4 Evidence and Powers of Attorney Act 1940 is of little relevance today.

If it is an enduring power, and an order has been made under s 8 EPAA 1985, which deals with the functions of the court with respect to a registered power, the registrar must be supplied with a copy of the order or an office copy or copy certified pursuant to r 214. Rule 217(1) provides that a certified copy means a copy of a document which a conveyancer, and such other persons as the register may permit, has certified on its face to be a true copy of the original and endorsed with his name and address.

Conveyancer means a solicitor or a licensed conveyancer or a Fellow of the Institute of Legal Executives.

Proof of non-revocation of the power

13.5   If the transaction between the donee of the power of attorney and the person dealing with him is completed within twelve months of the date when the power came into force, the registrar will not usually require any additional evidence to the effect that the power has not been revoked. It will be recalled that s 5(2) Powers of Attorney Act 1971 provides that where a power of attorney has been revoked and a person, without knowledge of the revocation, deals with the donee of the power, the transaction between them shall, in favour of that person, be as valid as if the power had then been in existence. Section 5(4) provides that where the interest of a purchaser depends on whether a transaction between the donee of a power of attorney and another person was valid by virtue of subs (2), it will be conclusively presumed in favour of a purchaser that that person did not at the material time know of the revocation of the power if the transaction between that person was completed within twelve months of the date on which the power came into operation. The registrar is protected by both these provisions; in addition, any person who deals with the attorney, and who is aware that the power has been revoked, is not entitled to indemnity if the register is rectified against him (para 5 Sch 8 Land Registration Act 2002).

If the transaction between the donee of the power of attorney and the person dealing with him is completed more than twelve months after the date on which the power came into operation, the registrar may require evidence that the power has not been revoked (r 62). This evidence may consist of a statutory declaration by the person dealing with the donee, or a certificate given by that person's conveyancer in Form 2 (Form 2 is reproduced in APPENDIX 1).

Rule 63 applies where the power is given under s 9 of the Trusts of Land and Appointment of Trustees Act 1996. Such powers are rarely granted, but if one is, then the registrar may require a statutory declaration by the person who dealt with the attorney or a certificate given by that person's conveyancer either in Form 3, or where evidence of non-revocation is required in Form 2. Forms 2 and 3 are reproduced in APPENDIX 1.

Joint tenants and tenants in common

13.6   Section 1 of the Trustee Delegation Act 1999 permits a trustee to delegate his functions, provided he has a beneficial interest in the land. However, s 7 requires that two persons must execute any transfer. Spouses or cohabitees who are joint proprietors can therefore delegate their functions by means of a power of attorney and the following options are open to them:

(a)   Co-owners can delegate their powers by means of an enduring power to the children of the donor, or the other co-owner and a child of the donor.

(b)   Section 7 does not apply to personalty, and so co-owners can grant each other enduring powers limited to the personal estate. A separate power – limited to the real estate – could then be granted to each other and a child. If one co-owner then becomes mentally incapable, the power can be registered, but there will be at least two people to sign any transfer so as to comply with s 7.

(c)   Another possibility is for both co-owners to appoint each other attorneys under enduring powers. If one becomes mentally incapable, the other can make use of s 8 TDA to appoint another trustee.

The section inserts a new section into s 36 Trustee Act 1925. Section 36(6A) confers on the donee of an enduring power a limited power to appoint a new trustee. The subsection applies to a person who is either –

•   both a trustee and attorney for the other trustee (if one other), or for both of the other trustees (if two others), under a registered power; or

•   attorney under a registered power for the trustee (if one), or for both or each of the trustees (if two or three) (s 36(6A)).

Thus a trustee who is one of two trustees, and is appointed attorney by the other trustee, can appoint another trustee. Similarly a trustee who is one of three trustees and is appointed attorney by the other two trustees can appoint a fourth. An attorney who is not a trustee can also exercise this power, but must have been appointed by all the trustees. Note that all the powers must be registered.

The attorney must as attorney under the power intend –

(a)   to exercise any function of the trustee or trustees by virtue of s 1(1) Trustee Delegation Act 1999; or

(b)   to exercise any function of the trustee or trustees in relation to any land, capital proceeds of a conveyance of land or income from land by virtue of its delegation to him under s 25 Trustee Delegation Act 1999 or the instrument (if any) creating the trust (s 36(6B) Trustee Act).

Thus the attorney must intend to exercise any trustee function, but it is immaterial whether the power is granted under s 1 Trustee Delegation Act 1999, or s 25 Trustee Act as substituted.

Section 36(6D) states that s 36(6A) is subject to any contrary intention expressed in the instrument creating the power of attorney (or, where more than one, any of them) or the instrument (if any) creating the trust, and has effect subject to the terms of those instruments.

Spouses or cohabitees could make use of this power to appoint each other as attorneys. If one becomes mentally incapable, the one retaining capacity can appoint another trustee. If the co-owned house is then sold, the transfer can be executed by the spouse retaining capacity in his or her personal capacity, as attorney for the spouse lacking capacity and the additional trustee, thereby satisfying the requirements of s 7.

The question of delegation by trustees, and the position with regard to pre-TDA powers is explored in more detail in CHAPTER 9.

How can a purchaser be satisfied that a trustee has a beneficial interest in the land? Section 2 provides that a purchaser need not do anything else as long as the donee signs a statement that the donor has a beneficial interest in the property either when doing the act in question or within three months of doing it.

III. Grants of representation to an attorney

Effect of mental incapacity on existing grants

13.7   If a sole executor or administrator, or the sole surviving executor or administrator, appoints an attorney under an enduring power, and then becomes mentally incapable, the attorney cannot continue with the administration of the estate, even if the power has been registered.

Similarly, if one of two or more executors or administrators becomes mentally incapable having appointed an attorney under an enduring power, the attorney cannot take over the administration of the estate. (See Practice Direction [1986] 2 All ER 41.)

Procedure on an application by an attorney

13.8   If a donor of an enduring or ordinary power of attorney is entitled to apply for a grant of probate or letters of administration, his attorney can apply for administration for the use and benefit of the donor under r 31(1) Non-Contentious Probate Rules 1987 (SI 1987 No 2024), provided he has authority to do so under the power; a general power gives such authority. The grant may be limited until further representation be granted, or in such other way as the registrar may direct.

If an attorney is applying on behalf of a donor who is an executor, notice of the application must be given to any other executor unless such notice is dispensed with by the registrar (r 31(2)), but the rules do not require an attorney acting on behalf of a donor who is entitled to a grant of letters of administration to give notice to other persons who are equally entitled to apply for a grant of letters of administration.

If the donor was appointed an executor, the attorney will be given a grant of letters of administration with the will annexed. The donor of the power, or if more than one executor was appointed, another executor, can apply for a grant of probate, and if that grant is made, the grant of letters of administration with the will annexed will terminate.

Even if there is a grant to an attorney, it will still be necessary to comply with s 114(2) Supreme Court Act 1981. This provides that where under a will or intestacy, any beneficiary is a minor, or a life interest arises, any grant of administration by the High Court must be made either to a trust corporation (with or without an individual) or to no fewer than two individuals unless it appears to the court to be expedient in all the circumstances to appoint an individual as sole administrator.

An attorney applying for a grant should lodge with the Probate Registry the instrument creating the power of attorney, or alternatively a copy certified in accordance with s 3 Powers of Attorney Act 1971.

If the donor is mentally incapable, and the attorney is acting under an enduring power, r 31(3) requires the application to be made in accordance with r 35. Rule 35(1) provides that, unless the registrar otherwise directs, no grant will be made under the rule unless all the persons entitled in the same degree as the donor have been cleared off. Rule 22(1) lays down the order of priority for a grant of letters of administration; if there is anyone in the same class as the donor, r 35 does not apply until all the persons in that class have been cleared off.

Rule 35(2) provides that where a registrar is satisfied that a person entitled to a grant is by reason of mental incapacity incapable of managing his own affairs, administration for his use and benefit, limited until further representation be granted or in such other way as the registrar may direct, may be granted in the following order of priority:

- to the person authorised by the Court of Protection to apply for a grant;

- where there is no person so authorised, to the lawful attorney of the incapable person acting under a registered enduring power of attorney;

- where there is no such attorney entitled to act, or if the attorney renounces administration for the use and benefit of the incapable person, to the person entitled to the residuary estate of the deceased.

If the enduring power is registered, no further proof of mental incapacity is required.

If it is a situation where two administrators are required because either a beneficiary is a minor or a life interest arises, and if there is only one person competent and willing to take a grant under the rule, administration may be granted to such person jointly with any other person nominated by him, unless a registrar otherwise directs (r 35(3)).

Under r 35(5), notice of an intended application under this rule must be given to the Court of Protection.

For a fuller discussion of these matters readers are referred to *Butterworth's Wills, Probate and Administration Service*, Division D.

Summary

13.9

- The donee of a power of attorney can execute a document in his own name.

- The existence or terms of a power of attorney can be proved by the production of the original or a certified copy, or if it is an enduring power which has been registered, an office copy.

- If an order has been made under s 8 EPAA 1985, if the title is registered, the registrar must be supplied with a copy of the order, or an office copy or a certified copy.

- If the transaction between the donee of the power of attorney and the person dealing with him is completed more than twelve months after the date on which the power came into operation, the person dealing with the donee will have to make a statutory declaration. A certificate may be accepted.

- The donee of an ordinary or enduring power may have authority to take out a grant of probate or letters of administration if the donor would have been entitled to do so.

Chapter 14

Procedure in the Court of Protection

14.1   It may be that a person becomes mentally incapable without having executed an enduring power of attorney. In these circumstances, if it is desired to deal with the property of that person, it will be necessary to apply to the Court of Protection.

Previous regulations provided for a division of functions between the Public Trust Office and the Court of Protection. New regulations, which came into force on 1 April 2001, provide that all applications are to be made to the Court of Protection.

Extent of the powers of the Court of Protection

14.2   Section 95(1) Mental Health Act 1983 provides that the judge may, with respect to the property and affairs of a patient, do or secure the doing of all such things as appear necessary or expedient:

(a)   for the maintenance or other benefit of the patient,

(b)   for the maintenance or other benefit of members of the patient's family,

(c)   for making provision for other persons or purposes for whom or which the patient might be expected to provide if he were not mentally disordered, or

(d)   otherwise for administering the patient's affairs.

'Family' in s 95(1)(b) means persons for all of whom the patient might *prima facie* be expected to make some provision, and does not include collateral relatives such as nephews and nieces. Such people must bring themselves within s 95(1)(c) as persons for whom the patient might be expected to provide if he were not mentally disordered (per Cross J in *Re DML [1965] 2 All ER 129* at pages 131–132).

Section 96(1) confers wide powers on the judge to make orders or give directions or authorities for:

(a)   the control (with or without the transfer or vesting of property or the payment into or lodgement in the Supreme Court of money or securities) and the management of any property of the patient;

(b)   the sale, exchange, charging or other disposition of or dealing with any property of the patient;

(c) the acquisition of any property in the name or on behalf of the patient;

(d) the settlement of any property of the patient, or the gift of any property of the patient to any such persons or for any such purposes as are mentioned in paragraph (b) and (c) of s 95(1) above;

(e) the execution for the patient of a will making any provision (whether by way of disposing of property or exercising a power or otherwise) which could be made by a will executed by the patient if he were not mentally disordered;

(f) the carrying on by a suitable person of any profession, trade or business of the patient;

(g) the dissolution of a partnership of which the patient is a member;

(h) the carrying out of any contract entered into by the patient;

(i) the conduct of legal proceedings in the name of the patient or on his behalf;

(j) the reimbursement out of the property of the patient, with or without interest, of money applied by any person either in payment of the patient's debts (whether legally enforceable or not) or for the maintenance or other benefit of the patient or members of his family or in making provision for other persons or purposes for whom or which he might be expected to provide if he were not mentally disordered;

(k) the exercise of any power (including a power to consent) vested in the patient whether beneficially, or as guardian or trustee, or otherwise.

How will the court exercise its powers? In *Re C [1960] 1 All ER 393* a receiver had been appointed for a patient, and then discharged. The patient had then dissipated quite a large sum of money. A receiver had then been appointed, and it was proposed to make an irrevocable settlement of his property. This was authorised under broadly similar powers in the Law of Property Act 1925 to those contained in the Mental Health Act 1983. Danckwerts J, at page 396, said: 'This is a case where it is proper and desirable that the court should restrain the patient if he comes out into the world again, so that he is not able to squander his property to his own detriment.'

In *M v Lester [1966] 1 All ER 207* the infant plaintiff suffered brain damage, and was awarded damages of £15,000. It was directed that the money should be invested under the supervision of the Court of Protection, and that application for the appointment of a receiver should be made.

A settlement can also be ordered even if it will result in a saving of tax (*Re CWM [1951] 2 All ER 707*).

Section 96(3) provides that if a settlement has been made, it can be varied if:

(a) a material fact was not disclosed when the settlement was made; or

(b) there has been a substantial change in circumstances.

This power to vary can only be exercised whilst the patient is alive.

The procedure in the Court of Protection is governed by the Court of Protection Rules 2001, SI 2001 No 824 ('CPR 2001') as amended. Readers are warned not to confuse these rules with SI 2001 No 825, which is concerned with the registration of enduring powers of attorney.

When can an application be made for the appointment of a receiver?

14.3   The court can appoint a receiver if a person is incapable, by reason of mental disorder, of managing and administering his property and affairs (s 94 Mental Health Act 1983). Section 1(2) Mental Health Act 1983 defines mental disorder as meaning mental illness, arrested or incomplete development of mind, psychopathic disorder and any other disorder or disability of mind.

Exercise of the court's functions

14.4   Rule 3 CPR 2001 provides that where any function is expressed by the rules to be exercisable by the court then, subject to the provisions of the Mental Health Act 1983, that function may be exercised:

(a)   by a judge;

(b)   by the Master of the Court of Protection;

(c)   to the extent to which he is authorised under s 94 Mental Health Act 1983, by any nominated officer.

Rule 2(1) CPR 2001 defines 'judge' as the Lord Chancellor or a nominated judge.

Rule 11 CPR 2001 provides that where in the opinion of the court an application ought to be made for the appointment or discharge of a receiver or for the exercise of any other function with respect to the property and affairs of a patient, and there appears to be no other suitable person able and willing to make the application, or the court for any other reason thinks fit, the court may direct that the application be made by an officer of the court or, if he consents, by the Official Solicitor.

Exercise of jurisdiction of the court

14.5   Rule 6 CPR 2001 gives the court a wide discretion as to how the jurisdiction is exercised. It provides that, except where the rules otherwise provide, the jurisdiction of the court may be exercised:

(a)   without fixing an appointment for a hearing;

(b)   by the court of its own motion or at the instance or on the application of any person interested;

(c)   whether or not any proceedings have been commenced in the court with respect to the patient.

Form of application

14.6   Rule 7 CPR 2001 provides that a first application to the court for the appointment of a receiver is now made by the submission of a Receiver's Declaration. An application to the court respecting the exercise of any of its other jurisdiction in relation to a patient may be by letter unless the court directs that formal application must be made. In this situation, Form A must be used.

If the application is urgent, the court may dispense with the need for an application in writing (r 7(3)).

Rule 34(1) CPR 2001 provides that on the issue of a first application for the appointment of a receiver for a patient, or for a short order or direction under r 8 authorising any person to do any act or carry out any transaction on behalf of a patient without appointing him a receiver, the applicant must file a medical certificate and evidence of family and property, unless the court otherwise directs.

A medical certificate is defined as a certificate by a medical practitioner that the patient is incapable, by reason of mental disorder, of managing and administering his property and affairs. Evidence of family and property means a certificate or, if the court so orders in a particular case, an affidavit, giving particulars of the patient's relatives, property and affairs and of the circumstances giving rise to the application. The relevant form is now called the Statement of Client's Assets and Income.

Upon receipt of an application under r 7, the court fixes a date for the hearing of the application. However, it need not do so if it considers that the application can properly be dealt with without a hearing – and once a hearing date has been fixed, it can be cancelled on the same grounds (r 9).

It may be that application is made in respect of a husband and wife, or brothers and sisters. Rule 10 provides that the court may allow one application to be made in respect of two or more patients or may consolidate applications relating to two or more patients, if in the opinion of the court the proceedings relating to them can be more conveniently dealt with together.

The court may allow or direct an applicant to amend his application. The amendment may be effected by making in writing the necessary alterations to the application, but if the amendments are so numerous or of such a nature or length that written alterations would be difficult or inconvenient to read, a fresh application amended as authorised or direction may be issued (r 51).

There is also provision for a short order or direction without the appointment of a receiver where it appears to the court that the property of the patient does not exceed £16,000 in value, or it is otherwise appropriate to proceed under this rule, and that it is not necessary to appoint a receiver (r 8(1)). Rule 8(3) CPR 2001 provides that a short order or direction under this rule is an order directing an officer of the court or some other suitable person named in the order or direction to deal with the patient's property, or any part, or with his affairs, in any manner authorised by the Mental Health Act 1983 and specified in the order or direction.

Notification of application for the appointment of a receiver

14.7   Rule 24 is concerned with 'relevant applications', which are defined in r 24(1) as an application for any order, direction or certificate exercising the court's jurisdiction in respect of a patient, including an application for the appointment of a receiver. Rule 24(1A) provides that where a relevant application is made, the applicant, or such other person as the court may direct, shall give notice to the patient in accordance with paragraphs (1D) to (1F).

Rule 24(1D) provides that notice under paragraph (1A) shall consist of notice –

(a)   that an application has been made;

(b)   of the effect, if made, of:

    (i)   the appointment of a receiver, in the case of a first application for appointment of a receiver; or

    (ii)   such other order, direction or certificate as may have been applied for;

(c)   of the identity of the applicant and, if different, that of any proposed receiver;

(d)   of any hearing fixed by the court; and

(e)   of such information as the court may direct.

Rule 24 (1E) provides that notice under paragraph (1A) must be given to the patient personally.

Where the court has fixed a hearing, the time limits set out in r 19(5) apply to the giving of notice under paragraph (1A). Rule 19(5) provides that notice of the hearing shall be given –

•   in the case of a first application for the appointment of a receiver, or an application under r 16, not less than ten clear days; and

•   in the case of any other application, not less than two clear days before the date fixed for the hearing.

Paragraph (1A) does not apply where a relevant application ('the previous relevant application') has already been made in respect of the same patient, unless there has been any finding by the court since the previous relevant application was made that the patient is capable of managing and administering his property and affairs, or where an enduring power of attorney created by the patient has been registered, and the registration has not been cancelled (r 24(1B)). Rule 24(1BB) also provides that para (1A) does not apply to a relevant application where the court is of the opinion that it is necessary to make an immediate order directing or authorising any person to do any act or carry out any transaction on behalf of a patient, and directs that notice to the patient may be dispensed with. This is subject to para 1(c) which provides that para (1A) applies if the relevant application is a first application for the appointment of a receiver.

Rule 24(2) provides that where the patient is a minor, notification must be given to his parent or guardian or, if he has no parent or guardian, to the person with parental responsibility within the meaning of the Children Act 1989 (r 24(2)).

Next of kin may also have to be notified of the application. Rule 25(1) provides that where an applicant proposes to make an application for the appointment of a receiver or a new receiver, the applicant must give notice of his intention to do so to:

(a) all relatives of the patient who have the same or a nearer degree of relationship to the patient than the applicant or proposed receiver; and

(b) such other persons as the court may specify who appear to the court to be interested.

The court can direct that such notification be dispensed with.

Rule 25(2) CPR 2001 provides that for the purposes of the rule, notice of intention to make an application is given if the person concerned is notified, in such manner as the court directs, of the identities of the patient, the applicant and the proposed receiver and supplied with such additional information as the court may direct.

Rule 19(5) provides that notice of the hearing must be given not less than ten clear days before the date fixed for the hearing.

Rule 26 deals with certificates of service – this is dealt with in para 14.8.

Service of notice of the hearing

14.8   Rule 19 CPR 2001 provides that an applicant must give notice of the hearing of an application to:

(a)   the receiver for a patient, unless he is the applicant; and

(b)   such other persons as appear to the court to be interested and as the court may specify;

except where the rules provide otherwise or the court directs otherwise.

If the application is under s 54 Trustee Act 1925, which applies when the patient is also a trustee, or under s 96(1)(k) Mental Health Act 1983 which is concerned with the exercise of any power vested in the patient whether beneficially or as guardian or trustee or otherwise, r 19(3) provides that notice of hearing must also be given to every person who, according to the practice of the Chancery Division, would have been required to be served with the summons if the application had been made to the High Court.

In the case of a first application for the appointment of a receiver, r 19(5) provides that notice of the hearing of an application must be given not less than ten clear days before the date fixed for the hearing. The notice is given by means of a notification letter. In the case of any other application, notice must be given at least two clear days before. Rule 19(6) provides that notice of a hearing is to be given to the person concerned in such manner as the court may direct.

Rule 20 provides that except where the rules otherwise provide, any document required by the rules to be served on any person must be served by:

(a)   delivering it to him personally;

(b)   sending it to him by first class post or through a document exchange at his last known address; or

(c)   by transmitting it to him at his last known address by fax or other electronic means.

Under r 21 a solicitor acting for the person to be served can accept service on behalf of that person by endorsing on the document or a copy of it a statement to the effect that he accepts service on behalf of that person. If it is impracticable to serve any document in accordance with r 20, the court may make an order for substituted service of the document by taking such steps as the court may direct to bring it to the notice of the person to be served (r 22). Normally personal service of a first application for the appointment of a receiver is required.

Rule 23 provides that any document required to be served on a person who is a minor but is not also a patient must be served on his parent or guardian or, if he has no parent or guardian, on the person with parental responsibility as defined in s 3 Children Act 1989.

In the case of a patient, the document must be served:

(a)   on his receiver; or, if he has no receiver,

(b)   on the person acting in pursuance of an order or direction made under r 8 (which is concerned with short orders or directions without the appointment of a receiver); or, if there is no such person,

(c)   on an attorney acting under a registered power of attorney; or, if there is no such attorney,

(d)   on the person with whom he resides or in whose care he is.

Under r 23(2) the court has power to order that a document has been duly served on such a person.

Rule 26(1) provides that a certificate of service shall be filed as soon as practicable after the service of a document has been effected in accordance with these rules –

(a)   in the case of notice given under r 24(1A), unless the court directs otherwise;

(b)   otherwise if the court so directs.

Rule 26(1A) provides that a certificate of service under paragraph (1) shall show where, when and how and by whom service was effected and, in relation to a notice given under r 24(1A), shall also contain a certificate as to whether or not the patient appeared, to the person giving it, to understand the notice.

Representation of the patient

14.9   Rule 12(1) CPR 2001 provides that if a receiver has been appointed, any application on behalf of the patient must be made by the receiver in his own name, unless the court otherwise directs. Rule 12(2) provides that subject to any directions given by the court, a patient for whom a receiver has been appointed may be represented by the receiver at any hearing relating to the patient or of which the patient has been given notice.

It may be that the interests of the patient cannot be adequately represented by the receiver. In this situation, the court may direct that the Official Solicitor shall act as solicitor if he consents.

Urgent applications

14.10   Section 98 Mental Health Act 1983 provides that where it is represented to the judge, and he has reason to believe, that a person may be incapable, by reason of mental disorder, of managing and administering his property and affairs, and the judge is of the opinion that it is necessary to make immediate provision for any of the matters referred to in s 95 (see 14.2 above), then pending the determination of the question whether that person is so incapable, the judge may exercise in relation to the property and affairs of that person any of the powers conferred on him in relation to the property and affairs of a patient.

Rule 6 provides that, except where the rules otherwise provide, any function may be exercised:

(a)   without fixing an appointment for a hearing;

(b)   by the court of its own motion or at the instance or on the application of any person interested;

(c)   whether or not any proceedings have been commenced in the court with respect to the patient.

Evidence

14.11   Rule 27 CPR 2001 provides that except where the rules otherwise provide, evidence in proceedings under the rules shall be given by affidavit evidence. Rule 28(1) provides that the court may accept and act upon a statement of facts or such other evidence, whether oral or written, as the court considers sufficient, although not given on oath. It does not matter that the evidence would not be admissible in a court of law apart from this rule. Rule 28(2) provides that the court may give directions as to the manner in which a statement of facts or other written evidence is to be given but, subject to such directions, any such statement or other evidence must be:

(a)   drawn up in numbered paragraphs and dated; and

(b)   signed by the person by whom it is made or given.

Rule 30 provides that any person who has made an affidavit, or given a certificate or other written evidence for use in proceedings, may be ordered by the court to attend for cross-examination.

Normally any affidavit, certificate or other written evidence must be filed in the court before it can be used in any proceedings under the rules. However, the court may make an order on the basis of such evidence before it is filed if the person tendering it undertakes to file it before the order is drawn up (r 32). Rule 32(2) provides that every affidavit, certificate or other written evidence must be endorsed with the name and address of the solicitor, if any, for the person on whose behalf it is filed.

Rule 33 provides that evidence used in any proceedings can be used in a subsequent stage of those proceedings or in any other proceedings relating to the same patient or to another member of the patient's family.

Rule 48(1) provides that the court may allow or direct any person to take out a witness summons in Form B requiring the person named therein to attend before the court and give oral evidence or produce any document. Rule 48(3) provides that a witness summons must be served personally on the witness. Service must be a reasonable time before the day fixed for attendance, and the witness is entitled to the same conduct money and payment for expenses and loss of time as if he had been summoned to attend the trial of an action in the High Court.

Rule 50 authorises the judge or Master to make an order for the patient's attendance at such time and place as he may direct for examination by the Master, a visitor or any medical practitioner. See also 14.17 below.

Hearing of proceedings

14.12   Rule 37 CPR 2001 provides that every application shall be heard in chambers unless, in the case of an application for hearing by a judge, the judge otherwise directs. Rule 38 provides that the court may determine which persons should be entitled to attend at any stage of the proceedings relating to the patient.

Rule 39 provides that if two or more persons are represented by the same legal adviser, the court may require them to be separately represented. Rule 40 applies when the function of the court is not being exercised by a judge, and requires the court to refer to the judge any proceedings or any question arising in any proceedings which ought by virtue of any enactment or in its opinion to be considered by the judge. The Master can give such directions as he thinks fit. Rule 41 authorises the judge to refer any proceedings before him or any question arising therein to the Master for inquiry and report.

Receivers

14.13   Rule 42 CPR 2001 authorises the court to make immediate provision in relation to the property and affairs of a patient. This can be done by a certificate directing or authorising any person named therein to do any act or carry out any transaction specified in the certificate. Alternatively, the court can appoint an interim receiver for the patient. Subject to any directions given by the court, such appointment continues until further order.

An order appointing an interim receiver shall, unless the court otherwise directs, be served upon the patient within such time as the court may specify. The patient may, within such time as the order may specify, apply under r 54 for the reconsideration of the order by the court or, if the order was made by a judge, apply to have the order set aside.

Usually a draft order will be prepared and sent to the solicitor for the applicant for approval.

Rule 43(1) provides that where a receiver is appointed for a patient, or where the court orders, directs or authorises any named person ('the named person') to deal with a patient's property or any part of it or affairs, the court may allow the receiver or named person remuneration for his services at such amount or at such rate as it considers reasonable and proper. If remuneration is allowed, then it is a debt due to the receiver or named person from the patient and his estate. This provision also applies if use is made of the short order or direction under r 8.

Once a patient has died, it is not possible to ask for remuneration, unless the court has during the receivership directed that remuneration shall be allowed, and the request is made within six years from the date of the discharge of the receiver.

It is possible for two or more persons to be appointed receivers, and the court can direct that the receivership should continue in favour of the surviving or continuing receiver(s).

Rule 46(1) provides that where:

(a)   an order is made on a first application appointing a receiver for a patient or directing or authorising any person to do any act or carry out any transaction on behalf of a patient without appointing him a receiver, or

(b)   an order or direction with respect to a patient's property is made under r 8 (short procedure – see 14.6 above),

the order or direction is not to be entered until the expiration of ten clear days after the patient has been notified of the application. This means that the order or direction will not be effective until ten days after the patient has been notified of the application. This rule does not apply to any order for interim provision under r 42.

Security

14.14   Rule 56 CPR 2001 requires a receiver to give security for the due performance of his duties, and this security must be given before the receiver acts, unless the court allows it to be given subsequently. This obligation does not apply if the Official Solicitor or an officer of the court is appointed as receiver. Rule 57 provides that subject to any directions of the court, security may be given in any of the following ways, or a combination of such ways:

(a)   by a bond approved by the court and given by the person giving security and also by –

(i)   an insurance company, group of underwriters, or bank approved by the court; or

(ii)   two personal sureties approved by the court; or

(b)   in such other manner as the court may approve.

Rule 58 provides that any security given by lodgment of money or stock shall be dealt with in accordance with the terms of the direction filed when the lodgment was made.

Rule 60 provides that every person who has given security by a bond shall, whenever his accounts are passed or the court so directs, satisfy the court:

(a)   that any premiums payable in respect of the bond have been duly paid, or

(b)   if the bond was given by personal sureties, that each surety is living and within the jurisdiction and has neither been adjudicated bankrupt nor compounded with his creditors.

If the court is not so satisfied, it may require new security to be given or may give such other direction as he thinks fit.

Rule 59 provides that where a receiver is authorised or directed to give new security, and:

(a)   the new security has been completed, and

(b)   he has paid or secured to the satisfaction of the court any balance due from him,

the former security shall be discharged, unless the court otherwise directs.

Investments

14.15   The court has developed investment policies. The investments which will be permitted depend *inter alia* on the period for which investment is required, and the amount of money involved.

Accounts

14.16   It is clearly essential for a receiver to keep accounts. Rule 61(1) CPR 2001 obliges every receiver annually, and on the death or recovery of the patient for whom he has been appointed receiver, and at any other time as the court may direct, to deliver his accounts to the court within such time and in such manner as the court shall direct. Rule 61(3) provides that on the passing of any accounts, the court shall make proper allowance out of the patient's estate, including an allowance in respect of the reasonable and proper costs of the receiver in passing the accounts. Rule 61(4) provides that the court may direct that a receiver need not account under this rule or may dispense with the passing of any accounts at any time at which they would otherwise require to be passed. If any money is due from the receiver, it should be paid into court to the credit of the proceedings and invested in such manner as the court may direct, or be invested or otherwise dealt with by the receiver in such manner as the court may direct (r 62).

If the receiver defaults in these obligations, the court may disallow any remuneration which would otherwise be due to the receiver. If the receiver has defaulted in paying into court or investing or otherwise dealing with any money, he may be charged interest at such rate as the court may determine for the period of his default (r 63).

Rule 64 provides that unless otherwise directed, any money ordered to be paid by a receiver for maintenance shall be paid out of income, and any costs ordered to be paid by a receiver may, when taxed or fixed, be paid out of any monies coming into his hands, after providing for any maintenance and fees payable under these rules.

On the death or recovery of the patient, the receiver must deliver his final account to the court within such a time and in such manner as the court shall direct (r 65(1)). If the receiver is discharged or dies, the receiver or, in the case of his death, his personal representatives, must deliver a final account to the court within such time as the court shall direct (r 65(2)). Rule 65(3) provides that the court will pass the final account of a receiver from the date of the receiver's last account or, if no account of his has previously been passed, from the date of his appointment, unless in the opinion of the court the passing of such accounts may properly be dispensed with.

If a balance is found due from a receiver or his estate, he or his personal representatives must pay it into court or otherwise deal with it as the court may direct. If a balance is found due to the receiver or his estate, it must be paid to him or his personal representatives by the patient or out of the patient's estate (r 65(4) and (5)). Rule 65(6) provides that on payment of any balance found due from a receiver, or if no balance is found due from him, or the passing of his accounts has been dispensed with under r 65(1), the security of the receiver shall be discharged.

Enquiries

14.17   Section 102 Mental Health Act 1983 provides for three panels of visitors: medical, legal and general. Members are appointed by the Lord Chancellor, and medical visitors must be registered medical practitioners who appear to the Lord Chancellor to have special knowledge and experience of cases of mental disorder. Legal visitors must be barristers or solicitors of not less than ten years' standing.

Visitors may interview the patient in private, and a medical visitor may carry out in private a medical examination of the patient, and may require the production of and inspect any medical records relating to the patient.

Rule 67(1) provides that where a court has reason to believe that a receiver should be appointed for a patient or that any other power conferred on the court should be exercised with respect to the property and affairs of the patient, the court may direct:

(a) a medical or legal visitor or, if he consents, the Official Solicitor, or any other appropriate person to visit the patient and report to the court whether it is desirable in the interests of the patient that an application should be made for that purpose, and in the case of a report by a medical or legal visitor, whether there is any other matter which the court should consider before exercising its functions in relation to a patient's property and affairs; or

(b) a medical visitor to visit the patient and report to the court on the capacity of the patient to manage and administer his property and affairs.

On receiving any such report, the court may, if it thinks fit:

(a) direct an application to be made pursuant to r 11 (see 14.4 above); or

(b) if the report is by a medical visitor and the court is satisfied that the patient is incapable, by reason of mental disorder, of managing and administering his property and affairs, make an order appointing a receiver or exercising any other power conferred on the court with respect to the patient's property and affairs.

The court may inspect the property of the patient, or direct an officer of the court or, if he consents, the Official Solicitor or any other appropriate person to inspect the property, make any necessary enquiries and report to the court (r 68).

Rule 69 empowers the court to make or cause to be made such enquiries as it thinks fit as to any dealings with the patient's property before the commencement of the proceedings and as to the mental capacity of the patient at the time of such dealing. The court can also make enquiries as to whether the patient has executed any testamentary document, and make what other enquiries it considers necessary or expedient for the proper discharge of its functions under the Mental Health Act or the Court of Protection Rules (rr 70 and 71).

Custody and disposal of funds and other property

14.18 Rule 72 CPR 2001 deals with the situation where any furniture or effects of a patient are allowed by the court to remain in the possession of, or are deposited with, any person. That person must sign and file an inventory of the furniture or effects and an undertaking not to part with them except on a direction under seal.

Rule 73 empowers the court to order some proper person to transfer stock in the name of the patient or receiver to the receiver, a new receiver, or into court.

What happens if a patient dies or recovers? Rule 74(1) provides that on the death or recovery of a patient the court may order any money, securities or other property belonging to the patient, or forming part of his estate, or remaining under the control of or held under the directions of the court, to be paid, transferred, delivered or released to the person who appears to be entitled thereto. If the patient dies, and his estate is less than £5,000 after allowing for the debts and funeral expenses, the court may if it thinks fit provide for the payment of the funeral expenses, and then order that the balance should be transferred either to the personal representatives of the deceased or to the person who appears to be entitled to apply for a grant of representation (r 74(3)).

Sale of land

14.19   It may be necessary to sell the house in which the patient lived. For example, it may be that the patient is living with relatives, or is in hospital, and the patient's house has not been lived in for some time. If the sale has not already been authorised by the court, it is necessary to apply to the court for a direction permitting the sale. Once a purchaser has been found a certificate of value must be lodged; in some circumstances, for example if the receiver is purchasing the property, an affidavit of value will have to be filed. There is no need to submit the contract or transfer to the court for approval.

After completion, the solicitor for the receiver must submit a completion statement to the court. The balance of the purchase price is to be placed on deposit.

Co-ownership

14.20   Frequently the house will be vested in the name of the patient and the patient's spouse as trustees holding on trust for themselves as joint tenants or tenants in common. Section 36(1) Trustee Act 1925 provides that where a trustee is unfit to act or is incapable of acting, then:

(a)   the person(s) nominated for the purpose of appointing new trustees by the instrument creating the trust; or

(b)   if there is no such person, or no such person able and willing to act, then the surviving or continuing trustee(s) for the time being, or the personal representatives of the last surviving or continuing trustee,

may by writing appoint one or more other persons (whether or not the person exercising the power) to be a trustee or trustees in the place of the unfit or incapable trustee.

The number of trustees must not be increased beyond four (s 34(2)).

Section 36(6A) (inserted by Trustee Delegation Act 1999) provides that a person who is both a trustee and an attorney for the other trustee or trustees, or an attorney for all the trustees under a registered power, may appoint new trustees. (For a more detailed discussion of s 36(6A) please see 8.21 above.)

Section 36(9) Trustee Act 1925 provides that where a trustee is incapable, by reason of mental disorder within the meaning of the Mental Health Act 1983, of exercising his functions as trustee and is also entitled in possession to some beneficial interest in the trust property, he may not be replaced as trustee without the leave of the Court of Protection. If a receiver has been appointed, then application can be by letter to the court.

Section 41 Trustee Act 1925 empowers the court to appoint new trustees; it is specifically authorised to do so if a trustee is incapable of exercising his functions as a trustee by reason of mental disorder within the meaning of the Mental Health Act 1983.

Rule 16 provides that no person other than a co-trustee, or other person with power to appoint a new trustee, may make an application to the court under s 36(9) Trustee Act 1925 for leave to appoint a new trustee in place of a patient.

Section 54(2) Trustee Act 1925 applies *inter alia* where a patient is a trustee under an express, implied or constructive trust, and is also beneficially entitled, for example where spouses are co-owners. If a receiver appointed by the Court of Protection is acting for him, or an application for the appointment of a receiver has been made but not determined, the Court of Protection has concurrent jurisdiction with the High Court in relation to the trust property. This does not apply to a trust which is subject to an order for administration made by the High Court.

Rule 15 CPR 2001 provides that an application to the court under s 54(2) may be made only by:

(a)   the receiver for the patient; or

(b)   any person who has made an application for the appointment of a receiver which has not yet been determined; or

(c)   a continuing trustee; or

(d)   any other person who, according to the practice of the Chancery Division, would have been entitled to make the application if it had been made in the High Court.

Rule 19(3) provides that notice of hearing must also be given to every person who, according to the practice of the Chancery Division, would have been required to be served with the summons if the application had been made to the High Court.

(See PN8 issued by the Court of Protection.)

Can the receiver benefit persons other than the patient?

14.21   The provisions of s 95 Mental Health Act 1983 are set out at the beginning of this chapter.

In *Re WJGL [1965] 3 All ER 865* the court was concerned with a similar provision in the Mental Health Act 1959. The question was whether the court should authorise a lifetime settlement, and it was held that it should. Cross J said at pages 871–872:

'It seems to me . . . that I must assume that the patient becomes a sane man for a sufficient time to review the situation but knows that after a brief interval of sanity he will once more be as he was before. On that footing he would see himself a bachelor of sixty-eight who will never marry or have a family . . .. He would know that he will never have any friends, other than H.J.S. and the receiver, or any interests.'

The judge made further assumptions, and then continued:

'Making those very curious assumptions I have no doubt that the patient would execute an irrevocable settlement of a substantial part of his property; on the other hand, I do not think that it follows from those assumptions that he would leave himself no more than he could foresee that he was likely to need.'

Retirement of the receiver

14.22   A receiver may wish to retire through ill health or old age. In this situation, application should be made to the court.

Death of the receiver

14.23   The personal representatives of a deceased receiver should notify the court immediately. A final account may have to be prepared.

Recovery of the patient

14.24   It may be that the patient will recover, in which event application can be made for an order determining the proceedings. Medical evidence that the patient has recovered will be required.

Rule 35(1) CPR 2001 provides that where at any stage of proceedings relating to a patient the court has reason to believe that the patient has recovered, it may require medical evidence of the recovery to be furnished by such person as it thinks appropriate.

In *Re WLW [1972] 2 All ER 433* there was a conflict of evidence as to whether the patient had recovered. The report of a medical visitor had been disclosed, and it was held that the visitor could be cross-examined about the report. Goff J said at page 438:

'Accordingly, in my judgment, although the judge has a discretion it can only be exercised so as to refuse cross-examination where, on the facts of the particular case, it would be injurious to the patient and such cases could only be rare and exceptional.'

Death of the patient

14.25   The powers of the receiver terminate with the death of the patient. However, the receiver will have to produce a final account.

Rule 35(1) CPR 2001 provides that where at any stage of proceedings relating to a patient, the court has reason to believe that the patient has died, it may require evidence of the death to be furnished by such person as it thinks appropriate.

The court will release funds to the personal representatives once final directions have been given. Funds for the payment of funeral accounts, Inheritance Tax and the fees payable to the Probate Registry can be released.

Time limits

14.26   Rule 4(1) CPR 2001 provides that where a period of time fixed by the rules or by any order or direction of the court for doing an act expires on a day on which the appropriate office for doing that act is closed and for that reason the act cannot be done on that day, the act shall be in time if done on the next day on which that office is open.

Rule 4(2) provides that where the act is required to be done within a specified period after or from a specified date, the period begins immediately after that date. Rule 4(3) provides that where any period of time fixed as mentioned in r 4(1) is less than six days, any day on which the appropriate office is closed shall not be included in the computation of that period.

Rule 5 empowers the court to extend or abridge time.

Power of the court to intervene

14.27   The court has power to intervene if it is dissatisfied with the conduct of any proceedings or the carrying out of any order (r 49(1)). Rule 49(2) empowers the court to direct any person to make any application and to conduct any proceedings and carry out any directions which the court may specify. If the Official Solicitor consents, he can be appointed to act as solicitor for the patient in the proceedings in place of any solicitor previously acting for him.

Fees

14.28   Rules 76–83 and the Appendix to the CPR 2001 prescribe the fees payable. In general terms, a fee is payable on the commencement of any proceedings, annually and for transactions.

Costs

14.29   It will be remembered that r 43 CPR 2001 provides for the remuneration of the receiver (see 14.13 above). Rule 84(1) provides that any other costs are in the discretion of the court – the court may order them to be paid by the patient or charged on or paid out of his estate or paid by any other person attending or taking part in the proceedings.

Rule 87(1) provides that no receiver for a patient, other than the Official Solicitor, is entitled at the expense of the patient's estate to employ a solicitor or other professional person to do any work not usually requiring professional assistance. The court can authorise payment in this situation. Where two or more persons having the same interest in relation to the matter to be determined attend any hearing by separate legal representatives, they will not be allowed more than one set of costs of the hearing unless the court certifies that the circumstances justify separate representation.

Is it possible to avoid an application for the appointment of a receiver?

14.30   The procedure for dealing with small estates has already been mentioned (see 14.6 above). If the patient has no assets, it will frequently be unnecessary to apply to the court for the appointment of a receiver. For example, it may be that a pension can be paid to the relatives of a mentally disordered person. In addition, if an enduring power has been granted, application will not be necessary.

Money due for past maintenance

14.31   Rule 36 CPR 2001 provides that the amount due to any public authority for the past maintenance of a patient may, unless the court otherwise directs, be proved by the filing of an account certified under the hand of the proper officer of the authority.

Copies of documents

14.32   Any person who has filed an affidavit is entitled to a copy of it (r 75(1)). The person having the conduct of the proceedings is entitled on request to be supplied with a copy of any order, certificate, authority, direction or other document made, given or prepared by the court in the proceedings (r 75(2)). The court may direct otherwise under both sub-rules.

Rule 75(3) provides that any other person may, on request, be supplied with a copy of any such document as is mentioned in r 75(1) or (2), if the court is satisfied that he has good reason for requiring it and that it is not reasonably practicable for him to obtain it from the person entitled to bespeak a copy from the court.

Are relatives entitled to see documents in the possession of the Official Solicitor? In *Re E (mental health patient) [1985] 1 All ER 609* the Official Solicitor had successfully brought a claim against an area health authority on behalf of a patient. The parents of the patient were not satisfied with the award, and requested the Official Solicitor to release the papers relating to the case. The Court of Appeal confirmed that the paramount consideration was the interest and benefit of the patient (page 615). Stephenson LJ said at pages 616–617:

'. . . where, as here, the papers of which the patient seeks inspection are in the custody of the Official Solicitor in connection with litigation in which he has been authorised by the Court of Protection, . . ., or in which he is, as he is entitled to be under the Rules of the Supreme Court, the next friend of a patient whose property is being administered by the Court of Protection, a parent of this patient has no absolute right to see those papers, although they are the patient's property, but must obtain the authority of the Court of Protection to order disclosure of them as necessary or expedient for the benefit of the patient. The right course is . . . for the Vice-Chancellor . . . to inspect the papers himself, thereafter allowing inspection by the father's solicitors of any papers not really harmful to the patient'.

Consent to medical treatment

14.33   The Court of Protection has no power to agree to medical treatment on behalf of a patient. However, the High Court has jurisdiction under RSC O 15 r 16, or has inherent jurisdiction, to make a declaration as to the legality of a particular operation (*F v West Berkshire Health Authority and another (Mental Health Act Commission intervening) [1989] 2 All ER 545*).

Relationship between the Court of Protection and the Chancery Division

14.34   Does the Chancery Division have power to deal with the estates of persons suffering from mental disorder? The answer is to a large extent in the negative. The matter was raised in *Re K's Settlement Trusts [1969] 2 Ch 1* where X was entitled under various trusts to a large sum of money on attaining majority. X, whose mental age was unlikely to exceed fifteen, lived abroad. Trustees applied to the Chancery Division for an order that the capital should be retained until a specified date. They also requested an order that the income should be paid to the testamentary guardians of X so that it could be applied for his maintenance and benefit. It was held that the Chancery Division only had jurisdiction if three conditions were satisfied:

- Proceedings in the Court of Protection are not contemplated.

- The income is so small that it will all be used in the maintenance of the beneficiary.

- The Chancery Division must already be seised of the case.

Even if the conditions are satisfied, the jurisdiction is discretionary.

Can a creditor enforce a judgment against the patient?

14.35   Section 95(2) Mental Health Act 1983 provides that the requirements of the patient must first be considered and that the rules of law restricting the enforcement by a creditor of rights against property under the control of the judge in lunacy apply to the property under the control of the judge. However, the interests of creditors must be considered, together with the desirability of making provision for obligations of the patient notwithstanding that they may not be legally enforceable.

A creditor cannot levy execution against the goods of the patient, but the court will make an order for the payment of maintenance for the patient, although not for the spouse of the patient, and this will be without prejudice to any charge or priority the creditor may have acquired by lodging his writ of fi fa with the sheriff (*In re Winkle [1894] 2 Ch 519*).

Effect of bankruptcy of the patient

14.36   A patient can be made bankrupt, but the trustee in bankruptcy stands in the shoes of the debtor, and cannot obtain a better title. The Court of Protection controls the property of the patient, although if the patient recovers, control will then vest in the trustee in bankruptcy (*Re A Debtor [1941] 3 All ER 11*).

Divorce

14.37   It may be desirable for a patient to begin proceedings for divorce. This issue was discussed in *Re W [1970] 2 All ER 502*, where sections of the Mental Health Act 1959 similar to those in the Mental Health Act 1983 were considered.

Section 95(1) Mental Health Act 1983, which re-enacts s 102(1) Mental Health Act 1959, provides:

'The judge may, with respect to the property and affairs of a patient, do or secure the doing of all such things as appear necessary or expedient –

(a)   for the maintenance or other benefit of the patient;

(b)   for the maintenance or other benefit of members of the patient's family;

(c)   for making provision for other persons or purposes for whom or which the patient might be expected to provide if he were not mentally disordered; or

(d)   otherwise for administering the patient's affairs.'

It was held that 'benefit . . . is not restricted to material benefit, but that it is of wide significance comprehending whatever would be beneficial in any respect, material or otherwise' (Ungoed-Thomas J at page 505). At page 507 he said:

'Various aspects of "benefit", or factors in assessing "benefit", were discussed before me: (1) breakdown of marriage; (2) religion; (3) public policy; (4) children; (5) financial consequences; (6) the effect of the Divorce Reform Act 1969. These are of course all clearly factors to be taken into consideration in deciding whether or not, on balance, the presentation of a petition is for the "benefit" of the objects sought by the Act to be benefited, having regard to the order of priority laid down by the Act. The weight to be attached to the different factors will vary with the circumstances as variously as the circumstances themselves will vary . . .'.

The spouse of a patient may wish to apply for financial provision from the estate of a patient. This can be done (*Re CL v CFW [1928] P 223*).

Preservation of interests in the patient's property

14.38   It may be that a person would have been entitled to some property of the patient, which is disposed of under the Act. In these circumstances, the disappointed beneficiary takes the same interest, if and so far as circumstances allow, in any property belonging to the estate of the deceased which represents the property disposed of (s 101 Mental Health Act 1983).

Reviews and appeals

14.39   Rule 54(1) CPR 2001 provides that any person who is aggrieved by a decision of the court made on an unattended hearing may apply to the court within fourteen days of the date on which the decision was given to have the decision reviewed by the court. On the hearing of the application the court may either confirm or revoke the previous decision or make any other order or decision which it thinks fit (r 54(3)). Note that no appeal lies from a decision under r 83, which deals with the remission, postponement and exemption of fees (r 54(2)).

Rule 55 provides for appeals from decisions made after an attended hearing. The appellant must within fourteen days:

(a)   serve a notice of appeal in Form C on –

  (i)   every person who appeared, or was represented, before the court when the order or decision was made or given, and

  (ii)   any other person whom the court may direct; and

(b)   lodge a copy of the notice at the court office.

The time and place at which the appeal is to be heard is fixed by the court. Notice of the time and place so fixed is sent to the appellant who must immediately send notice of it to every person who has been served with notice of the appeal (r 55(3)). Rule 55(4) provides that no evidence further to that given at the hearing shall be filed in support of or in opposition to the appeal without leave of the court.

Representation by solicitors

14.40   Problems can sometimes arise if more than one solicitor is instructed. For example, two relatives of a mentally disordered person may instruct different solicitors. According to a Practice Direction issued by the Court of Protection on 9 August 1995 the solicitor who makes the first application will be regarded as acting for the patient or the donor of an enduring power, until there is an objection to the application, or another application is received. The first solicitor must then choose whether to represent the first applicant or the patient. If the solicitor chooses to represent the first applicant, it will be necessary for the court to decide if the patient should be represented by another solicitor. The Official Solicitor may be appointed if he agrees.

Summary

14.41

- The Court of Protection has wide powers to deal with the property of a mentally disordered person.

- Application for the appointment of a receiver must be supported by a medical certificate and a certificate of family and property.

- There is a short procedure for small estates.

- A person appointed as receiver must give security.

- A receiver must keep accounts.

- Visitors may be asked to make further enquiries.

Chapter 15

Wills for mentally disordered persons

Testamentary capacity of the donor of a power of attorney

15.1   The mere fact that a donor has granted an ordinary or enduring power will not prevent him making a valid will, provided he has the necessary testamentary capacity. In *Banks v Goodfellow (1870) LR 5 QB 549* at page 565 Cockburn CJ stated:

> 'It is essential ... that a testator shall understand the nature of the act and its effects; shall understand the extent of the property of which he is disposing; shall be able to comprehend and appreciate the claims to which he ought to give effect; and, with a view to the latter object, that no disorder of the mind shall poison his affections, pervert his sense of right, or prevent the exercise of his natural faculties – that no insane delusion shall influence his will in disposing of his property and bring about a disposal of it which, if the mind had been sound, would not have been made.'

If an enduring power is granted, the donee must apply for registration of the power if he has reason to believe that the donor is or is becoming mentally incapable (s 4(1) EPAA 1985). Even if the power is registered, if the donor recovers his mental capacity, he can make a valid will, even though the registration has not been cancelled. It is possible that the donor might still have the capacity to make a will even though the donee is under a duty to apply for registration because the donor is becoming mentally incapable. A donor may have good days when he has capacity to make a will, and bad days when he lacks capacity.

Wills under the Mental Health Act 1983

Jurisdiction

15.2   An attorney under an ordinary power or an enduring power of attorney cannot make a will on behalf of the donor of the power. If the donor lacks capacity to make a will, application can be made to the Court of Protection, which is empowered by s 96(1) Mental Health Act 1983 to:

> 'make orders and give directions or authorities for ... (e) the execution for the patient of a will making any provision (whether by way of disposing of

property or exercising a power or otherwise) which could be made by a will executed by the patient if he were not mentally disordered.'

Under s 94(2) Mental Health Act 1983, the judge can exercise his functions 'where after considering medical evidence, he is satisfied that a person is incapable, by reason of mental disorder, of managing and administering his property and affairs'.

Section 96(4) provides that the power of a judge to make or give an order, direction or authority for the execution of a will for a patient must not be exercised unless the judge has reason to believe that the patient is incapable of making a valid will for himself.

There is no need to apply for the appointment of a receiver at the same time as an application for a statutory will (see PD Lewis, *The Law Society's Gazette* (29 April 1987) at page 1219).

Beneficiaries

15.3   This is dealt with in s 95(1) Mental Health Act 1983. The will can benefit members of the patient's family, and also persons for whom the patient might be expected to provide if he were not mentally disordered. 'Family' is not defined in the 1983 Act, but it does not include collateral relatives such as nephews and nieces (*Re DML [1965] 2 All ER 129*). Relatives such as a spouse, issue or parents are clearly members of the family, but other relatives will have to prove that they are persons for whom the patient might have been expected to provide had he not been mentally disordered.

Principles

15.4   In *Re D (J) [1982] Ch 237* at pages 243, 244, it was held that the judge will apply the following five principles in deciding what will should be made for the patient:

   (i)   'it is to be assumed that the patient is having a brief lucid interval at the time when the will was made';

  (ii)   'during the lucid interval the patient has a full knowledge of the past and a full realisation that as soon as the will is executed he or she will relapse into the actual mental state that previously existed, with the prognosis as it actually is';

 (iii)   'it is the actual patient who has to be considered and not a hypothetical patient';

 (iv)   'during the hypothetical lucid interval, the patient is to be envisaged as being advised by competent solicitors';

  (v)   'in all normal cases the patient is to be envisaged as taking a broad brush to the claims on his bounty, rather than an accountant's pen'.

In *Re C (Spinster and Mental Patient) [1991] 3 All ER 866*, the patient had always been mentally incapable. Hoffmann J said that 'the court must assume that she would have been a normal decent person, acting in accordance with contemporary standards of morality'.

If appropriate, application can be made for a will in order to save tax (*Re L (WJG) [1966] 1 Ch 135*).

Applications to the court

15.5   The procedure is governed by the Court of Protection Rules 2001 (SI 2001 No 824) and Practice Notes issued by the Court of Protection.

Rule 18 provides that applications can be made by:

(i) the receiver for the patient; or

(ii) any person who has made an application for the appointment of a receiver which has not been determined; or

(iii) any person who under any known will of the patient or under his intestacy may become entitled to any property of the patient or any interest therein; or

(iv) any person for whom the patient might be expected to provide if he were not mentally disordered; or

(v) an attorney acting under a registered enduring power; or

(vi) any other person whom the court may authorise to make it.

Rule 19 deals with who should be given notice of the hearing, and the time limits for doing so. It provides:

'(1) Except where these rules provide otherwise or the court directs otherwise, the applicant shall give notice of the hearing of an application in accordance with the following provisions of this rule.

(2) Where a receiver has been appointed for a patient he shall, unless he is the applicant, be given notice of the hearing of any application relating to the patient ...

(4) Notice of the hearing of the application shall also be given to such other persons who appear to the court to be interested as the court may specify ...'.

Rule 19(5) provides that notice of the hearing of an application for the execution of a will of the patient must be given not less than two clear days before the date fixed for the hearing.

If the court thinks that the interests of the patient are not adequately represented by the receiver, the court can direct the Official Solicitor to act as solicitor for the patient, provided that the Official Solicitor consents (r 13).

It may be that no notice is appropriate. In *Re Davey [1980] 3 All ER 342* an elderly lady made a will benefiting seventeen named persons. Subsequently, a psychiatrist examined her, and concluded that she was incapable of managing her own affairs. She then married a forty-eight-year-old man who worked at the nursing home where she lived; the effect of the marriage was to revoke the will, and the man would have been entitled to a substantial part of the estate under the intestacy rules. The matter came to the attention of the Court of Protection on 17 December 1979, and on 20 December 1979 the court directed the execution of a will in the same form as the original one. It was held that it was not necessary for notice to have been given to the man. Fox J said at page 348:

'No doubt in the normal case the court would generally insist on the joinder of a person who was adversely affected by the relief sought, but in circumstances of urgency the position may be different. The deputy master quite clearly directed his mind to the question of whether Mr Davey should be joined as a respondent and decided against it on the ground of delay. In the circumstances I think that that was a reasonable view for the deputy master to take.'

Rule 20 CPR 2001 provides for the following modes of service of a document:

(a)   personal delivery to the person to be served;

(b)   sending it by first class post or through a document exchange to the last known address of the person to be served; or

(c)   transmitting it to him at his last known address by fax or other electronic means.

A solicitor can accept service (r 21). Under r 23(1)(b) if the patient is required to be served, service must be made on his receiver, or if there is no receiver, on the person acting in pursuance of an order or direction made under r 8, or, if there is no such person, on an attorney acting under a registered power of attorney, or, if there is no such attorney, on the person with whom he resides or in whose care he is.

Evidence

15.6   An affidavit must be filed. Practice Note 9 provides details of the information which should be included.

Execution of the will

15.7   The judge may authorise a person to execute a will on behalf of a patient. Under s 97(1)(a) Mental Health Act 1983, the will must be signed by the authorised person with the name of the patient, and with his own name, in the presence of two or more witnesses present at the same time. In addition, the will must be attested and subscribed by those witnesses in the presence of the authorised person, and sealed with the Official Seal of the Court of Protection.

Summary

15.8

- The donor of an enduring power can execute a will provided he has the necessary capacity.

- The donee of a power of attorney cannot make a will for the donor.

- If the donor of a power lacks capacity to execute a will, application can be made to the Court of Protection for the execution of a will.

- The beneficiaries under such a will can be members of the patient's family, and also persons for whom the patient might be expected to provide.

Chapter 16

Capacity and power to make gifts

16.1   The question of capacity can arise in three contexts: whether the donor has capacity to grant an enduring power of attorney; whether the donor has the capacity to make gifts in his or her lifetime; and whether the donor has capacity to make a will. There may also be issues as to whether an attorney under an enduring power of attorney can make lifetime gifts.

The tests for capacity differ according to whether the donor is proposing to grant an enduring power of attorney, to make lifetime gifts, or to make gifts by will.

However, if there is any doubt about capacity, a medical report should be obtained, and ideally the doctor should be asked to witness the relevant document.

Some of the issues discussed in this chapter have been considered in other chapters, but for convenience have also been included here.

Capacity of donor to grant an enduring power

16.2   Frequently solicitors are asked to draft enduring powers of attorney for clients who are verging on mental incapacity. People do not usually become mentally incapable overnight. It is usually a gradual decline into incapacity. At what point does someone become mentally incapable of granting an EPA?

In *Re K; Re F [1988] 1 All ER 358* donors executed enduring powers. At the time the powers were executed both donors were verging on mental incapacity to manage their own affairs, but they understood the nature and effect of the enduring power. Hoffmann J held that both powers were valid.

Hoffmann J pointed out that the Enduring Powers of Attorney Act 1985 (EPAA 1985) did not specify the mental capacity needed to execute a power of attorney. A power of attorney is normally revoked by the subsequent mental incapacity of the donor, but Hoffmann J rejected the view that a person suffering from mental incapacity which would have revoked a power could not validly create one.

He said at pages 362, 363:

> 'In practice it is likely that many enduring powers will be executed when symptoms of mental incapacity have begun to manifest themselves. These symptoms may result in the donor being mentally incapable in the statutory sense that she is unable on a regular basis to manage her property

and affairs. But, as in the case of Mrs F, she may execute the power with full understanding and with the intention of taking advantage of the Act to have her affairs managed by an attorney of her choice rather than having them put in the hands of the Court of Protection. I can think of no reason of policy why this intention should be frustrated.'

He then went on to define what degree of understanding is involved. He said:

'Plainly one cannot expect that the donor should have been able to pass an examination on the provisions of the 1985 Act. At the other extreme, I do not think that it would be sufficient if he realised only that it gave [the donee of the power] power to look after his property. Counsel as *amicus curiae* helpfully summarised the matters which the donor should have understood in order that he can be said to have understood the nature and effect of the power: first, if such be the terms of the power, that the attorney will be able to assume complete authority over the donor's affairs; second, if such be the terms of the power, that the attorney will in general be able to do anything with the donor's property which the donor could have done; third, that the authority will continue if the donor should be or become mentally incapable; fourth, that if he should be or become mentally incapable, the power will be irrevocable without confirmation by the court.'

In *Re W [2000] 1 All ER 175*, an enduring power of attorney was challenged on the ground that the donor did not have capacity to grant it. The judge held that as he was not satisfied that the donor did not have capacity, the power should be registered.

At page 178 the judge said:

'I am not satisfied on the evidence that Mrs W did not have this understanding. This does not mean that I am satisfied that she did have it.'

What the judge meant was that the onus was on the person approving registration to prove that the donor did not have capacity; if they could not discharge the onus, the power would be registered, even though there might be doubts about the capacity of the donor.

The decision has been confirmed on appeal [2001] 4 All ER 88.

Capacity to make gifts

16.3   In *Re Beanie (deceased) [1978] 1 WLR 770* an elderly lady suffered from dementia. She lived in her house with her eldest daughter. Shortly after being admitted to hospital, she signed a deed of gift transferring the house to the eldest daughter. The gift was set aside.

The judge said:

> 'The degree or extent of understanding required in respect of any instrument is relative to the particular transaction which it is to effect . . . Thus, at one extreme, if the subject matter and value of a gift are trivial in relation to the donor's other assets, a low degree of understanding will suffice. But, at the other, if its effect is to dispose of the donor's only asset of value and thus, for practical purposes, to pre-empt the devolution of his estate under the [donor's] will or . . . intestacy, then the degree of understanding required is as high as that required for a will, and the donor must understand the claims of all potential donees and the extent of the property to be disposed of.'

Capacity to make a will

16.4   The test for mental capacity to make a will has three elements:

— *The testator must understand the nature and effect of his acts*

This does not mean that the testator must have a degree in the law of wills. What it means is that the testator must understand that they are signing a document which will dispose of their property on death. They do not need to understand the exact way in which it will operate in great detail.

— *The testator must have an idea about the extent of his estate*

This does not mean that the testator must know exactly how much they own down to the last penny. What it means is that the testator must have a general idea about how much they actually own.

— *The testator must have an idea about the claims to which he ought to give effect*

The testator must have some idea of the relatives or other dependants they need to consider. This does not mean that they need to be able to list all their relatives. Neither does it mean that someone who is aware of all his relatives must benefit them. A testator who considers all his relatives and decides to leave all his property to charity can still have the capacity to make a will. On the other hand if the testator makes a will benefiting a charity and forgets that he has children, the will will be invalid.

With the great majority of clients there is no doubt that they do have capacity.

Mental incapacity can take various forms. If you are asked to draft a will for someone who is suffering from delusions, for example that they are a prominent public figure, it does not mean that they cannot make a will. The delusions may not affect their ability to make a will. They may still be able to satisfy the three requirements for capacity to make valid will. Even though the client may believe that he is a well-known public figure, if he is aware of what a will is, knows he has a spouse and children, and has some idea of his assets, the will will still be valid.

More often than not the question of mental incapacity arises in connection with elderly people where there is usually a gradual decline into mental incapacity. In the early stages, it is probable that such a person will still have the capacity to make a will, but in the latter stages capacity will be lacking.

What is the position if there is a valid will, but the testator enters into transactions which have the effect of depriving beneficiaries under the will of gifts they would have otherwise received? In *Special Trustees for Great Ormond Street Hospital for Children v Rushin; sub nom Morris, in the estate of Morris deceased [2001] WTLR 1137* under the will of M, a charity was the residuary beneficiary. M entered into various transactions with R, which were challenged by the charity after her death. There was evidence that she was suffering from senile dementia.

It was held that the transactions should be set aside because M did not have capacity, or if she did, there was a presumption of undue influence, which had not been rebutted.

It is thus clear that a donor making large gifts which will impact on the will must have a clear understanding of what they are doing and the effect on the will.

Powers of attorney to make gifts

16.5   An attorney under an ordinary power has no power to make gifts, but s 3(5) EPAA 1985 authorises an attorney to make gifts in certain circumstances. It provides that, subject to any conditions or restrictions contained in the instrument, an attorney under an enduring power, whether general or limited, may (without obtaining any consent) dispose of the property of the donor by way of gift to the following extent but no further:

(a)   he may make gifts of a seasonal nature or at a time, or on an anniversary, of a birth or marriage, to persons (including himself) who are related or connected with the donor; and

(b)   he may make gifts to any charity to whom the donor made or might be expected to make gifts,

provided that the value of each such gift is not unreasonable having regard to all the circumstances and in particular the size of the donor's estate. This power is without prejudice to the power conferred by s 3(4).

There is no definition of 'related' or 'connected' in the EPAA 1985. In many cases, it will be clear that the person to be benefitted is related or connected, but there could be problems in deciding if an acquaintance is connected with the donor. Note also that the gift must be of a seasonal nature, or made on an anniversary of a birth or marriage. With charities, the attorney can clearly benefit a charity which the donor has supported in the past, but it might be difficult to justify a gift to a charity which the donor has never supported. However, it would probably be in order to benefit, say, a charity for the relief of cancer if a relative or friend of the donor had died from that disease, even though the donor had not contributed to such a charity in the past.

The value of any gift must not be unreasonable having regard to the circumstances and the size of the estate. Gifts of £5, £10, or £20 are probably in order, unless the estate is very small. A gift of £1,000 out of an estate in excess of £500,000 is clearly permissible, but if the estate is under £10,000, it is probably unreasonable. A gift to a close relative with whom the donor has had no contact for many years is also probably unreasonable.

The court has no power to order the attorney to make gifts. In *Re R [1990] 2 WLR 1219,* the applicant was employed by R as a cook and housekeeper and lived in R's flat. R gave her nephew an enduring power of attorney, and shortly afterwards she moved to a nursing home. The enduring power of attorney was registered, and the nephew terminated the employment of the applicant, and required her to give up possession of the flat. The applicant alleged that R had promised to provide for her for the rest of her life, and that she had worked for less than the market rate for her services. She applied for provision from R's estate. The application was unsuccessful. Vinelott J said at pages 1222 and 1223:

> 'It is quite plain, and it is not in dispute, that the only authority that the Court of Protection could have to give directions to the attorney, requiring him to make provision for the applicant, would have to be found, if at all, in s 8(2)(b)(i). The case put by the applicant's counsel is that the subparagraph does give the court unrestricted power to direct an attorney to dispose of any part of the property of the donor by way of gift or in recognition of some moral obligation, unaccompanied by any legal obligation.

> I find that an impossible view. Of course the word "disposal" is, in some contexts, capable of being given a very wide meaning, and could include a disposition by way of gift. But it seems to me that in the context of section 8 it cannot have been intended that it should bear that wide meaning. It is in a paragraph, (b), which is plainly concerned with administrative matters: the management of the donor's property; the rendering of accounts and the determination of the remuneration of the attorney. These are all part of the jurisdiction which the court is given to supervise the conduct of the attorney and to see that he is exercising his powers of management and administration properly. It would be remarkable, in a paragraph directed to matters of that sort, to find an unrestricted power given to the court to dispose of the whole of the donor's property by way of gift . . .'.

However, the court can sanction gifts on the application of, amongst others, a receiver or an attorney acting under a registered enduring power of attorney (see Practice Note 9).

Factors to be taken into account when advising about gifts

16.6   Frequently the motivation for a gift is a desire to save inheritance tax or to prevent the proceeds sale of the home of the donor being used to pay care home fees.

As far as inheritance tax is concerned, a gift by parents of their house to children will be ineffective for inheritance tax purposes if they continue living there as they will be deemed to have reserved a benefit in that house, and the full value of the house will be subject to inheritance tax on their death. There are various schemes designed to save inheritance tax, but almost all involve tying up the house so that it might be difficult if the parents want to sell and move to another property, and there is always the risk that the scheme will not work at the end of the day.

As far as care home fees are concerned, if the parents give the house to the children, and have to go into a care home, it is possible that the value of the house will be included in an assessment of the means of the parents. In addition, it is possible that action could be taken under various provisions in order to set aside the gift.

Solicitors are referred to guidelines concerning gifts of property prepared by the Mental Health and Disability Committee of the Law Society (see APPENDIX 6).

Summary

16.7

- The test of whether a donor is mentally capable of granting an EPA is very strict.

- However, the onus is on the person opposing registration to prove that the donor did not have capacity. If that person cannot prove that the donor lacked capacity, the EPA will be registered.

- Different tests apply to decide if a person is capable of making lifetime gifts, wills or granting enduring powers of attorney.

Appendices

Contents

Appendix 1

Forms

Contents

A1.1

ENDURING POWER OF ATTORNEY

Part A: About using this form

1. **You may choose one attorney or more than one.** If you choose one attorney then you must delete everything between the square brackets on the first page of the form. If you choose more than one, you must decide whether they are able to act:
   - Jointly (that if, they must all act together and cannot act separately) or
   - Jointly and severally (that is, they can all act together but they can also act separately if they wish).
   On the first page of the form, show what you have decided by crossing out one of the alternatives.

2. **If you give your attorney(s) general power** in relation to all your property and affairs, it means that they will be able to deal with your money or property and may be able to sell your house.

3. **If you don't want your attorney(s) to have such wide powers,** you can include any restrictions you like. For example, you can include a restriction that your attorney(s) must not act on your behalf until they have reason to believe that you are becoming mentally incapable; or a restriction as to what your attorney(s) may do. Any restrictions you choose must be written or typed where indicated on the second page of the form.

4. **If you are a trustee** (and please remember that co-ownership of a home involves trusteeship), you should seek legal advice if you want your attorney(s) to act as a trustee on your behalf.

5. **Unless you put in a restriction preventing it** Your attorney(s) will be able to use any of your money or property to make any provision which you yourself might be expected to make for their own needs or the needs of other people. Your attorney(s) will also be able to use your money to make gifts, but only for reasonable amounts in relation to the value of your money and property.

6. **Your attorney(s) can recover the out-of-pocket expenses** of acting as your attorney(s). If your attorney(s) are professional people, for example solicitors or accountants, they may be able to charge for their professional services as well. You may wish to provide expressly for remuneration of your attorney(s) (although if they are trustees they may not be allowed to accept it).

7. **If your attorney(s) have reason to believe** that you have become or are becoming mentally incapable of managing your affairs, your attorney(s) will have to apply to the Court of Protection for registration of this power.

8. **Before applying to the Court of Protection for registration** of this power, your attorney(s) must give written notice that that is what they are going to do, to you and your nearest relatives as defined in the Enduring Powers of Attorney Act 1985. You or your relatives will be able to object if you or they disagree with registration.

9. **This is a simplified explanation** of what the Enduring Powers of Attorney Act 1985 and the Rules and Regulations say. If you need more guidance, you or your advisers will need to look at the Act itself and the Rules and Regulations. The Rules are the Court of Protection (Enduring Powers of Attorney) Rules 1986 (Statutory Instrument 1986 No. 127). The Regulations are the Enduring Powers of Attorney (Prescribed Form) Regulations 1990 (Statutory Instrument 1990 No. 1376).

10. **Note to Attorney(s)**
    After the power has been registered you should notify the Court of Protection if the donor dies or recovers.

11. **Note to Donor**
    Some of these explanatory notes may not apply to the form you are using if it has already been adapted to suit your particular requirements.

YOU CAN CANCEL THIS POWER AT ANY TIME BEFORE IT HAS TO BE REGISTERED

Part B: To be completed by the 'donor' (the person appointing the attorney(s))

Don't sign this form unless you understand what it means

Please read the notes in the margin which follow and which are part of the form itself.

Donor's name and address.

I _____

of _____

Donor's date of birth.

born on _____

appoint _____

See note 1 on the front of this form. If you are appointing only one attorney you should cross out everything between the square brackets. If appointing more than two attorneys please give the additional name(s) on an attached sheet.

of _____

• [and _____

of _____

Cross out the one which does not apply (see note 1 on the front of this form).

• jointly

• jointly and severally]

to be my attorney(s) for the purpose of the Enduring Powers of Attorney Act 1985

Cross out the one which does not apply (see note 2 on the front of this form). Add any additional powers.

• with general authority to act on my behalf

• with authority to do the following on my behalf:

If you56 don't want the attorney(s) to have general power, you must give details here of what authority you are giving the attorney(s).

in relation to

Cross out the one which does not apply.

• all my property and affairs:

• the following property and affairs:

Part B: continued

Please read the notes in the margin
which follow and which are part of
the form itself.
If there are restrictions or conditions,
insert them here; if not, cross out
these words if you wish (see note 3 on
the front of this form).

- subject to the following restrictions and conditions:

If this form is being signed at your
direction:-

- the person signing must not be an
  attorney or any witness (to Parts B or
  C).
- you must add a statement that this
  form has been signed at your
  direction.
- a second witness is   necessary
  (please see below).

Your signature (or mark).

I intend that this power shall continue even if I become mentally incapable

I have read or have had read to me the notes in Part A which are part of, and
explain, this form.

Signed by me as deed _____
and delivered

Date.

Someone must witness your
signature.
Signature of witness.

on _____

Your attorney(s) cannot be your
witness. It is not advisable for your
husband or wife to be your witness.

in the presence of _____

Full name of witness_____

Address of witness_____

_____

_____

A second witness is only necessary if
this form is being signed by you
personally but at your direction (for
example, if a physical disability
prevents you from signing).
Signature of second witness.

in the presence of _____

Full name of witness _____

Address of witness _____

_____

_____

Part C: To be completed by the attorney(s)

Note:1. This form may be adapted to provide for execution by a corporation

2. If there is more than one attorney additional sheets in the form as shown below must be added to this Part C

Please read the notes in the margin which follow and which are part of the form itself.

Don't sign this form before the donor has signed Part B or if, in your opinion, the donor was already mentally incapable at the time of signing Part B.

If this form is being signed at your direction:-
• the person signing must not be an attorney or any witness (to Parts B or C).
• you must add a statement that this form, has been signed at your direction.
• a second witness is necessary (please see below).

Signature (or mark) of attorney.

Date.

Signature of witness.

The attorney must sign the form and his signature must be witnessed. The donor may not be the witness and one attorney may not witness the signature of the other.

A second witness is only necessary if this form is not being signed by you personally but at your direction (for example, if a physical disability prevents you from signing).
Signature of second witness.

I understand that I have a duty to apply to the Court for the registration of this form under the Enduring Powers of Attorney Act 1985 when the donor is becoming or has become mentally incapable.

I also understand my limited power to use the donor's property to benefit persons other than the donor.

I am not a minor

Signed by me as a deed
and delivered _____

on _____

in the presence of _____

Full name of witness _____

Address of witness _____

_____

_____

in the presence of _____

Full name of witness _____

Address of witness _____

_____

_____

A1.2

Form EP1

Court of Protection
Enduring Powers of Attorney Act

Notice of intention to apply for registration

To ....

Of ....

This form may be adapted for use by three or more attorneys.	**TAKE NOTICE THAT** I .... of ....
Give the name and address of the donor.	and I .... of ....
It will be necessary for you to produce evidence in support of your objection. If evidence is available please send it with your objection, the attorney(s) will be given an opportunity to respond to your objection.	The attorney(s) of .... of .... intend to apply to the Court of Protection for registration of the enduring power of attorney appointing me (us) attorney(s) and made by the donor on the..
The grounds upon which you can object are limited and are shown at 2 overleaf.	1. If you wish to object to the proposed registration you have 4 weeks from the day on which this notice is given to you to do so in writing. Any objections should be sent to the Court of Protection and should contain the following details: • Your name and address • Any relationship to the donor • If you are not the donor, the name and address of the donor • The name and address of the attorney • The grounds for objecting to the registration of the enduring power

Note. The instrument means the enduring power of attorney made by the donor which it is sought to register.	2. The grounds on which you may object are: ■ That the power purported to have been created by the instrument is not valid as an enduring power of attorney. ■ That the power created by the instrument no longer subsists. ■ That the application is premature because the donor is not yet becoming mentally incapable. ■ That fraud or undue pressure was used to induce the donor to make the power. ■ That the attorney is unsuitable to be the donor's attorney (having regard to all the circumstances and in particular the attorney's relationship to or connection with the donor).

The attorney(s) does not have to be a relative. Relatives are not entitled to know of the existence of the enduring power of attorney prior to being given this notice.

Note. This is addressed only to the donor	3. You are informed that while the enduring power of attorney remains registered, you will not be able to revoke it until the Court of Protection confirms the revocation.

Note. This notice should be signed by every one of the attorneys who are applying to register the enduring power of attorney	Signed..Dated.................. Signed..Dated..................

Forms

A1.3

Form EP2

Rule 3

Court of Protection

Enduring Powers of Attorney Act 1985

Application for Registration

IMPORTANT: Please complete the form in BLOCK CAPITALS using a black ballpoint pen. For circled options please completely fill-in the appropriate choice.

Part One - The Donor

Please state the full name and present address of the donor. State the donor's first name in 'Forename 1' and the donor's other forenames/initials in 'Other Forenames'. If the donor's address on the enduring power of attorney is different give that one too. If necessary, complete several parts of the address on each Address line shown.

Mr ○   Mrs ○   Ms ○   Miss ○   Other ○   If Other, please specify here.

Last Name:

Forename 1:

Other Forenames:

Address 1:

Address 2:

Address 3:

Town/City:

County:

Postcode:

Address on the enduring power of attorney (if different from above):

Address 1:

Address 2:

Town/City:

County: Postcode:

You can find the donor's date of birth in Part B of the enduring power of attorney.

Donor Date of Birth: *If the exact date is unknown please state the year of birth*

D D   M M   Y Y Y Y

Part Two - Attorney One

Please state the full name and present address of the attorney. If applicable, include the Company Name in 'Address 1'.

Mr ○   Mrs ○   Ms ○   Miss ○   Other ○   *If Other, please specify here:*

Last Name:

Forename 1:

Other Forenames:

Continued overleaf

Part Two - Attorney One cont'd

Address 1:

Address 2:

Address 3:

Town/City:

County:

Postcode: DX No.
                   (solicitors only):

DX Exchange
(solicitors only):

Attorney
Date of Birth: Occupation:
                D D   M M   Y Y Y Y

                                        Daytime   (STD Code):
                                        Tel No.:

Email Address:

Relationship to donor:
                Other   No   Other
Spouse Child   Relation   Relation Solicitor Professional   If 'Other Relation' or 'Other Professional', specify relationship:
  ○   ○   ○   ○   ○   ○

Part B of the enduring power of attorney states whether the attorney is to act jointly, jointly and severally, or alone.

                                    Jointly   Jointly and Severally   Alone
Appointment *(please fill the appropriate circle)*:   ○   ○   ○

Part Three - Attorney Two

Please state the full name and present address of the second attorney. If applicable, include the Company Name in 'Address 1'.

Mr   Mrs   Ms   Miss   Other
 ○   ○   ○   ○   ○   *If Other, please specify here:*

Last Name:

Forename 1:

Other
Forenames:

Address 1:

Address 2:

Address 3:

Town/City:

County:

Postcode: DX No.
                   (solicitors only):

DX Exchange
(solicitors only)

Continued overleaf

Forms

Part Three - Attorney Two cont'd

Attorney Date of Birth: ☐☐ ☐☐ ☐☐☐☐

D D M M Y Y Y Y

Occupation: _____

Daytime Tel No.: _____

Email Address: _____

Relationship to donor:

Spouse	Child	Other Relation	No Relation	Solicitor	Other Professional
○	○	○	○	○	○

If 'Other Relation' or 'Other Professional', specify relationship: _____

Part Four - Attorney Three

Please state the full name and present address of the third attorney. If applicable, include the Company Name in 'Address 1'.

Mr	Mrs	Ms	Miss	Other
○	○	○	○	○

If Other, please specify here: ☐☐☐☐☐☐☐☐☐☐☐☐☐☐☐

Last Name: ☐☐☐☐☐☐☐☐☐☐☐☐☐☐☐☐☐☐☐☐☐☐☐

Forename 1: ☐☐☐☐☐☐☐☐☐☐☐☐☐☐☐☐☐☐☐☐☐☐☐

Other Forenames: ☐☐☐☐☐☐☐☐☐☐☐☐☐☐☐☐☐☐☐☐☐☐☐

Address 1: ☐☐☐☐☐☐☐☐☐☐☐☐☐☐☐☐☐☐☐☐☐☐☐

Address 2: ☐☐☐☐☐☐☐☐☐☐☐☐☐☐☐☐☐☐☐☐☐☐☐

Address 3: ☐☐☐☐☐☐☐☐☐☐☐☐☐☐☐☐☐☐☐☐☐☐☐

Town/City: ☐☐☐☐☐☐☐☐☐☐☐☐☐☐☐☐☐☐☐☐☐☐☐

County: ☐☐☐☐☐☐☐☐☐☐☐☐☐☐☐☐☐☐☐☐☐☐☐

Postcode: ☐☐☐☐ ☐☐☐

DX No. (solicitors only): ☐☐☐☐☐☐☐☐☐☐☐☐☐

DX Exchange (solicitors only): ☐☐☐☐☐☐☐☐☐☐☐☐☐☐☐☐☐☐

Attorney Date of Birth: ☐☐ ☐☐ ☐☐☐☐

D D M M Y Y Y Y

Occupation: _____

Daytime Tel No: _____

Email Address: _____

Relationship to donor:

Spouse	Child	Other Relation	No Relation	Solicitor	Other Professional
○	○	○	○	○

If 'Other Relation' or 'Other Professional', specify relationship: _____

If there are additional attorneys, please complete the above details in the 'Additional Information' section (at the end of this form).

Part Five - The Enduring Power of Attorney

The date is the date that the donor signed the enduring power of attorney.
You can find this in Part B of the enduring power of attorney.

I (We) the attorney(s) apply to register the enduring power of attorney made by the donor under the above Act, the original of which accompanies this application.

I (We) have reason to believe that the donor is or is becoming mentally incapable.

Date of enduring
power of attorney:

D D   M M   Y Y Y Y

To your knowledge, has the donor made
any other enduring power of attorney?   Yes ○   No ○

If 'Yes', please give details below including registration date if applicable:

Part Six - Notice of Application to Donor

Notice must be given personally to the donor. It should be made clear if someone other than the attorney(s) gives the notice.

I (We) have given notice of the application to register in the prescribed form (EP1) to the donor personally.

If someone other than the attorney gives notice to the donor please complete the name, address and date details below:

Full Name:	
Address 1:	
Address 2:	
Town/City:	
County:	Postcode:

On this date:

D D   M M   Y Y Y Y

Part Seven - Notice of Application to Relatives

If there are no relatives entitled to notice please ensure that the circle is filled below.

Please fill-in the circle if no relatives are entitled to notice: ○

I (We) have given notice to register in the prescribed form (EP1) to the following relatives of the donor:

Name	Relationship to Donor	Address

Date notice given:

D D   M M   Y Y Y Y

Name	Relationship to Donor	Address

Date notice given:

D D   M M   Y Y Y Y

Name	Relationship to Donor	Address

Date notice given:

D D   M M   Y Y Y Y

Name	Relationship to Donor	Address

Date notice given:

D D   M M   Y Y Y Y

Continued overleaf

Part Seven - Nature of Application to Relatives cont'd

If there are additional relatives please complete the Relative Name, Relationship, Address and Date details in the 'Additional Information' section (at the end of this from).

Name	Relationship to Donor	Address

Date notice given:

D D   M M   Y Y Y Y

Part Eight - Nature of Application to Co-Attorney(s)

Do not complete this section if it does not apply. If there are additional co-attorneys please complete the Attorney Name, Relationship, Address and Date details in the 'Additional Information' section (at the end of this form).

Are all the attorneys applying to register?   Yes ○   No ○

If no, I (We) have given notice to my (our) co-attorney(s) as follows:

Name	Relationship to Donor	Address

Date notice given:

D D   M M   Y Y Y Y

Name	Relationship to Donor	Address

Date notice given:

D D   M M   Y Y Y Y

Part Nine - Fees

Guidelines on remission postponement of fees can be obtained from the Court of Protection.

Have you enclosed a cheque for the registration fee for this application?   Yes ○   No ○

Do you wish to apply for postponement or remission of the fee?   Yes ○   No ○

If yes, please give details below:

Part Ten - Declaration

Note: The application should be signed by all attorneys who are making the application. This must not pre-date the date(s) when the notices were given.

I (We) certify that the above information is correct and that to the best of my (our) knowledge and belief I (We) have complied with the provisions of the Enduring Powers of Attorney Act 1985 and all of the Rules and Regulations.

Signed: _____   Dated:

D D   M M   Y Y Y Y

Signed: _____   Dated:

D D   M M   Y Y Y Y

Signed: _____   Dated:

Continued overleaf

D D   M M   Y Y Y Y

Part Eleven - Correspondence Address

Please state the address to which the correspondence should be sent if this is different to the address of Attorney One. State the full name and present address. If applicable, include the Company Name in Address Line 1.

Mr ○   Mrs ○   Ms ○   Miss ○   Other ○   *If Other, please specify here:*

Last Name:

Forename 1:

Other Forenames:

Address 1:

Address 2:

Address 3:

Town/City:

County:

Postcode: DX No. (solicitors only):

DX Exchange (solicitors only):

Daytime Tel No.:   (STD Code):

Email Address:

Part Twelve - Additional Information

Please write down any additional information to support this application in the space below. If necessary attach additional paper to the end of this form.

A1.4

Form EP3
Court of Protection
Enduring Powers of Attorney Act 1985

In the matter of a power given by

If this application is being made prior to an application for registration the original enduring power of attorney should accompany this application.	....(a donor) to.. (attorney) and..(attorney) General Form of Application

	I ....
Note. Give details of the order or directions that you are seeking	of... and I..
State under which subsection of the Enduring Powers of Attorney Act 1985 or which rule of the Court of Protection (Enduring Powers of Attorney) Rules 2001 this application is made	Apply for an order or directions that.................................. ....
Note. Give details of the grounds on which you are seeking the orders or directions	And for any other directions which are necessary as a result of my/our application. The grounds on which I/we make this application are:
Evidence in support should accompany this application.	....
Note. The application should be signed by all the applicants or their solicitors	Signed..Dated.................. Signed..Dated.................. Address where notices should be sent............................... ....

A1.5

Form EP4

No.....................

Court of Protection
Enduring Powers of Attorney Act 1985

Application for search/office copy

I (we)..

of...

....

> Note. Give the full name (if known) of the person who is the subject of your enquiry

apply to be informed by the Court of Protection whether an enduring power of attorney has been registered (or whether registration of an enduring power of attorney is pending) in the

Name of...

Alternative name..

Address (if known)...

....

Alternative address..

....

I (we) enclose the prescribed fee of £.................................

> Note. Please fill in if applicable.

Please supply me (us) with an office copy of the power.

- My/our reasons for requesting a copy from the Court of

  Protection are...

  ....

  ....

- It is not reasonably practicable to obtain a copy from the

  attorney because..

  ....

  ....

Signed..

Dated..

A1.6

Form EP5

No..................

Court of Protection
Enduring Powers of Attorney Act 1985

Certificate of result of search

Your reference ....

In reply to your enquiry made on ....

☐ The following enduring power of attorney is registered
against the donor's name you give:

Donor's name ....

Attorney's name ....

Power made by donor on ....

Registered on ....

☐ There is an application pending for registration of the
following enduring power of attorney:

Donor's name ....

Attorney's name ....

Power made by donor on ....

☐ There was an enduring power of attorney registered
against the donor's name you give but the registration has
been cancelled:

Donor's name ....

Attorney's name ....

Power made by donor on ....

Registered on ....

Date cancelled...

☐ There is no enduring power of attorney registered against
the donor's name (......................) you give.

Signed..

Dated ....

A1.7

Form EP6

No.....................

Court of Protection
Enduring Powers of Attorney Act 1985

In the matter of a power given by

.... a donor

Witness summons

To...

of...

....

you are ordered to attend before

....

at..

....

on the........................ day of.....................................20...................

at.........................o'clock to:

- Give evidence in this matter
- Bring with you and produce at the hearing the documents listed below:

....

....

....

....

....

....

Dated..

This summons was issued at the request of

....

Solicitors for the...

of..

....

Forms

A1.8

No...........................

Court of Protection
Enduring Powers of Attorney Act 1985

In the matter of...

.... a donor

Notice of appeal

I (we)...

of...

....

| Note. If you are appealing against only part of the order/decision write down which part | Wish to appeal to a judge against the order/decision of the Court made in this matter on the.................................... 20........ |

I (we) intend to ask that the order/decision may be

| Note. Tick the box that applies. | |

☐   discharged

☐   varied in the following way:

| Note. Give details of the new order/decision you are asking to be made. | |

| Note. The form should be sent to the Court of Protection. | Signed .... |

Dated ....

Solicitors for the appellant(s)..

....

of ....

....

To the appellant(s): You will be sent notice of the time, date and place of this appeal.

Appendix 2

Precedents

Contents

A2.1   General power of attorney under the Powers of Attorney Act 1971

This general power of attorney is made this .... day of .... 20 ....

by (*name of donor of power*) ....

of ....

I appoint ....

of ....

[or .... of .... and ....

of ....

jointly or jointly and severally] to be my attorney[s] in accordance with section 10 of the Powers of Attorney Act 1971.

In Witness whereof (the donor) has hereunto set his hand and seal the day and year above written.

Signed as a deed and delivered: ....

Witness: ....

© *Crown Copyright*

A2.2 Limited power of attorney authorising sale of a house and the purchase and mortgage of another house

This limited power of attorney is made this .... day of .... 20 ....

by ....

of ....

I appoint ....

of ....

to do all or any of the following acts:

    1.   To sign a contract and execute a conveyance or transfer for the sale of .... at a price of not less £ ....

    2.   To pay to .... such money as is necessary to redeem the charge or charges or mortgage or mortgages in their favour.

    3.   To sign a contract and execute a conveyance or transfer for the purchase of .... at a price not exceeding £ ....

    4.   To execute a charge or mortgage of .... in favour of the .... for an amount not exceeding £ ....

    5.   To draw whatever cheques shall be necessary.

    6.   To do such other acts as shall be necessary to complete the sale, redemption of the existing charges or mortgages, the purchase and mortgage or charge.

Signed as a deed and delivered: ....

Witness: ....

A2.3 Limited power of attorney authorising the redemption of an existing mortgage and the remortgage of the property

Opening – as in precedent 2.

1. To pay to .... such money as is necessary to redeem the charge or charges or mortgage or mortgages in their favour on ....

2. To draw whatever cheques shall be necessary for this purpose in favour of ....

3. To execute a charge or mortgage on the security of in favour of ...

4. To do such other acts as shall be necessary to complete the redemption of the existing charges or mortgages and to complete the charge or mortgage in favour.

Signed as a deed and delivered: ....

Witness: ....

A2.4   Limited power of attorney authorising the grant of a lease

Opening – as in precedent 2.

1.   To grant a lease of [insert address of property] for a term not exceeding .... years on such terms as my attorney thinks fit.

2.   To receive the rent and to apply the rent in discharge of the obligations of the landlord.

3.   To take such proceedings as may be necessary to recover any rent or to enforce any of the obligations imposed on the tenant or to recover possession of the property.

Signed as a deed and delivered: ....

Witness: ....

A2.5 Form 1 – Certificate as to execution of power of attorney (rule 61)

Date of power of attorney: ....

Donor of power of attorney: ....

Donee of power of attorney: ....

....I/We: of

....

certify that

- the power of attorney ('the power') is in existence [and is made under (*state statutory provision under which the power is made if applicable*)],

- the power is dated (*insert date*),

- I am/we are satisfied that the power is validly executed as a deed and authorises the attorney to execute the document on behalf of the donor of that power, and

- I/we hold [the instrument creating the power] or [a copy of the power by means of which its contents may be proved under section 3 of the Powers of Attorney Act 1971] *or* [a document which under section 4 of the Evidence and Powers of Attorney Act 1940 or section 7(3) of the Enduring Powers of Attorney Act 1985 is sufficient evidence of the contents of the power].

Signature of conveyancer ....

Date ....

A2.6   Statutory declaration/certificate as to non-revocation for powers more that 12 months old at the date of the disposition for which they are used (rule 62)

Date of power of attorney: ....

Donor of power of attorney: ....

....I/We of

....

do solemnly and sincerely [declare] *or* [certify] that at the time of completion of the ....

to me/us/my client/I/we/my client had no knowledge —

- of a revocation of the power, or

- of the death or bankruptcy of the donor or, if the donor is a corporate body, its winding up or dissolution, or

- of any incapacity of the donor or, if the donor is a corporate body, its winding up or dissolution, or

- of any incapacity of the donor where the power is not a valid enduring power, or

Where the power is in the form prescribed for an enduring power —

- that the power was not in fact a valid enduring power, or

- of an order or direction of the Court of Protection which revoked the power, or

- of the bankruptcy of the attorney, or

Where the power was given under section 9 of the Trusts Land and Appointment of Trustees Act 1996 —

- of an appointment of another trustee of the land in question, or

- of any other event which would have the effect of revoking the power, or

- of any lack of good faith on the part of the person(s) who dealt with the attorney,

- that the attorney was not a person to whom the functions of the trustees could be delegated under section 9 of the Trusts Land and Appointment of Trustees Act 1996, or

Where the power is expressed to be given by way of security —

- that the power was not in fact given by way of security, or

- of any revocation of the power with the consent of the attorney, or

- of any other event which would have had the effect of revoking the power.

Where a certificate is given —

Signature of conveyancer ....

Date .... or

Where a statutory declaration is made —

And I/We make this solemn declaration conscientiously believing the same to be true and by virtue of the provisions of the Statutory Declarations Act 1835.

Signature of Declarant(s) ....Date ....

DECLARED at .... before me, a person entitled to administer oaths.

Name ....

Address ....

Qualification ....

Signature...

A2.7 Form 3 – Statutory declaration certificate in support of power delegating trustees' functions to a beneficiary (rule 63)

Date of power of attorney: ....

Donor of power of attorney: ....

I/We ....of

....

do solemnly and sincerely [declare] *or* [certify] that at the time of completion of the ....to me/us/my/client/I/we/my client had no knowledge —

- of any lack of faith on the part of the person(s) who dealt with the attorney, or

- that the attorney was not a person to whom the functions of the trustees could be delegated under section 9 of the Trusts of Land and Appointment of Trustees Act 1996.

Where a certificate is given —

Signature of conveyancer ....Date ...., or

Where a Statutory Declaration is made —

And I/we make this solemn declaration conscientiously believing the same to be true and by virtue of the provisions of the Statutory Declarations Act 1835.

Signature of Declarants(s) ....Date ....

DECLARED at ....before me, a person entitled to administer oaths.

Name ....

Address ....

Qualification ....

Signature ....

A2.8 Delegation of trusts by power of attorney under section 25 Trustee Act 1925

This general trustee power of attorney is made this .... day of .... 20 ....

by [name of one donor] of [address of donor] as trustee of [name or details of any trust].

I appoint [name of one donee] of [address of donee] to be my attorney [if desired, the date on which the delegation commences or the period for which it continues (or both)] in accordance with section 25(5) of the Trustee Act 1925.

[To be executed as a deed].

© Crown Copyright

A2.9   Notice under section 25 Trustee Act 1925 as substituted by Trustee Delegation Act 1999

To ....

of ....

By a power of attorney coming into force on the . day of . 20 ., and expiring on the . day of . 20 ., I delegated the execution or exercise of the trusts powers and discretions vested in me, excluding ...., for a period of .... months to ....

of ....

The power has been given because I (*state reason*).

A2.10   Extension of powers in respect of shareholdings

Clauses to be incorporated in ordinary or enduring powers:

To permit a suitably qualified person to exercise the asset management functions of the attorney. Such asset management functions to comprise the asset management functions of trustees is defined in s 15(5) of the Trustee Act 2000.

To permit shares to be held in the name of a nominee without being liable for any losses.

Appendix 3

A3.1: Powers of Attorney Act 1971

Arrangement of sections

Schedules

1 Execution of powers of attorney

(1) An instrument creating a power of attorney shall be [executed as a deed by] the donor of the power.

(2) . . .

(3) This section is without prejudice to any requirement in, or having effect under, any other Act as to the witnessing of instruments creating powers of attorney and does not affect the rules relating to the execution of instruments by bodies corporate.

NOTES

Amendment
Sub-s (1): words in square brackets substituted by the Law of Property (Miscellaneous Provisions) Act 1989, s 1, Sch 1, para 6(a).
   Sub-s (2): repealed by the Law of Property (Miscellaneous Provisions) Act 1989, ss 1, 4, Sch 1, para 6(b), Sch 2.

2 . . .

NOTES

Amendment
Repealed by the Supreme Court Act 1981, s 152(4), Sch 7.

3 Proof of instruments creating powers of attorney

(1) The contents of an instrument creating a power of attorney may be proved by means of a copy which—

  (a) is a reproduction of the original made with a photographic or other device for reproducing documents in facsimile; and

  (b) contains the following certificate or certificates signed by the donor of the power or by a solicitor [duly certificated notary public] or stockbroker, that is to say—

    (i) a certificate at the end to the effect that the copy is a true and complete copy of the original; and

    (ii) if the original consists of two or more pages, a certificate at the end of each page of the copy to the effect that it is a true and complete copy of the corresponding page of the original.

(2) Where a copy of an instrument creating a power of attorney has been made which complies with subsection (1) of this section, the contents of the instrument may also be proved by means of a copy of that copy if the further copy itself complies with that subsection, taking references in it to the original as references to the copy from which the further copy is made.

(3) In this section ["duly certificated notary public" has the same meaning as it has in the Solicitors Act 1974 by virtue of section 87(1) of that Act and]

"stockbroker" means a member of any stock exchange within the meaning of the Stock Transfer Act 1963 or the Stock Transfer Act (Northern Ireland) 1963.

(4) This section is without prejudice to section 4 of the Evidence and Powers of Attorney Act 1940 (proof of deposited instruments by office copy) and to any other method of proof authorised by law.

(5) For the avoidance of doubt, in relation to an instrument made in Scotland the references to a power of attorney in this section and in section 4 of the Evidence and Powers of Attorney Act 1940 include references to a factory and commission.

NOTES

Amendment
Sub-ss (1), (3): words in square brackets inserted by the Courts and Legal Services Act 1990, s 125(2), Sch 17, para 4.
Modification
References to solicitors etc modified to include references to bodies recognised under the Administration of Justice Act 1985, s 9, by the Solicitors' Incorporated Practices Order 1991, SI 1991/2684, arts 4, 5, Sch 1.

4 Powers of attorney given as security

(1) Where a power of attorney is expressed to be irrevocable and is given to secure—

> (a) a proprietary interest of the donee of the power; or

> (b) the performance of an obligation owed to the donee,
> then, so long as the donee has that interest or the obligation remains undischarged, the power shall not be revoked—

>> (i) by the donor without the consent of the donee; or

>> (ii) by the death, incapacity or bankruptcy of the donor or, if the donor is a body corporate, by its winding up or dissolution.

(2) A power of attorney given to secure a proprietary interest may be given to the person entitled to the interest and persons deriving title under him to that interest, and those persons shall be duly constituted donees of the power for all purposes of the power but without prejudice to any right to appoint substitutes given by the power.

(3) This section applies to powers of attorney whenever created.

5 Protection of donee and third persons where power of attorney is revoked

(1) A donee of a power of attorney who acts in pursuance of the power at a time when it has been revoked shall not, by reason of the revocation, incur any liability (either to the donor or to any other person) if at that time he did not know that the power had been revoked.

(2) Where a power of attorney has been revoked and a person, without knowledge of the revocation, deals with the donee of the power, the transaction between them shall, in favour of that person, be as valid as if the power had then been in existence.

(3) Where the power is expressed in the instrument creating it to be irrevocable and to be given by way of security then, unless the person dealing with the donee knows that it was not in fact given by way of security, he shall be entitled to assume that the power is incapable of revocation except by the donor acting with the consent of the donee and shall accordingly be treated for the purposes of subsection (2) of this section as having knowledge of the revocation only if he knows that it has been revoked in that manner.

(4) Where the interest of a purchaser depends on whether a transaction between the donee of a power of attorney and another person was valid by virtue of subsection (2) of this section, it shall be conclusively presumed in favour of the purchaser that that person did not at the material time know of the revocation of the power if—

    (a)   the transaction between that person and the donee was completed within twelve months of the date on which the power came into operation; or

    (b)   that person makes a statutory declaration, before or within three months after the completion of the purchase, that he did not at the material time know of the revocation of the power.

(5) Without prejudice to subsection (3) of this section, for the purposes of this section knowledge of the revocation of a power of attorney includes knowledge of the occurrence of any event (such as the death of the donor) which has the effect of revoking the power.

(6) In this section "purchaser" and "purchase" have the meaning specified in section 205 (1) of the Law of Property Act 1925.

(7) This section applies whenever the power of attorney was created but only to acts and transactions after the commencement of this Act.

6 Additional protection for transferees under stock exchange transactions

(1) Without prejudice to section 5 of this Act, where—

    (a)   the donee of a power of attorney executes, as transferor, an instrument transferring registered securities; and

    (b)   the instrument is executed for the purposes of a stock exchange transaction,

it shall be conclusively presumed in favour of the transferee that the power had not been revoked at the date of the instrument if a statutory declaration to that effect is made by the donee of the power on or within three months after that date.

(2) In this section "registered securities" and "stock exchange transaction" have the same meanings as in the Stock Transfer Act 1963.

7 Execution of instruments etc by donee of power of attorney

[(1) If the donee of a power of attorney is an individual, he may, if he thinks fit—

    (a)   execute any instrument with his own signature, and]

    (b)   do any other thing in his own name,
by the authority of the donor of the power; and any document executed or thing done in that manner shall be as effective as if executed or done by the donee with the signature . . . , or, as the case may be, in the name, of the donor of the power.

(2) For the avoidance of doubt it is hereby declared that an instrument to which subsection (3) . . . of section 74 of the Law of Property Act 1925 applies may be executed either as provided in [that subsection] or as provided in this section.

(3) This section is without prejudice to any statutory direction requiring an instrument to be executed in the name of an estate owner within the meaning of the said Act of 1925.

(4) This section applies whenever the power of attorney was created.

NOTES

Amendment
Sub-ss (1), (2): words omitted repealed and words in square brackets substituted by the Law of Property (Miscellaneous Provisions) Act 1989, ss 1, 4, Sch 1, para 7, Sch 2.

8 Repeal of s 129 of Law of Property Act 1925

NOTES

Amendment
This section repeals the Law of Property Act 1925, s 129 (which contained provisions in respect of powers of attorney granted by married women).

9 ...

NOTES

Amendment
Repealed by the Trustee Delegation Act 1999, s 12, Schedule.
   Date in force: 1 March 2000 (in relation to powers of attorney created after that date): see SI 2000/216, art 2.

10 Effect of general power of attorney in specified form

(1) Subject to subsection (2) of this section, a general power of attorney in the form set out in Schedule 1 to this Act, or in a form to the like effect but expressed to be made under this Act, shall operate to confer—

(a)   on the donee of the power; or

(b)   if there is more than one donee, on the donees acting jointly or acting jointly or severally, as the case may be,

authority to do on behalf of the donor anything which he can lawfully do by an attorney.

(2) [Subject to section 1 of the Trustee Delegation Act 1999, this section] does not apply to functions which the donor has as a trustee or personal representative or as a tenant for life or statutory owner within the meaning of the Settled Land Act 1925.

NOTES

Amendment
Sub-s (2): words "Subject to section 1 of the Trustee Delegation Act 1999, this section" in square brackets substituted by the Trustee Delegation Act 1999, s 3.
    Date in force: 1 March 2000: see SI 2000/216, art 2.

11   Short title, repeals, consequential amendments, commencement and extent

(1) This Act may be cited as the Powers of Attorney Act 1971.

(2) The enactments specified in Schedule 2 to this Act are hereby repealed to the extent specified in the third column of that Schedule.

(3) . . .

(4) This Act shall come into force on 1st October 1971.

(5) Section 3 of this Act extends to Scotland and Northern Ireland but, save as aforesaid, this Act extends to England and Wales only.

NOTES

Amendment
Sub-s (3): in part amends the Law of Property Act 1925, s 125(2); remainder repealed by the Supreme Court Act 1981, s 152(4), Sch 7.

SCHEDULE 1
FORM OF GENERAL POWER OF ATTORNEY FOR PURPOSES OF SECTION 10

Section 10

THIS GENERAL POWER OF ATTORNEY is made this ..... day of ..... 19 .. by AB of

I appoint CD of (*or* CD of .... and EF of .... jointly *or* jointly and severally) to be my attorney(s) in accordance with section 10 of the Powers of Attorney Act 1971.

IN WITNESS etc,

[*Schedule 2 concerns repeals and is not reproduced.*]

A3.2: Enduring Powers of Attorney Act 1985

Arrangement of sections

Enduring powers of attorney

1 Enduring power of attorney to survive mental incapacity of donor

(1) Where an individual creates a power of attorney which is an enduring power within the meaning of this Act then—

(a) the power shall not be revoked by any subsequent mental incapacity of his; but

(b) upon such incapacity supervening the donee of the power may not do anything under the authority of the power except as provided by subsection (2) below or as directed or authorised by the court under section 5 unless or, as the case may be, until the instrument creating the power is registered by the court under section 6; and

(c) section 5 of the Powers of Attorney Act 1971 (protection of donee and third persons) so far as applicable shall apply if and so long as paragraph (b) above operates to suspend the donee's authority to act under the power as if the power had been revoked by the donor's mental incapacity.

(2) Notwithstanding subsection (1)(b) above, where the attorney has made an application for registration of the instrument then, until the application has been initially determined, the attorney may take action under the power—

(a) to maintain the donor or prevent loss to his estate; or

(b) to maintain himself or other persons in so far as section 3(4) permits him to do so.

(3) Where the attorney purports to act as provided by subsection (2) above then, in favour of a person who deals with him without knowledge that the attorney is acting otherwise than in accordance with paragraph (a) or (b) of that subsection, the transaction between them shall be as valid as if the attorney were acting in accordance with paragraph (a) or (b).

2 Characteristics of an enduring power

(1) Subject to subsections (7) to (9) below and section 11, a power of attorney is an enduring power within the meaning of this Act if the instrument which creates the power—

(a) is in the prescribed form; and

(b) was executed in the prescribed manner by the donor and the attorney; and

(c) incorporated at the time of execution by the donor the prescribed explanatory information.

(2) The Lord Chancellor shall make regulations as to the form and execution of instruments creating enduring powers and the regulations shall contain such provisions as appear to him to be appropriate for securing—

    (a)   that no document is used to create an enduring power which does not incorporate such information explaining the general effect of creating or accepting the power as may be prescribed; and

    (b)   that such instruments include statements to the following effect—

        (i)   by the donor, that he intends the power to continue in spite of any supervening mental incapacity of his;

        (ii)   by the donor, that he read or had read to him the information explaining the effect of creating the power;

        (iii)   by the attorney, that he understands the duty of registration imposed by this Act.

(3) Regulations under subsection (2) above—

    (a)   may include different provision for cases where more than one attorney is to be appointed by the instrument than for cases where only one attorney is to be appointed; and

    (b)   may, if they amend or revoke any regulations previously made under that subsection, include saving and transitional provisions.

(4) Regulations under subsection (2) above shall be made by statutory instrument which shall be subject to annulment in pursuance of a resolution of either House of Parliament.

(5) An instrument in the prescribed form purporting to have been executed in the prescribed manner shall be taken, in the absence of evidence to the contrary, to be a document which incorporated at the time of execution by the donor the prescribed explanatory information.

(6) Where an instrument differs in an immaterial respect in form or mode of expression from the prescribed form the instrument shall be treated as sufficient in point of form and expression.

(7) A power of attorney cannot be an enduring power unless, when he executes the instrument creating it, the attorney is—

    (a)   an individual who has attained eighteen years and is not bankrupt; or

    (b)   a trust corporation.

(8) . . .

(9) A power of attorney which gives the attorney a right to appoint a substitute or successor cannot be an enduring power.

(10) An enduring power shall be revoked by the bankruptcy of the attorney whatever the circumstances of the bankruptcy.

(11) An enduring power shall be revoked on the exercise by the court of any of its powers under Part VII of the Mental Health Act 1983 if, but only if, the court so directs.

(12) No disclaimer of an enduring power, whether by deed or otherwise, shall be valid unless and until the attorney gives notice of it to the donor or, where section 4(6) or 7(1) applies, to the court.

(13) In this section "prescribed" means prescribed under subsection (2) above.

NOTES

Amendment
Sub-s (8): repealed by the Trustee Delegation Act 1999, s 12, Schedule.
   Date in force: 1 March 2000 (in relation to powers of attorney created after that date): see SI 2000/216, art 2.
Subordinate Legislation
Enduring Powers of Attorney (Welsh Language Prescribed Form) Regulations 2000, SI 2000/289.

3 Scope of authority etc of attorney under enduring power

(1) An enduring power may confer general authority (as defined in subsection (2) below) on the attorney to act on the donor's behalf in relation to all or a specified part of the property and affairs of the donor or may confer on him authority to do specified things on the donor's behalf and the authority may, in either case, be conferred subject to conditions and restrictions.

(2) Where an instrument is expressed to confer general authority on the attorney it operates to confer, subject to the restriction imposed by subsection (5) below and to any conditions or restrictions contained in the instrument, authority to do on behalf of the donor anything which the donor can lawfully do by an attorney.

(3) . . .

(4) Subject to any conditions or restrictions contained in the instrument, an attorney under an enduring power, whether general or limited, may (without obtaining any consent) act under the power so as to benefit himself or other persons than the donor to the following extent but no further, that is to say—

   (a)   he may so act in relation to himself or in relation to any other person if the donor might be expected to provide for his or that person's needs respectively; and

   (b)   he may do whatever the donor might be expected to do to meet those needs.

(5) Without prejudice to subsection (4) above but subject to any conditions or restrictions contained in the instrument, an attorney under an enduring power,

whether general or limited, may (without obtaining any consent) dispose of the property of the donor by way of gift to the following extent but no further, that is to say—

> (a)　he may make gifts of a seasonal nature or at a time, or on an anniversary, of a birth or marriage, to persons (including himself) who are related to or connected with the donor, and

> (b)　he may make gifts to any charity to whom the donor made or might be expected to make gifts,

provided that the value of each such gift is not unreasonable having regard to all the circumstances and in particular the size of the donor's estate.

NOTES

Amendment

Sub-s (3): repealed by the Trustee Delegation Act 1999, s 12, Schedule, with effect in accordance with the provisions contained in s 4 thereof.

　Date in force: 1 March 2000: see SI 2000/216, art 2.

Action on actual or impending incapacity of donor

4　Duties of attorney in event of actual or impending incapacity of donor

(1) If the attorney under an enduring power has reason to believe that the donor is or is becoming mentally incapable subsections (2) to (6) below shall apply.

(2) The attorney shall, as soon as practicable, make an application to the court for the registration of the instrument creating the power.

(3) Before making an application for registration the attorney shall comply with the provisions as to notice set out in Schedule 1.

(4) An application for registration shall be made in the prescribed form and shall contain such statements as may be prescribed.

(5) The attorney may, before making an application for the registration of the instrument, refer to the court for its determination any question as to the validity of the power and he shall comply with any direction given to him by the court on that determination.

(6) No disclaimer of the power shall be valid unless and until the attorney gives notice of it to the court.

(7) Any person who, in an application for registration, makes a statement which he knows to be false in a material particular shall be liable—

> (a)　on conviction on indictment, to imprisonment for a term not exceeding two years or to a fine, or both; and

> (b)　on summary conviction, to imprisonment for a term not exceeding six months or to a fine not exceeding the statutory maximum, or both.

(8) In this section and Schedule 1 "prescribed" means prescribed by rules of the court.

5   Functions of court prior to registration

Where the court has reason to believe that the donor of an enduring power may be, or may be becoming, mentally incapable and the court is of the opinion that it is necessary, before the instrument creating the power is registered, to exercise any power with respect to the power of attorney or the attorney appointed to act under it which would become exercisable under section 8(2) on its registration, the court may exercise that power under this section and may do so whether the attorney has or has not made an application to the court for the registration of the instrument.

6   Functions of court on application for registration

(1) In any case where—

(a)   an application for registration is made in accordance with section 4(3) and (4), and

(b)   neither subsection (2) nor subsection (4) below applies,
the court shall register the instrument to which the application relates.

(2) Where it appears to the court that there is in force under Part VII of the Mental Health Act 1983 an order appointing a receiver for the donor but the power has not also been revoked then, unless it directs otherwise, the court shall not exercise or further exercise its functions under this section but shall refuse the application for registration.

(3) Where it appears from an application for registration that notice of it has not been given under Schedule 1 to some person entitled to receive it (other than a person in respect of whom the attorney has been dispensed or is otherwise exempt from the requirement to give notice) the court shall direct that the application be treated for the purposes of this Act as having been made in accordance with section 4(3), if the court is satisfied that, as regards each such person—

(a)   it was undesirable or impracticable for the attorney to give him notice; or

(b)   no useful purpose is likely to be served by giving him notice.

(4) If, in the case of an application for registration—

(a)   a valid notice of objection to the registration is received by the court before the expiry of the period of five weeks beginning with the date or, as the case may be, the latest date on which the attorney gave notice to any person under Schedule 1, or

(b) it appears from the application that there is no one to whom notice has been given under paragraph 1 of that Schedule, or

(c) the court has reason to believe that appropriate inquiries might bring to light evidence on which the court could be satisfied that one of the grounds of objection set out in subsection (5) below was established,

the court shall neither register the instrument nor refuse the application until it has made or caused to be made such inquiries (if any) as it thinks appropriate in the circumstances of the case.

(5) For the purposes of this Act a notice of objection to the registration of an instrument is valid if the objection is made on one or more of the following grounds, namely—

(a) that the power purported to have been created by the instrument was not valid as an enduring power of attorney;

(b) that the power created by the instrument no longer subsists;

(c) that the application is premature because the donor is not yet becoming mentally incapable;

(d) that fraud or undue pressure was used to induce the donor to create the power;

(e) that, having regard to all the circumstances and in particular the attorney's relationship to or connection with the donor, the attorney is unsuitable to be the donor's attorney.

(6) If, in a case where subsection (4) above applies, any of the grounds of objection in subsection (5) above is established to the satisfaction of the court, the court shall refuse the application but if, in such a case, it is not so satisfied, the court shall register the instrument to which the application relates.

(7) Where the court refuses an application for registration on ground (d) or (e) in subsection (5) above it shall by order revoke the power created by the instrument.

(8) Where the court refuses an application for registration on any ground other than that specified in subsection (5)(c) above the instrument shall be delivered up to be cancelled, unless the court otherwise directs.

Legal position after registration

7 Effect and proof of registration, etc

(1) The effect of the registration of an instrument under section 6 is that—

(a) no revocation of the power by the donor shall be valid unless and until the court confirms the revocation under section 8(3);

(b) no disclaimer of the power shall be valid unless and until the attorney gives notice of it to the court;

    (c)   the donor may not extend or restrict the scope of the authority conferred by the instrument and no instruction or consent given by him after registration shall, in the case of a consent, confer any right and, in the case of an instruction, impose or confer any obligation or right on or create any liability of the attorney or other persons having notice of the instruction or consent.

(2) Subsection (1) above applies for so long as the instrument is registered under section 6 whether or not the donor is for the time being mentally incapable.

(3) A document purporting to be an office copy of an instrument registered under this Act [or under the Enduring Powers of Attorney (Northern Ireland) Order 1987] shall, in any part of the United Kingdom, be evidence of the contents of the instrument and of the fact that it has been so registered.

(4) Subsection (3) above is without prejudice to section 3 of the Powers of Attorney Act 1971 (proof by certified copies) and to any other method of proof authorised by law.

NOTES

Amendment
Sub-s (3): words in square brackets inserted by the Enduring Powers of Attorney (Northern Ireland Consequential Amendment) Order 1987, SI 1987/1628, art 2.

8   Functions of court with respect to registered power

(1) Where an instrument has been registered under section 6, the court shall have the following functions with respect to the power and the donor of and the attorney appointed to act under the power.

(2) The court may—

    (a)   determine any question as to the meaning or effect of the instrument;

    (b)   give directions with respect to—

        (i)   the management or disposal by the attorney of the property and affairs of the donor;

        (ii)   the rendering of accounts by the attorney and the production of the records kept by him for the purpose;

        (iii)   the remuneration or expenses of the attorney, whether or not in default of or in accordance with any provision made by the instrument, including directions for the repayment of excessive or the payment of additional remuneration;

    (c)   require the attorney to furnish information or produce documents or things in his possession as attorney;

(d) give any consent or authorisation to act which the attorney would have to obtain from a mentally capable donor;

(e) authorise the attorney to act so as to benefit himself or other persons than the donor otherwise than in accordance with section 3(4) and (5) (but subject to any conditions or restrictions contained in the instrument);

(f) relieve the attorney wholly or partly from any liability which he has or may have incurred on account of a breach of his duties as attorney.

(3) On application made for the purpose by or on behalf of the donor, the court shall confirm the revocation of the power if satisfied that the donor has done whatever is necessary in law to effect an express revocation of the power and was mentally capable of revoking a power of attorney when he did so (whether or not he is so when the court considers the application).

(4) The court shall cancel the registration of an instrument registered under section 6 in any of the following circumstances, that is to say—

(a) on confirming the revocation of the power under subsection (3) above or receiving notice of disclaimer under section 7(1)(b);

(b) on giving a direction revoking the power on exercising any of its powers under Part VII of the Mental Health Act 1983;

(c) on being satisfied that the donor is and is likely to remain mentally capable;

(d) on being satisfied that the power has expired or has been revoked by the death or bankruptcy of the donor or the death, mental incapacity or bankruptcy of the attorney or, if the attorney is a body corporate, its winding up or dissolution;

(e) on being satisfied that the power was not a valid and subsisting enduring power when registration was effected;

(f) on being satisfied that fraud or undue pressure was used to induce the donor to create the power; or

(g) on being satisfied that, having regard to all the circumstances and in particular the attorney's relationship to or connection with the donor, the attorney is unsuitable to be the donor's attorney.

(5) Where the court cancels the registration of an instrument on being satisfied of the matters specified in paragraph (f) or (g) of subsection (4) above it shall by order revoke the power created by the instrument.

(6) On the cancellation of the registration of an instrument under subsection (4) above except paragraph (c) the instrument shall be delivered up to be cancelled, unless the court otherwise directs.

Protection of attorney and third parties

9 Protection of attorney and third persons where power invalid or revoked

(1) Subsections (2) and (3) below apply where an instrument which did not create a valid power of attorney has been registered under section 6 (whether or not the registration has been cancelled at the time of the act or transaction in question).

(2) An attorney who acts in pursuance of the power shall not incur any liability (either to the donor or to any other person) by reason of the non-existence of the power unless at the time of acting he knows—

    (a)   that the instrument did not create a valid enduring power; or

    (b)   that an event has occurred which, if the instrument had created a valid enduring power, would have had the effect of revoking the power; or

    (c)   that, if the instrument had created a valid enduring power, the power would have expired before that time.

(3) Any transaction between the attorney and another person shall, in favour of that person, be as valid as if the power had then been in existence, unless at the time of the transaction that person has knowledge of any of the matters mentioned in subsection (2) above.

(4) Where the interest of a purchaser depends on whether a transaction between the attorney and another person was valid by virtue of subsection (3) above, it shall be conclusively presumed in favour of the purchaser that the transaction was valid if—

    (a)   the transaction between that person and the attorney was completed within twelve months of the date on which the instrument was registered; or

    (b)   that person makes a statutory declaration, before or within three months after the completion of the purchase, that he had no reason at the time of the transaction to doubt that the attorney had authority to dispose of the property which was the subject of the transaction.

(5) For the purposes of section 5 of the Powers of Attorney Act 1971 (protection of attorney and third persons where action is taken under the power of attorney in ignorance of its having been revoked) in its application to an enduring power the revocation of which by the donor is by virtue of section 7(1)(a) above invalid unless and until confirmed by the court under section 8(3) above, knowledge of the confirmation of the revocation is, but knowledge of the unconfirmed revocation is not, knowledge of the revocation of the power.

(6) Schedule 2 shall have effect to confer protection in cases where the instrument failed to create a valid enduring power and the power has been revoked by the donor's mental incapacity.

(7) In this section "purchaser" and "purchase" have the meanings specified in section 205(1) of the Law of Property Act 1925.

Supplementary

10   Application of Mental Health Act provisions relating to the court

(1) The provisions of Part VII of the Mental Health Act 1983 (relating to the Court of Protection) specified below shall apply to persons within and proceedings under this Act in accordance with the following paragraphs of this subsection and subsection (2) below, that is to say—

- (a)   section 103 (functions of Visitors) shall apply to persons within this Act as it applies to the persons mentioned in that section;

- (b)   section 104 (powers of judge) shall apply to proceedings under this Act with respect to persons within this Act as it applies to the proceedings mentioned in subsection (1) of that section;

- (c)   section 105(1) (appeals to nominated judge) shall apply to any decision of the Master of the Court of Protection or any nominated officer in proceedings under this Act as it applies to any decision to which that subsection applies and an appeal shall lie to the Court of Appeal from any decision of a nominated judge whether given in the exercise of his original jurisdiction or on the hearing of an appeal under section 105(1) as extended by this paragraph;

- (d)   section 106 except subsection (4) (rules of procedure) shall apply to proceedings under this Act and persons within this Act as it applies to the proceedings and persons mentioned in that section.

(2) Any functions conferred or imposed by the provisions of the said Part VII applied by subsection (1) above shall be exercisable also for the purposes of this Act and the persons who are "within this Act" are the donors of and attorneys under enduring powers of attorney whether or not they would be patients for the purposes of the said Part VII.

(3) In this section "nominated judge" and "nominated officer" have the same meanings as in Part VII of the Mental Health Act 1983.

11   Application to joint and joint and several attorneys

(1) An instrument which appoints more than one person to be an attorney cannot create an enduring power unless the attorneys are appointed to act jointly or jointly and severally.

(2) This Act, in its application to joint attorneys, applies to them collectively as it applies to a single attorney but subject to the modifications specified in Part I of Schedule 3.

(3) This Act, in its application to joint and several attorneys, applies with the modifications specified in subsections (4) to (7) below and in Part II of Schedule 3.

(4) A failure, as respects any one attorney, to comply with the requirements for the creation of enduring powers, shall prevent the instrument from creating such a power in his case without however affecting its efficacy for that purpose as respects the other or others or its efficacy in his case for the purpose of creating a power of attorney which is not an enduring power.

(5) Where one or more but not both or all the attorneys makes or joins in making an application for registration of the instrument then—

    (a)   an attorney who is not an applicant as well as one who is may act pending the initial determination of the application as provided in section 1(2) (or under section 5);

    (b)   notice of the application shall also be given under Schedule 1 to the other attorney or attorneys; and

    (c)   objection may validly be taken to the registration on a ground relating to an attorney or to the power of an attorney who is not an applicant as well as to one or the power of one who is an applicant.

(6) The court shall not refuse under section 6(6) to register an instrument because a ground of objection to an attorney or power is established if an enduring power subsists as respects some attorney who is not affected thereby but shall give effect to it by the prescribed qualification of the registration.

(7) The court shall not cancel the registration of an instrument under section 8(4) for any of the causes vitiating registration specified in that subsection if an enduring power subsists as respects some attorney who is not affected thereby but shall give effect to it by the prescribed qualification of the registration.

(8) In this section—

    "prescribed" means prescribed by rules of the court; and

    "the requirements for the creation of enduring powers" means the provisions of section 2 other than subsections (10) to (12) and of regulations under subsection (2) of that section.

12   Power of Lord Chancellor to modify pre-registration requirements in certain cases

(1) The Lord Chancellor may by order exempt attorneys of such descriptions as he thinks fit from the requirements of this Act to give notice to relatives prior to registration.

(2) Subject to subsection (3) below, where an order is made under this section with respect to attorneys of a specified description then, during the currency of the order, this Act shall have effect in relation to any attorney of that description with the omission of so much of section 4(3) and Schedule 1 as requires notice of an application for registration to be given to relatives.

(3) Notwithstanding that an attorney under a joint or joint and several power is of a description specified in a current order under this section, subsection (2) above shall not apply in relation to him if any of the other attorneys under the power is not of a description specified in that or another current order under this section.

(4) The power to make an order under this section shall be exercisable by statutory instrument which shall be subject to annulment in pursuance of a resolution of either House of Parliament.

13 Interpretation

(1) In this Act—

"the court", in relation to any functions under this Act, means the authority having jurisdiction under Part VII of the Mental Health Act 1983;

"enduring power" is to be construed in accordance with section 2;

"mentally incapable" or "mental incapacity", except where it refers to revocation at common law, means, in relation to any person, that he is incapable by reason of mental disorder of managing and administering his property and affairs and "mentally capable" and "mental capacity" shall be construed accordingly;

"mental disorder" has the same meaning as it has in the Mental Health Act 1983;

"notice" means notice in writing;

"rules of the court" means rules under Part VII of the Mental Health Act 1983 as applied by section 10;

. . .

"trust corporation" means the Public Trustee or a corporation either appointed by the High Court or a county court (according to their respective jurisdictions) in any particular case to be a trustee or entitled by rules under section 4(3) of the Public Trustee Act 1906 to act as custodian trustee.

(2) Any question arising under or for the purposes of this Act as to what the donor of the power might at any time be expected to do shall be determined by assuming that he had full mental capacity at the time but otherwise by reference to the circumstances existing at that time.

NOTES

Amendment
Sub-s (1): definition omitted repealed by the Statute Law (Repeals) Act 1993.

14   Short title, commencement and extent

(1) This Act may be cited as the Enduring Powers of Attorney Act 1985.

(2) This Act shall come into force on such day as the Lord Chancellor appoints by order made by statutory instrument.

(3) This Act extends to England and Wales only except that section 7(3) and section 10(1)(b) so far as it applies section 104(4) of the Mental Health Act 1983 extend also to Scotland and Northern Ireland.

NOTES

Appointment
Commencement order: SI 1986/125.

SCHEDULE 1
NOTIFICATION PRIOR TO REGISTRATION

Section 4(3)

PART I DUTY TO GIVE NOTICE TO RELATIVES AND DONOR

Duty to give notice to relatives

1   Subject to paragraph 3 below, before making an application for registration the attorney shall give notice of his intention to do so to all those persons (if any) who are entitled to receive notice by virtue of paragraph 2 below.

2   (1) Subject to the limitations contained in sub-paragraphs (2) to (4) below, persons of the following classes (referred to in this Act as "relatives") are entitled to receive notice under paragraph 1 above—

(a)   the donor's husband or wife;

(b)   the donor's children;

(c)   the donor's parents;

(d)   the donor's brothers and sisters, whether of the whole or half blood;

(e)   the widow or widower of a child of the donor;

(f)   the donor's grandchildren;

(g)   the children of the donor's brothers and sisters of the whole blood;

(h)   the children of the donor's brothers and sisters of the half blood;

(i)   the donor's uncles and aunts of the whole blood; and

(j)   the children of the donor's uncles and aunts of the whole blood.

(2) A person is not entitled to receive notice under paragraph 1 above if—

(a)   his name or address is not known to the attorney and cannot be reasonably ascertained by him; or

(b)   the attorney has reason to believe that he has not attained eighteen years or is mentally incapable.

(3) Except where sub-paragraph (4) below applies, no more than three persons are entitled to receive notice under paragraph 1 above and, in determining the persons who are so entitled, persons falling within class (a) of sub-paragraph (1) above are to be preferred to persons falling with class (b) of that sub-paragraph, persons falling within class (b) are to be preferred to persons falling within class (c) of that sub-paragraph; and so on.

(4) Notwithstanding the limit of three specified in sub-paragraph (3) above, where—

(a)   there is more than one person falling within any of classes (a) to (j) of sub-paragraph (1) above, and

(b)   at least one of those persons would be entitled to receive notice under paragraph 1 above,

then, subject to sub-paragraph (2) above, all the persons falling within that class are entitled to receive notice under paragraph 1 above.

3   (1) An attorney shall not be required to give notice under paragraph 1 above to himself or to any other attorney under the power who is joining in making the application, notwithstanding that he or, as the case may be, the other attorney is entitled to receive notice by virtue of paragraph 2 above.

(2) In the case of any person who is entitled to receive notice under paragraph 1 above, the attorney, before applying for registration, may make an application to the court to be dispensed from the requirement to give him notice; and the court shall grant the application if it is satisfied—

(a)   that it would be undesirable or impracticable for the attorney to give him notice; or

(b)   that no useful purpose is likely to be served by giving him notice.

Duty to give notice to donor

4   (1) Subject to sub-paragraph (2) below, before making an application for registration the attorney shall give notice of his intention to do so to the donor.

(2) Paragraph 3(2) above shall apply in relation to the donor as it applies in relation to a person who is entitled to receive notice under paragraph 1 above.

PART II CONTENTS OF NOTICES

5   A notice to relatives under this Schedule—

    (a)   shall be in the prescribed form;

    (b)   shall state that the attorney proposes to make an application to the Court of Protection for the registration of the instrument creating the enduring power in question;

    (c)   shall inform the person to whom it is given that he may object to the proposed registration by notice in writing to the Court of Protection before the expiry of the period of four weeks beginning with the day on which the notice under this Schedule was given to him;

    (d)   shall specify, as the grounds on which an objection to registration may be made, the grounds set out in section 6(5).

6   A notice to the donor under this Schedule—

    (a)   shall be in the prescribed form;

    (b)   shall contain the statement mentioned in paragraph 5(b) above; and

    (c)   shall inform the donor that, whilst the instrument remains registered, any revocation of the power by him will be ineffective unless and until the revocation is confirmed by the Court of Protection.

PART III DUTY TO GIVE NOTICE TO OTHER ATTORNEYS

7   (1) Subject to sub-paragraph (2) below, before making an application for registration an attorney under a joint and several power shall give notice of his intention to do so to any other attorney under the power who is not joining in making the application; and paragraphs 3(2) and 5 above shall apply in relation to attorneys entitled to receive notice by virtue of this paragraph as they apply in relation to persons entitled to receive notice by virtue of paragraph 2 above.

(2) An attorney is not entitled to receive notice by virtue of this paragraph if—

    (a)   his address is not known to the applying attorney and cannot reasonably be ascertained by him; or

    (b)   the applying attorney has reason to believe that he has not attained eighteen years or is mentally incapable.

PART IV SUPPLEMENTARY

8 (1) For the purposes of this Schedule an illegitimate child shall be treated as if he were the legitimate child of his mother and father.

(2) Notwithstanding anything in section 7 of the Interpretation Act 1978 (construction of references to service by post), for the purposes of this Schedule a notice given by post shall be regarded as given on the date on which it was posted.

SCHEDULE 2
FURTHER PROTECTION OF ATTORNEY AND THIRD PERSONS

Section 9(6)

1 Where—

- (a) an instrument framed in a form prescribed under section 2(2) creates a power which is not a valid enduring power; and

- (b) the power is revoked by the mental incapacity of the donor, paragraphs 2 and 3 below shall apply, whether or not the instrument has been registered.

2 An attorney who acts in pursuance of the power shall not, by reason of the revocation, incur any liability (either to the donor or to any other person) unless at the time of acting he knows—

- (a) that the instrument did not create a valid enduring power; and

- (b) that the donor has become mentally incapable.

3 Any transaction between the attorney and another person shall, in favour of that person, be as valid as if the power had then been in existence, unless at the time of the transaction that person knows—

- (a) that the instrument did not create a valid enduring power; and

- (b) that the donor has become mentally incapable.

4 Section 9(4) shall apply for the purpose of determining whether a transaction was valid by virtue of paragraph 3 above as it applies for the purpose of determining whether a transaction was valid by virtue of section 9(3).

SCHEDULE 3
JOINT AND JOINT AND SEVERAL ATTORNEYS

Section 11(2), (3)

PART I JOINT ATTORNEYS

1 In section 2(7), the reference to the time when the attorney executes the instrument shall be read as a reference to the time when the second or last attorney executes the instrument.

2   In section 2(9) and (10), the reference to the attorney shall be read as a reference to any attorney under the power.

3   In section 5, references to the attorney shall be read as including references to any attorney under the power.

4   Section 6 shall have effect as if the ground of objection to the registration of the instrument specified in subsection (5)(e) applied to any attorney under the power.

5   In section 8(2), references to the attorney shall be read as including references to any attorney under the power.

6   In section 8(4), references to the attorney shall be read as including references to any attorney under the power.

PART II JOINT AND SEVERAL ATTORNEYS

7   In section 2(10), the reference to the bankruptcy of the attorney shall be construed as a reference to the bankruptcy of the last remaining attorney under the power; and the bankruptcy of any other attorney under the power shall cause that person to cease to be attorney, whatever the circumstances of the bankruptcy.

8   The restriction upon disclaimer imposed by section 4(6) applies only to those attorneys who have reason to believe that the donor is or is becoming mentally incapable.

Appendix 4

Trustee Act 2000

A4.1   Section 11 of the Act permits trustees to authorise any person to exercise any or all their delegable functions as an agent. Section 11(2) defines the delegable functions of the trustees as any function other than –

(a)   any function relating to whether or in what way any assets of the trust should be distributed,

(b)   any power to decide where any fees or other payment due to be made out of the trust funds should be made out of income or capital,

(c)   any power to appoint a person to be a trustee of a trust, or

(d)   any power conferred by any other enactment or the trust instrument which permits the trustees to delegate any of their functions or to appoint a person to act as a nominee or custodian.

Section 11(3) provides that in the case of a charitable trust, the trustees' delegable functions are –

(a)   any function consisting of carrying out a decision that the trustees have taken,

(b)   any function relating to the investment of assets subject to the trust (including, in the case of land acquired as an investment, managing the land and creating or disposing of an interest in the land),

(c)   any function relating to the raising of funds for the trust otherwise than by means of profits of a trade which is an integral part of carrying out the trust's charitable purpose,

(d)   any other function prescribed by an order made by the Secretary of State.

Section 12 of the Act deals with who may be appointed as an agent. The trustees can appoint one of their number, but they cannot appoint a beneficiary. If two or more persons are appointed as agents, they must exercise their functions jointly. A person may be appointed to act as the agent of the trustees even though he is also appointed to act as the nominee or custodian of the trustees.

Appendix 5

The following guidelines for solicitors, revised September 1999, were prepared by the Mental Health and Disability Committee of The Law Society, and are reproduced here with the kind permission of The Law Society.

© The Law Society 1999

ENDURING POWERS OF ATTORNEY

1. Introduction

1.1 The following guidelines are intended to assist solicitors in advising clients who wish to draw up an enduring power of attorney (EPA). They have been prepared by the Law Society's Mental Health and Disability Committee, after consultation with other Law Society committees and the Professional Ethics Division, in response to queries raised by practitioners.

1.2 Different considerations apply in relation to donors who make an EPA as a precautionary measure while they are still in the prime of life, and those who are of borderline mental capacity, where the EPA may need to be registered immediately. These guidelines set out general points for consideration, and their relevance will depend on the particular circumstances of individual cases.

1.3 The guidelines are based on the law in England and Wales. It should be noted that there is currently no internationally recognised form of EPA, and additional arrangements must be made for clients who have property in other jurisdictions.

2. Who is the client?

2.1 Where a solicitor is instructed to prepare an EPA, **the donor is the client** (The Law Society, *The Guide to the Professional Conduct of Solicitors* (8th edition, 1999) Principle 24 03 note 1).

A solicitor must not accept instructions where he or she suspects that those instructions have been given by a client under duress or undue influence *(ibid,* Principle 12 04).

When asked to prepare an EPA on written instructions alone, a solicitor should always consider carefully whether these instructions are sufficient, or whether he or she should see the client to discuss them *(ibid,* Principle 24 03 note 2).

2.2 Where instructions for the preparation of an EPA are received not from the client (ie the prospective donor), but from a third party purporting to represent that client, a solicitor should obtain written instructions from the client that he or she wishes the solicitor to act. In any case of doubt the solicitor should see the client alone or take other appropriate steps, both to confirm the instructions with the donor personally after offering appropriate advice, and also to ensure that the donor has the necessary capacity to make the power (see section 5 below). The solicitor must also advise the prospective donor without regard to the interests of the source from which he or she was introduced (*ibid*, Principle 12 04 and Principle 24 03, note 2).

2.3 Once the EPA has been executed and comes into effect, instructions may be accepted from the attorney but the solicitor continues to owe his/her duties to the donor (*ibid*, Principle 24 03, note 1). Before registration of the EPA, it may be advisable for the solicitor, where appropriate, to satisfy him/herself that the donor continues to have capacity and to confirm the instructions with the donor. See also the Practice Statement issued by Mrs A B Macfarlane, former Master of the Court of Protection, on 9 August 1995 (*The Law Society's Gazette*, 11 October 1995, p 21 or The Law Society *Professional Standards Bulletin No 15*, p 53), which clarifies solicitors' duties in acting for patients or donors and sets out procedures for dealing with conflicts of interest.

The attorney is the statutory agent of the donor, just as in receivership proceedings the receiver is the statutory agent of the patient (*Re E G* [1914] 1 Ch 927, CA).

3. Capacity to make an EPA

3.1 The solicitor should be satisfied that, on the balance of probabilities, the donor has the mental capacity to make an EPA. Many EPAs are made when the donors are already losing capacity. Consequently they could be unaware of the implications of their actions and are more likely to be vulnerable to exploitation.

3.2 If there is any doubt about the donor's capacity, a medical opinion should be obtained. The solicitor should inform the doctor of the test of capacity laid down in *Re K, Re F* [1988] 1 All ER 358, 363 (see Appendix A attached, and *Assessment of Mental Capacity Guidance for doctors and lawyers* issued by the Law Society and the British Medical Association (1995)). If the doctor is of the opinion that the donor has capacity, he or she should make a record to that effect and witness the donor's signature on the EPA (*Kenward v Adams* [1975] The Times, 29 November 1975).

4. Risk of Abuse

4.1 The Master of the Court of Protection has estimated that financial abuse occurs in 10 to 15 per cent of cases of registered EPAs and even more often with unregistered powers (Denzil Lush, *Solicitors Journal,* 11th September 1998). When advising clients of the benefits of EPAs, the solicitor should also inform them of the risks of abuse, particularly the risk that the attorney could misuse the power. Throughout these guidelines, an attempt has been made to identify possible risk areas and to suggest ways of preventing abuse, which the solicitor should discuss with the donor. Written information for clients on both the benefits and risks of EPAs whether in a brochure or correspondence may also be helpful.

4.2 During the initial stages of advising a client, the solicitor should consider the following points

(i) There may be circumstances when an EPA may not be appropriate, and a later application for receivership, with oversight of the Court of Protection, may be preferable. This may be advisable, for example

- where there are indications of persistent family conflicts suggesting that an EPA may be contested, or

- where the assets are more substantial or complex than family members are accustomed to handle, or

- in cases where litigation may lead to a substantial award of damages for personal injury.

(ii) The solicitor should consider discouraging the use of an unregistered EPA as an ordinary power of attorney, particularly for vulnerable elderly clients. Instructions to this effect could be included in the instrument itself (see paragraph 5.3 below) or the donor could be advised to lodge the power with the solicitor, with strict instructions that it is not to be used until the donor becomes or is becoming incapable.

5. Taking instructions

The solicitor should take full and careful instructions from the donor, and ensure that the following matters, where applicable, are considered by the donor when giving instructions.

5.1 Choice of attorney

The choice of attorney is clearly a personal decision for the donor, but it is important for the solicitor to advise the donor of the various options available, and to stress the need for the attorney to be absolutely trustworthy, since on appointment the attorney's actions will be subject to little supervision or scrutiny (see section 4 above). The donor should be advised that the appointment of a sole attorney may provide greater opportunity for abuse and exploitation than appointing more than one attorney (see below).

The solicitor should ask questions about the donor's relationship with the proposed attorney and whether the attorney has the skills required to manage the donor's financial affairs. The donor should also consider the suitability of appointing a family member or someone independent of the family, or a combination of both.

More than one attorney

Where more than one attorney is to be appointed, they must be appointed to act either 'jointly' or 'jointly and severally' (Enduring Powers of Attorney Act 1985, s 11(1)).

One of these two alternatives must be chosen and the other crossed out. Failure to cross out one of these alternatives on the prescribed form makes the power invalid, and this is one of the commonest reasons for the Court of Protection or Public Trust Office refusing to register an EPA.

The differences between a 'joint' and 'joint and several' appointment should be explained to the donor

- In addition to the explanatory information in the prescribed form to the effect that joint attorneys must all act together and cannot act separately, the donor should be advised that a joint appointment will terminate if any one of the attorneys disclaims, dies, or becomes bankrupt or mentally incapable. However, joint appointments may provide a safeguard against possible abuse, since each attorney will be able to oversee the actions of the other(s).

- Similarly, in addition to the explanatory information in the prescribed form to the effect that joint and several attorneys can all act together but can also act separately if they wish, the donor should be advised that, where there is a joint and several appointment, the disclaimer, death, bankruptcy and incapacity of one attorney will not automatically terminate the power.

The donor may have to make difficult choices as to which family member(s) to appoint as his or her attorney. It is possible to allow some flexibility, as in the following examples

i) The donor may wish to appoint a family member and a professional to act jointly and severally with, for example, the family member dealing with day-to-day matters, and the professional dealing with more complex affairs.

ii) The donor may wish to appoint his or her spouse as attorney, with provision for their adult child(ren) to take over as attorney(s) should the spouse die or become incapacitated. One way to achieve this is for the donor to execute two EPAs the first appointing the spouse as attorney, and the second appointing the child(ren) with a provision that it will only come into effect if the first power is terminated for any reason. Alternatively, the donor could appoint everyone to act jointly and severally, with an informal understanding that the children will not act while the spouse is able to do so.

iii)   The donor may wish to appoint his or her three adult children as attorneys to act jointly and severally, with a proviso that anything done under the power should be done by at least two of them. This could be achieved by careful wording of the EPA document or by an accompanying statement or letter of wishes, which although not directly enforceable, would provide a clear indication as to how the donor wishes the power to be operated.

5.2   General or limited authority

The donor must be clear whether the EPA is to be a general power, giving the attorney authority to manage all the donor's property and affairs, or whether the authority is to extend only to part of his or her property and affairs. Any restrictions to the power should be carefully drafted and should have regard to the provisions of the Enduring Powers of Attorney Act 1985 (see also paragraphs 5.6 and 5.11 below).

The solicitor should also discuss with the donor what arrangements should be made for the management of those affairs which are not covered by the EPA. Donors should be advised that if they leave a 'gap', so that part of their affairs are not covered by the EPA, it may be necessary for the Court of Protection to intervene and appoint a receiver.

5.3   When the power is to come into operation

The donor must understand when the power is to come into operation. If nothing is said in the instrument, it will take effect immediately, and can be used as an ordinary power of attorney. The donor should be advised of the risk of abuse of an unregistered power, unless s/he is in a position to supervise and authorise use of the power.

If the donor does not want the power to take effect immediately and would prefer it to be held in abeyance until the onset of his or her incapacity, he or she must expressly say so in the EPA. The donor may also wish to include a specific condition that a statement from a doctor confirming lack of capacity must accompany the application to register the EPA.

In such circumstances, it may be preferable to state that the power will not come into operation until the need arises to apply to register the EPA, rather than state that it will not come into operation until it is registered. Pending completion of the registration formalities, the attorney has limited powers, and it may be better for the attorney to have these powers, rather than none at all.

5.4 Gifts

Section 3(5) of the Enduring Powers of Attorney Act 1985 gives the attorney limited authority to make gifts of the donor's money or property

- The recipient of the gift must be either an individual who is related to or connected with the donor, or a charity to which the donor actually made gifts or might be expected to make gifts if s/he had capacity.

- The timing of the gift must occur within the prescribed parameters. A gift to charity can be made at any time of the year, but a gift to an individual must be of a seasonal nature, or made on the occasion of a birth or marriage, or on the anniversary of a birth or marriage.

- The value of the gift must be not unreasonable having regard to all the circumstances and in particular the size of the donor's estate.

The donor cannot confer wider authority on the attorney than that specified in section 3(5), but it is open to the donor to restrict or exclude the authority which would otherwise be available to the attorney under that subsection. This possibility should be specifically discussed with the donor, since improper gifting is the most widespread form of abuse in attorneyship. The donor may wish to specify in the power the circumstances in which the attorney may make gifts of money or property.

Section 3(5) applies to both registered and unregistered EPAs, but not to those which are in the course of being registered. Where an application to register the EPA has been made , the attorney cannot make *any* gifts of the donor's property until the power has been registered.

If the EPA is registered, the Court of Protection can authorise the attorney to act so as to benefit himself or others, otherwise than in accordance with section 3(5), provided that there are no restrictions in the EPA itself (Enduring Powers of Attorney Act 1985, s 8(2)(e)).

Solicitors must also take account of Principle 15 05 of the Guide to Professional Conduct (*op cit,* 1999) concerning gifts to solicitors.

5.5 Delegation by the attorney

It is a basic principle of the law of agency that a delegate cannot delegate his or her authority. Alternatively, this could be expressed as a duty on the part of an agent to perform his or her functions personally.

Like any other agent, an attorney acting under an EPA has an implied power to delegate any functions which are of a purely ministerial nature, which do not involve or require the exercise of any confidence or discretion, and which the donor would not expect the attorney to attend to personally.

Any wider power of delegation must be expressly provided for in the EPA itself for example, transferring the donor's assets into a discretionary investment management scheme operated by a stockbroker or bank.

5.6 Investment business

Unless the power is restricted to exclude investments as defined by the Financial Services Act 1986, the attorney may need to consider the investment business implications of his/her appointment. A solicitor who is appointed attorney under an EPA is likely to be conducting investment business and if so, will need to be authorised under the Financial Services Act. In addition, the solicitor will need to consider whether the Solicitors Investment Business Rules 1995 apply.

The Financial Services and Markets Bill due to come into effect in approximately mid-2000, is likely to change the definition of investment business and affect the need for authorisation. The detailed position, at the time of writing, is unclear and solicitors will need to keep this aspect under review.

5.7 Trusteeships held by the donor

The solicitor should ask whether the donor holds

- any trusteeships, and

- any property jointly with others

Section 3(3) of the Enduring Powers of Attorney Act 1985 has been repealed by the Trustee Delegation Act 1999 with effect from 1st January 2000. Section 4 of the 1999 Act contains detailed transitional provisions which affect existing EPAs, both registered and unregistered.

The general rule is that any trustee functions delegated to an attorney (whether under an ordinary power or an enduring power) must comply with the provisions of section 25 of the Trustee Act 1925, as amended by the 1999 Act.

However, section 1(1) of the 1999 Act provides an exception to this general rule. An attorney can exercise a trustee function of the donor if it relates to land, or the capital proceeds or income from land, in which the donor has a beneficial interest. This is, of course, subject to any provision to the contrary contained in the trust instrument or the power of attorney itself.

5.8 Solicitor-attorneys

Where a solicitor is appointed as attorney, or where it is intended that a particular solicitor will deal with the general management of the donor's affairs, it is recommended that the solicitor's current terms and conditions of business (including charging rates and the frequency of billing) be discussed with and approved by the donor at the time of granting the power.

Since the explanatory information on the prescribed form of EPA is ambiguous about the remuneration of professional attorneys, it is recommended that a professional charging clause be included in the power for the avoidance of doubt.

Where a solicitor is appointed sole attorney (or is reasonably likely to become the sole attorney), or where two or more solicitors in the same firm are appointed and there is no external attorney, the donor should be informed of the potential problems of accountability if he or she should become mentally incapacitated. If necessary, arrangements could be made for the solicitor's costs to be approved or audited by an independent third party in the event of the donor's incapacity.

In a number of cases solicitor-attorneys have disclaimed when it became apparent that the donor's assets were insufficient to make the attorneyship cost-effective. The Law Society's view is that, if solicitors intend to disclaim in such circumstances, they should not take on the attorneyship in the first place, or should warn the donor of this possibility at the time of making the power.

Further guidance is given in the Guide to Professional Conduct (*op cit,* Principle 24 03, Notes 5,6,7). Solicitors are also reminded that any commission earned should be paid to the donor (see Annex 14G of the Guide to Professional Conduct).

5.9 The donor's property and affairs

It may be helpful for solicitors to record and retain information relating to the donor's property and affairs, even where they are not to be appointed as an attorney themselves. The Law Society's *Personal Assets Log,* which is sometimes used when taking will-drafting instructions, could be suitably adapted for this purpose. In addition, there are certain requirements under the Solicitors' Investment Business Rules where solicitors safeguard and administer documents of title to investments eg share certificates.

5.10 Notification of intention to register the EPA

Solicitors should explain to the donor that the attorney has a duty to notify the donor in person, and at least three members of the donor's family, of his or her intention to register the EPA with the Public Trust Office if the attorney has reason to believe that the donor is, or is becoming mentally incapable.

It may be helpful to obtain a list of the names and addresses of the relatives at the time the EPA is granted. If the donor would like other members of the family, or friends or close associates to be notified in addition to those on the statutory list, details could be included in the EPA itself or in a separate letter.

In any event, solicitors should encourage donors to tell their family that they have made an EPA and perhaps explain why they have chosen the attorney(s). This may help to guard against the possibility of abuse by the attorney and may also reduce the risk of conflict between family members at a later stage.

5.11 Disclosure of the donor's will

Solicitors are under a duty to keep their clients' affairs confidential (The Law Society, *The Guide to the Professional Conduct of Solicitors* (8th edition, 1999) Principle 16 01). However, the attorney(s) may need to know about the contents of the donor's will in order to avoid acting contrary to the testamentary intentions of the donor (for example, by the sale of an asset specifically bequeathed, when other assets that fell into residue could be disposed of instead).

The question of disclosure of the donor's will should be discussed at the time of making the EPA, and instructions should be obtained as to whether disclosure is denied, or the circumstances in which it is permitted. For example, the donor may agree that the solicitor can disclose the contents of the will to the attorney, but only if the EPA is registered and the solicitor thinks that disclosure of the will is necessary or expedient for the proper performance of the attorney's functions.

Principle 24 03, note 4 of the Guide *(ibid)* gives guidance where the EPA is registered and is silent on the subject of disclosure. Advice may also be sought from the Professional Ethics Division or from the Public Trust Office (see section 13 below).

The attorney also has a common law duty to keep the donor's affairs (including the contents of a will) confidential.

5.12 Medical evidence

It may be worth asking the donor to give advance consent in writing authorising the solicitor to contact the donor's GP or any other medical practitioner if the need for medical evidence should arise at a later date (for example, on registration of the power, or, after the power has been registered, to assess whether the donor has testamentary capacity).

5.13 Safeguards against abuse

Solicitors should discuss with the donor appropriate measures to safeguard against the power being misused or exploited. This could include notifying other family members of the existence of the power, and how the donor intends it to be used.

The solicitor could also consider offering an auditing service, by inserting a clause into the power requiring the attorney to produce to the solicitor, on a specified date each year, an account of his/her actions as attorney during the last 12 months. If the attorney failed to render a satisfactory account, the solicitor could apply for registration of the power to be cancelled on the grounds of the attorney's unsuitability. Again a charging procedure for this service must be agreed with the donor in advance.

6. Drawing up the EPA

6.1 The prescribed form

An EPA must be in the form prescribed by the Enduring Powers of Attorney (Prescribed Form) Regulations in force at the time of its execution by the donor.

There have been three sets of regulations and the periods during which they have been in force are

- 1986 Regulations   10 March 1986 to 30 June 1988
- 1987 Regulations   1 November 1987 to 30 July 1991
- 1990 Regulations   31 July 1991 onwards

Solicitors should ensure that existing EPAs are in the form prescribed on the date they were executed by the donors and that the form they are currently using is the one prescribed by the Enduring Powers of Attorney (Prescribed Form) Regulations 1990 (SI 1990 No 1376).

6.2   Provided the prescribed form is used, it does not matter whether it is a printed form from a law stationers or whether it is transcribed onto a word-processor, although a law stationer's form is more easily recognisable by third parties. What is essential, however, is that there should be no unauthorised departure from the prescribed form. So, where the donor is to be offered an EPA which is not on a law stationer's form, the solicitor should be absolutely certain that the form complies with the prescribed form regulations. Use of inaccurate or incomplete word-processed forms are common reasons for refusal to register an EPA.

Part A ('About using this form') and the marginal notes must be included in the EPA because the Enduring Powers of Attorney Act requires the prescribed explanatory information to be incorporated in the instrument at the time of execution by the donor (section 2(1) and 2(2) and Regulation 2(1) of the 1990 Regulations).

6.3   Completing the form

Solicitors should ensure that where alternatives are provided on the form (for example for 'joint' or 'joint and several' appointments, or to specify the extent of the authority granted), the required deletions are made by crossing out the options not chosen by the donor.

There is space on the prescribed form to provide details of two attorneys. Where it is intended to appoint three attorneys, the details of the third attorney may be included in the main document, fitted in to the space after the details of the second attorney.

Where more than three attorneys are to be appointed, details of the first two attorneys should be given in the main document, followed by the words, 'and (see additional names on attached sheet)' and the details given on a sheet to be attached to the main document marked clearly 'Names of additional attorneys'.

6.4 About 10% of EPAs are refused registration because of a defect in the form or the wording of the instrument. In some cases, registration may be possible after the filing of further evidence to overcome the defect. Solicitors who have assisted a donor in drawing up an EPA which is subsequently refused registration because of a defect that is material may be liable for the additional costs of receivership, since at that point the donor may not have the capacity to execute a new EPA.

7. Executing the power

7.1 An EPA must be executed by both the donor and the attorney(s). The donor must execute Part B of the prescribed form. The attorney must execute Part C. Where more than one attorney is appointed, each of them must complete a *separate* Part C, the additional sheets having been added and secured to the EPA document beforehand. One Part C cannot be 'shared' by more than one attorney.

The donor must execute the EPA before the attorney(s), because the attorney(s) cannot accept a power which has not yet been conferred. However, execution by the donor and attorney(s) need not take place simultaneously. There is no reason why execution by the attorney(s) should not occur at a later date, provided it happens before the donor loses capacity. It is often advisable for the attorney(s) to sign as soon as possible after the donor.

7.2 Execution by the donor and the attorney(s) must take place in the presence of a witness, but not necessarily the same witness, who must sign Part B or Part C of the prescribed form, as the case may be, and give his or her full name and address.

There are various restrictions as to who can act as a witness, and in particular

- the donor and attorney must not witness each other's signature,

- one attorney cannot witness the signature of another attorney,

- the marginal notes to Part B of the prescribed form warn that it is not advisable for the donor's spouse to witness his or her signature – this is because of the rules of evidence relating to compellability, and

- at common law, a blind person cannot witness another person's signature.

7.3   If the donor or attorney is physically disabled and unable to sign, he or she may make a mark, and the attestation clause should be adapted to explain this. Alternatively, the donor or an attorney may authorise another person to sign the EPA at his or her direction, in which case it must be signed by that person in the presence of two witnesses, as described in the marginal notes.

Although the Enduring Powers of Attorney (Prescribed Form) Regulations 1990 do not expressly state that, where someone executes the EPA at the direction of the donor or attorney, he or she must do so in the presence of the donor or attorney, it is essential that the power be executed in their presence in order to comply with section 1(3) of the Law of Property (Miscellaneous Provisions) Act 1989.

If the donor is blind, this should be stated in the attestation clause so that, if an application is made to register the EPA, the Public Trust Office can make enquiries as to how the donor was notified of the intention to register.

8.   Copies of an EPA

8.1   The contents of an EPA can be proved by means of a certified copy. In order to comply with the provisions of section 3 of the Powers of Attorney Act 1971, a certificate should appear at the end of each page of the copy stating that it is a true and complete copy of the corresponding page of the original. The certificate must be signed by the donor, or a solicitor, or a notary public or a stockbroker.

9.   Notification of intention to register the EPA

9.1   When it is necessary to give notice of the attorney's intention to register the power, the prescribed form of notice (Form EP1) must be used. The donor must be personally served with this notice, and the donor's relatives must be given notice by first class post.

It may be helpful, in the case of the relatives, to send the notice with an accompanying letter explaining the circumstances because, in the absence of such an explanation, there may be cause for concern. Giving an appropriate explanation and information at this stage may prevent the application from becoming contentious.

Although there is no statutory requirement to do so, a copy of the EPA could also be sent to the relatives, in view of the fact that one of the grounds on which they can object to registration is that the power purported to have been created by the instrument is not valid as an enduring power.

9.2   As stated above, the notice of intention to register (Form EP1) must be given to the donor personally. The notice need not be handed to the donor by the attorney. It can be given to the donor by an agent (perhaps a solicitor) acting on the attorney's behalf, and the name of the person who gives notice to the donor must be stated on Form EP2.

Many attorneys, both relatives and professionals, find it distressing to have to inform donors of the implications of their failing mental capacity. Schedule 1 to the Enduring Powers of Attorney Act 1985 makes provision for the attorney to apply to the Public Trustee for dispensation from the requirement to serve notice on anyone entitled to receive it, including the donor.

However, the Public Trustee is reluctant to grant such a dispensation because it is the donor's right, and the right of entitled relatives, to be informed and to have an opportunity to object to registration. A dispensation is only likely to be granted in relation to the donor where there is clear medical evidence to show that notification would be detrimental to the donor's health, and in the case of relatives, only in exceptional circumstances.

10.   Statutory wills

10.1   An attorney cannot execute a will on the donor's behalf because the Wills Act 1837 requires a will to he signed by the testator personally or by someone in his or her presence and at his or her direction.

Where a person lacks testamentary capacity, the Court of Protection can order the execution of a statutory will on his or her behalf. The Court's will-making jurisdiction is conferred by the Mental Health Act 1983 – not the Enduring Powers of Attorney Act 1985 – but can be invoked where there is a registered EPA. An application for an order authorising the execution of a statutory will should be considered by solicitors where there is no will or where the existing will is no longer appropriate due to a change of circumstances. In statutory will proceedings, the Official Solicitor is usually asked to represent the testator.

10.2   The Court will require recent medical evidence showing that the donor

- is incapable, by reason of mental disorder, of managing and administering his or her property and affairs. This evidence should be provided on Form CP3 because, in effect, the Court needs to be satisfied that the donor is a 'patient' for the purposes of the Mental Health Act, and

- is incapable of making a valid will for himself or herself.

The Court's procedure notes PN9 and PN9(A) explain the Court's requirements. Guidance on the relevant tests of capacity can be found in the Law Society/BMA publication *Assessment of Mental Capacity Guidance for doctors and lawyers* (1995).

11. Support for attorneys

11.1 Section 4(5) of the Enduring Powers of Attorney Act 1985 provides that the attorney may, before making an application for the registration of the EPA, refer to the Court any question as to the validity of the power. However, such an application can only be made when the attorney has reason to believe that the donor is, or is becoming, mentally incapable. The Court will not determine any question as to the validity of an unregistered power in any other circumstances.

11.2 Under section 8 of the Act, the Court of Protection has various functions with respect to registered powers. However, the Court should not be seen as being available to 'hold the hand' of the attorney, who should in normal circumstances be able to act in the best interests of the donor, taking advice where necessary from a solicitor or other professional adviser. It should be noted that, although the Court may interpret the terms of an EPA or give directions as to its exercise, it does not have power to extend or amend the terms of the EPA as granted by the donor.

12. Where abuse is suspected

12.1 If solicitors suspect that an attorney may be misusing an EPA or acting dishonestly and the donor is unable to take action to protect him or herself, they should try to facilitate the remedies that the donor would have adopted if able to do so. In the first instance, the Public Trust Office should be notified and guidance sought from the Court of Protection as to how to proceed. This might include

- an application to the Court of Protection under the Mental Health Act 1983 for an Order giving authority to take action to recover the donor's funds

- an application to the Court for registration of the power to be cancelled on the grounds of the attorney's unsuitability and for receivership proceedings to be instituted

- involvement of the police to investigate allegations of theft or fraud

- where residential care or nursing homes are involved, using the local authority complaints procedure or involving the relevant registration authority.

13. Further advice

13.1 Solicitors may obtain confidential advice on matters relating to professional ethics from the Law Society's Professional Ethics Division (0870 606 2577) and on practice issues from the Practice Advice Service (0870 606 2522). The Mental Health and Disability Committee is also willing to consider written requests from solicitors for comments on complex cases.

Information and advice can also be obtained from the Customer Services Unit of the Public Trust Office (0171 664 7300).

Further reading

Trevor Aldridge, *Powers of Attorney*, (8th Edition, 1991) Longman

Gordon R Ashton, *The Elderly Client Handbook,* (1994) The Law Society (2nd Edition due late 1999)

Gordon R Ashton, *Elderly People and the Law* (1995) Butterworths

Gordon R Ashton (Ed), *Butterworths Older Client Law Service* (1997) (looseleaf), Butterworths

Stephen Cretney and Denzil Lush, *Enduring Powers of Attorney* (4th Edition, 1996) Jordans

Anthony Donelly, *Court of Protection Handbook* (9th Edition, 1995) FT Law and Tax

Denzil Lush, *Elderly Clients A Precedent Manual* (1996) Jordans

Norman Whitehorn, *Heywood & Massey Court of Protection Practice* (12th Edition, 1991) Sweet & Maxwell

Law Society: guidelines for solicitors

Law Society, *The Guide to the Professional Conduct of Solicitors* (8th Edition, 1999)

Law Society/British Medical Association, *Assessment of Mental Capacity Guidance for Doctors and Lawyers* (1995) BMA (available from the Law Society Shop, £8.95)

Law Society Mental Health and Disability Sub-Committee, *Gifts of Property Implications for future liability to pay for long-term care* (1995) (published in Professional Standards Bulletin No 15, March 1996)

Information for Clients

Penny Letts, *Managing Other People's Money* (2nd Edition, 1998) Age Concern England

Public Trust Office, *Enduring Powers of Attorney* (1995), available free of charge from the Public Trust Office

Age Concern Factsheet No 22, *Legal arrangements for managing financial affairs,* available from Age Concern England

Appendix A

Capacity to make an Enduring Power of Attorney

A power of attorney signed by a person who lacks capacity is null and void, unless it can be proved that it was signed during a lucid interval. Shortly after the Enduring Powers of Attorney Act 1985 came into force, the Court of Protection received a considerable number of applications to register enduring powers which had only just been created. This raised a doubt as to whether the donors had been mentally capable when they signed the powers. The problem was resolved in the test cases *Re K, Re F* [1988] Ch 310, in which the judge discussed the capacity to create an enduring power.

Having stated that the test of capacity to create an enduring power of attorney was that the donor understood the nature and effect of the document, the judge in the case set out four pieces of information which any person creating an EPA should understand.

— first, if such be the terms of the power, that the attorney will be able to assume complete authority over the donor's affairs,

— secondly, if such be the terms of the power, that the attorney will be able to do anything with the donor's property which the donor could have done,

— thirdly, that the authority will continue if the donor should be or should become mentally incapable, and

— fourthly, that if he or she should be or should become mentally incapable, the power will be irrevocable without confirmation by the Court of Protection

It is worth noting that the donor need not have the capacity to do all the things which the attorney will be able to do under the power. The donor need only have capacity to create the EPA.

The implications of Re K, Re F

The judge in *Re K, Re F* also commented that if the donor is capable of signing an enduring power of attorney, but incapable of managing and administering his or her property and affairs, the attorney has an obligation to register the power with the Court of Protection straightaway. Arguably, the attorney also has a moral duty in such cases to forewarn the donor that registration is not merely possible, but is intended immediately.

The decision in *Re K, Re F* has been criticised for imposing too simple a test of capacity to create an enduring power. But the simplicity or complexity of the test depends largely on the questions asked by the person assessing the donor's capacity. For example, if the four pieces of basic relevant information described by the judge in *Re K, Re F* were mentioned to the donor and he or she was asked 'Do you understand this?' in such a way as to encourage an affirmative reply, the donor would probably pass the test with flying colours and, indeed, the test would be too simple. If, on the other hand, the assessor were specifically to ask the donor 'What will your attorney be able to do?' and 'What will happen if you become mentally incapable?' the test would be substantially harder. There is no direct judicial authority on the point, but it can be inferred from the decision in *Re Beaney (deceased)* [1978] 1 WLR 770, that questions susceptible to the answers 'Yes' or 'No' may be inadequate for the purpose of assessing capacity.

[Adapted from BMA/Law Society, *Assessment of Mental Capacity Guidance for Doctors and Lawyers*, (1995) BMA]

Appendix B

Checklist of Dos and Don'ts for Enduring Powers of Attorney

In taking instructions:

DO:

- Assess carefully the donor's capacity to make an EPA
- Advise the donor fully on both the benefits and the risks
- Discuss with the donor the suitability of the proposed attorney(s)
- Confirm instructions with the donor personally
- Clarify and specify arrangements relating to
    - disclosure of the donor's will
    - dealing with investment business
    - making gifts
    - payment of professional charges

DON'T:

- Forget that the donor is your client
- Act on the unconfirmed instructions of third parties
- Allow third parties to control your access to the donor

In preparing the EPA:

DO:

- Use the current prescribed form of EPA
- Clarify when the power is to take effect
- Ensure the power is executed by the donor while still competent
- Ensure the power is signed by the attorney(s) after the donor has signed
- Ensure the signatures of donor and attorney(s) are properly witnessed
- Ensure the power is dated

DON'T:

- Omit Part A of the form or any of the marginal notes
- Fail to make the required deletions where alternatives are offered on the form
- Include restrictions or instructions which are unclear or outside the scope of the Enduring Powers of Attorney Act 1985

In applying for registration:

DO:

- Notify the donor and the required relatives using Form EP1
- Apply for registration within 10 days of the notification of the last person required to be notified
- Enclose the original EPA with the application
- Insert on form EP2 the dates on which the people concerned were notified and the date of the application for registration
- Send the registration fee with the application
- Send medical evidence in support of any application to dispense with the requirement to serve notice on the donor

DON'T:

- Forget that Form EP1 must be given to the donor personally
- Fail to comply with specified time limit

Appendix 6

The following guidelines were prepared by the Mental Health and Disability Committee of The Law Society, and are reproduced here with the kind permission of The Law Society.

© The Law Society 2002

GIFTS OF PROPERTY:

IMPLICATIONS FOR FUTURE LIABILITY TO PAY FOR LONG TERM CARE

Guidelines for solicitors prepared by the Law Society's Mental Health and Disability Committee. Revised April 2002

1. Elderly people or those nearing retirement may seek advice from solicitors as to the advantages and disadvantages of transferring their home or other property to relatives, even though in some cases they still intend to live in the home. The solicitor's advice will of course vary, according to the individual circumstances of the client, their motivation for making such a gift, and what they are hoping to achieve by it.

2. The following guidelines are designed to assist solicitors, both to ensure that their clients fully understand the nature, effects, benefits, risks and foreseeable consequences of making such a gift, and also to clarify the solicitor's role and duty in relation to such transactions. In particular, consideration is given to the implications of making gifts of property on possible future liability for the payment of fees for residential or nursing home care. This area of law is still under review by the Government, so solicitors should be aware that the law may change.

3. Whilst these guidelines generally refer to the making of 'gifts' they apply with equal force to situations where the disposal of property at a significant undervalue is contemplated.

THE NEED FOR LEGAL ADVICE

4. The Law Society is aware of a number of non-solicitor legal advice services which are marketing schemes for elderly people to effect a gift of property with the intention of avoiding the value of that property being taken into account to pay for residential care. Some make unjustified claims as to the effectiveness of the schemes, or fail to take into account the individual circumstances of clients. Seldom do these schemes highlight the other risks involved in making a gift of the home to members of the family.

5.   These guidelines are also intended to assist solicitors to stress the need for clients to obtain proper legal advice, and to highlight the risks of using unqualified advisers.

Who is the client?

6.   The solicitor must first be clear as to who s/he is acting for, especially where relatives purport to be giving instructions on behalf of an elderly person. In most cases, it will be the elderly person who owns the home or property so if the solicitor is to act in a transfer the elderly person will be the client. This will be the assumption for the purpose of these guidelines. It is important to recognise that there is an inevitable conflict of interest between the elderly person and anyone who stands to gain from the transaction, so the elderly person should receive independent advice (see also paras 30-31 below).

7.   The solicitor acting for the elderly person should see the client alone, to satisfy 'him/herself that the client is acting freely, to confirm the client's wishes and intentions, and to gauge the extent, if any, of family or other influence (see Principle 12.05 of the *Guide to Professional Conduct of Solicitors* (1999)). It may be necessary to spend some time with the client, talking about wider issues, in order to evaluate these aspects, clarify the family circumstances, and assess whether the client has the mental capacity to make the gift (see Appendix A for details of the relevant test of capacity).

8.   If the client is not already known to the solicitor, it may also be advisable to check whether another solicitor has previously acted for the client, and if so, to seek the client's consent to contact that solicitor, in case there are factors to be taken into account which are not immediately apparent.

The client's understanding

9.   It is important to ensure that the client understands the nature of a gift, that this is what is intended and the long-term implications. Before making any such gift clients should in particular understand:

  •   that the money or property they intend to give away is theirs in the first place;

  •   why the gift is being made;

  •   whether it is a one-off, or part of a series of gifts;

  •   the extent of the gift in relation to the rest of their money and property;

  •   that they are making an outright gift rather than, say, a loan or acquiring a share in a business or property owned by the recipient;

  •   whether they expect to receive anything in return and, if so, how much, or on what terms. (For example: someone who is giving away their house might expect to be able to carry on living there rent free for the rest of their life: but who pays for the insurance and upkeep?);

- whether they intend the gift to take effect immediately, or at a later date – perhaps when they die, or go into residential care;

- that, if the gift is outright, they can't assume that the money or property would be returned to them on request;

- the effect that making the gift could have on their future standard of living;

- the effect that the gift could have on other members of the family who might have expected eventually to inherit a share of the money or property;

- the possibility that the recipient could die first, or become involved in divorce or bankruptcy proceedings, in which case the money or property given away could end up belonging to somebody else;

- that the donor and recipient could fall out and even become quite hostile to one another;

- whether they have already made gifts to the recipient or other people; and

- any other foreseeable consequences of making or not making the gift (some of which are considered below).

The client's objectives

10. The solicitor should establish why the gift of property is being contemplated, and whether the client's objectives will in fact be achieved by the making of the gift or could be achieved in some other way. In establishing the client's objectives, the following matters may be relevant:

   (i) If the objective is to ensure that a particular relative (eg a child) inherits the client's home rather than someone else, this can equally well be achieved by making a will.

   (ii) If the objective is to avoid inheritance tax on the death of the client, a rough calculation should be made of the client's likely estate to assess the amount of tax which may be payable, and whether other tax saving measures could be considered. The client might not appreciate that the value of the property, together with the remainder of the estate, may not exceed the level at which inheritance tax becomes payable.

   The client might also not be aware that if s/he intends to continue living in the home after giving it away, there may be no inheritance tax saving because of the 'reservation of benefit' rules. The consequence might also be to increase the liability to inheritance tax on the death of the relative to whom the gift has been made if s/he dies before the client. Again, other schemes to mitigate these vulnerabilities should be considered.

(iii) If the objective is to relieve the elderly client of the worry and responsibility of home ownership, other ways of achieving this should be discussed, such as making an Enduring Power of Attorney.

(iv) If the client volunteers that a significant part of his/her objective is to try to avoid the value of the home being taken into account in various forms of means-testing, the implications and possible consequences should be explained to the client. These matters are considered in the following paragraphs in relation to liability to pay for long-term care. Alternative measures should also be discussed. The solicitor may also need to consider her/his own position (see paras 28-31 below).

Other reasons for transferring the home

11. There may, of course, be good reasons for transferring the home, or a share in the home, to a relative or another person quite apart from the desire to avoid means-testing. If such reasons exist the transfer should be effected sooner rather than later and it would be worthwhile reciting the reason in the transfer deed. For example:

(a) the home has not been vested in the appropriate names in the first place (eg it was funded in whole or in part by a son or daughter but vested in the name of the parent);

(b) a daughter has given up a well paid job to live in the home and care for an infirm parent in the expectation of inheriting the home on the death of the parent;

(c) the parent has for some years been unable to meet the outgoings or pay for alterations or improvements to the home and these have been funded by a son in the expectation of inheriting the home on the death of the parent;

(d) the home comprises part of a family business (eg a farm) which would no longer be viable if the home was 'lost'.

12. If the home is already vested in the joint names of the infirm elderly person and another occupier, or can for justifiable reasons be transferred by the elderly person into joint names, the beneficial interest of the elderly person may, on a means assessment, have little value when subject to the continued rights of occupation of the co-owner.

Severance of a joint tenancy

13. If the home is vested in the joint names of an elderly couple it may be worth considering a severence of the joint tenancy with a view to preserv-

ing at least a one-half share for the family. Each spouse can then make a will leaving his or her one-half share to the children. This provides some protection in the event that a caring spouse dies before an infirm spouse but there may be vulnerability to a claim under the Inheritance (Provision for Family and Dependants) Act 1975. It is possible to sever the joint tenancy even after the infirm spouse has become mentally incapable.

IMPLICATIONS OF MAKING THE GIFT

14.   A proper assessment of the implications of making a gift of the home, both for the client and for her/his relative(s) can best be achieved by listing the possible benefits and risks. These may include the following:

Possible benefits

- a saving of inheritance tax, probate fees and costs on the death of the client. Although in most cases the existence of a potential liability for inheritance tax will mean that a gift of the home by itself will not avoid vulnerability to means-testing, the high value of homes particularly in London may create this situation;

- avoiding the need to sell the home to pay for charges such as residential care or nursing home fees, thus securing the family's inheritance;

- avoiding the value of the home being taken into account in means-testing for other benefits or services.

Possible risks

- the value of the home may still be taken into account under the anti-avoidance measures in relation to means-testing (see paras 15-27);

- the capital gains tax owner-occupier exemption will apply to the gift, but may be lost thereafter and there will be no automatic uplift to the market value of the home on the client's death;

- the client may never need residential or nursing home care (it has been estimated that less than 6% of people aged 75-85 need residential care), so the risks of giving away the home may outweigh any potential benefits to be achieved;

- if the client does eventually need residential or nursing home care but no longer has the resources to pay the fees him/herself because of the gift, the local authority may only pay for a basic level of care (eg a shared room in a home of its choice), so the client may be dependent on relatives to top up the fees if a better standard of care is desired;

- the relatives to whom the gift has been made may fail to keep their side of the understanding, whether deliberately or through no fault of their own. For example, they may:

— fail to support the client (eg by not topping up residential care fees)

— seek to move the client prematurely into residential care in order to occupy the home themselves or to sell it

— die suddenly without making suitable provision for the client

— run into financial difficulties because of unemployment or divorce or become bankrupt and in consequence be unable to support the client

- the home may be lost on the bankruptcy, divorce or death of the relative to whom it has been given, resulting in the client being made homeless if s/he is still living there;

- there may be no inheritance tax saving whilst the client continues to live in the home, yet there could be a liability for inheritance tax if the relative dies before the client;

- the relative to whom the home has been gifted may lose entitlement to benefits and/or services (eg social security benefits, legal aid) due to personal means-testing if not living in the home;

- the local authority may decide, having regard to the client's ownership of the notional capital value of the home, rather than the property itself (see paras 18-19 below), that s/he is not entitled to certain community care services, or even to be funded at all for residential care should this be needed.

Anti-avoidance measures

15. The client can be given no guarantees that there is a fool-proof way of avoiding the value of the home being taken into account in means-testing, since the anti-avoidance measures in the law enable some gifts to be ignored by the authorities and even set aside by the court. Not only are these measures subject to change from time to time, but it is also unclear how far the authorities will go in order to pursue contributions they believe to be owing to them.

16. In most cases, the intention behind making the gift is the most important factor. Where the intention is clearly to create or increase entitlement to financial support from the local authority, measures can be taken to impose a charge on the asset given away in the hands of the recipients or even to recover the asset itself. However, it is necessary that the authority concerned believe that this was a 'significant' part of the client's intention in making the gift. Using one of the marketed schemes (see para 4 above) which have been advertised specifically to help people to avoid local authority means-testing may make clear the client's intention.

CHARGES FOR RESIDENTIAL AND NURSING HOME CARE

17. At present, a major cause for concern among many older clients is the fear of having to sell their homes in order to pay for residential or nursing home care in the future, and they may wish to take steps to protect their families' inheritance. In giving advice on this matter, it is important that solicitors are familiar with the key points summarised in Appendix B, including:

- the eligibility criteria for NHS funded nursing home care;

- the charging and funding arrangements by local authorities for residential and nursing home care (when applicable);

- when care must be provided free of charge; and

- if charges may be made, the means-testing rules which apply

Implications of the 'notional capital' rule

18. Where the local authority believe that property has been given away by the client with the intention of creating or increasing entitlement to help with residential care fees, or nursing home fees where these are payable, then it may decide that the client has 'notional capital' equivalent in value to that of the property given away. If that notional capital value exceeds the capital cut off (currently £16,000, see Appendix B) the authority may decide that the client is not entitled to any assistance (or any continuing assistance) with the home care fees.

19. In such cases it would be the client who then had to take action if s/he wished to challenge the decision. This may involve the use of the local authority's complaints procedures, as well as the Ombudsman or a judicial review. These may all entail significant legal expense and anxiety for the client as the outcome could not be guaranteed. If a judicial review is necessary it would be the client who had to establish that the authority's decision was *Wednesbury* unreasonable (ie the burden of proof would be on the client). See *Robertson v Fife* (Court of Session) 12/1/2000 [http://www.scotscourt.gov.uk/index1.htm]

Enforcing payment of fees for residential and nursing home care

20. Having assessed someone as being in need of residential or nursing home care and then provided that care, the local authority cannot withdraw that provision simply because the resident does not pay assessed contributions. However, where charges may legally be made, the authority can take steps to recover contributions, and in assessing ability to pay, may take into account property that has been given away for the purpose of avoiding means-testing.

21. The enforcement provisions available to local authorities are as follows:

(i) taking proceedings in the Magistrates' Court to recover sums due as a civil debt (section 56, National Assistance Act 1948);

(ii) imposing a charge on any property belonging to the resident, with interest chargeable from the day after death (sections 22 and 24 HASSASSA Act 1983);

(iii) imposing a charge on property transferred by the resident within 6 months of going to residential care, or whilst in care, with the intention of avoiding contributions (section 21, HASSASSA Act 1983).

22. Once the debt for unpaid contributions reaches £750, insolvency proceedings could be taken to declare the resident bankrupt, whereupon transactions at an undervalue may be set aside within 2 years, or within 5 years if the person made bankrupt was insolvent at the time of the transaction, which is unlikely (sections 339-341 Insolvency Act 1986).

23. Under other provisions, a gift may be set aside without time limit and without bankruptcy, if the court is satisfied that the transfer was made for the purpose of putting assets beyond the reach of a potential creditor or otherwise prejudicing the creditor's interests (sections 423-425, Insolvency Act 1986). This provision is exceptionally wide, and the court has extensive powers to restore the position to that which it would have been had the gift not been made.

24. Although some local authorities have threatened to use insolvency proceedings, few have actually done so, perhaps because of lack of expertise or the prospect of bad publicity. However, with increasing pressures on local authority resources to provide community care services, there is no guarantee they will not do so in the future.

25. The burden of proof remains on the local authority to establish that the purpose behind the gift of the property was to avoid means-testing. But it may be difficult for the donor or his/her relatives to give evidence as to the donor's intentions, and if another purpose of the gift cannot be established or indicated the judge may conclude that it must have been to avoid means-testing.

26. The purpose of the gift will have been discussed in advance with the solicitor, and it would be prudent for the solicitor to retain evidence of the advice given in order to protect him/herself in the event of a subsequent family dispute or professional negligence claim. The file notes and correspondence will normally be covered by legal professional privilege or at least by the duty of confidentiality. The court will not usually order discovery of a solicitor's file unless there is *prima facie* evidence of fraud, but has done so in similar circumstances on the basis of public policy considerations *(Barclays Bank plc v Eustice* [1995] 1 WLR 1238). It is possible that a trustee in bankruptcy, or a local authority bringing proceedings under the Insolvency Act 1986, sections 423 – 425, may persuade the court to override privilege.

27. In *Yule v South Lanarkshire Council* [1999] 1 CCLR 546 Lord Philip held
     that a local authority was entitled to take account of the value of an elderly
     woman's home transferred to her daughter over 18 months before the
     woman entered residential care. The Court held that there was no time
     limit on local authorities when deciding whether a person had deprived
     themselves of assets for the purposes of avoiding residential care fees.

THE SOLICITOR'S DUTY

28. The solicitor's role is more than just drawing up and registering the
     necessary deeds and documents to effect the making of the gift. S/he has a
     duty to ensure that the client fully understands the nature, effect, benefits,
     risks and foreseeable consequences of making the gift. The solicitor has
     no obligation to advise the client on the wisdom or morality of the
     transaction, unless the client specifically requests this.

29. The Professional Ethics Division of the Law Society has advised that the
     solicitor should follow his/her client's instructions, provided that by
     doing so, the solicitor will not be involved in a breach of the law or a
     breach of the principles of professional conduct. Reference is made to
     Principle 12.02 of the *Guide to the Professional Conduct of Solicitors*
     (1999), which indicates when instructions must be refused. Solicitors will
     want to satisfy themselves in each individual case that no breach of the
     law is involved in the proposed transaction. Having advised the client as
     to the implications and possible consequences of making the gift, the
     decision whether or not to proceed remains with the client.

30. Solicitors must also be aware of the possible conflict of interest, or
     significant risk of such a conflict, between the donor and recipient of a
     gift. While there is no general rule of law that a solicitor should never act
     for both parties in a transaction where their interests might conflict,
     Principle 15.01 of the *Guide to the Professional Conduct of Solicitors*
     states: 'A solicitor or firm of solicitors should not accept instructions to
     act for two or more clients where there is a conflict or a significant risk of
     a conflict between the interests of the clients'. Given the potentially
     vulnerable position of an elderly client, the solicitor will have to consider
     carefully whether he can act for the donor and the recipient or whether
     there is an actual or significant risk of conflict. If the solicitor has initially
     advised the donor alone as to all the implications of the gift and is satisfied
     that there is no undue influence and that the donor has capacity, the
     solicitor may be able to act for both clients in the conveyancing.

31. If the solicitor is asked to act for both parties, the solicitor should make
     them both aware of the possibility of a conflict of interest and advise one
     of them to consider taking independent advice. S/he should also explain
     that as a result of any conflict of interest, a solicitor acting by agreement
     for both parties may be unable to disclose all that s/he knows to each of
     them or to give advice to one of them which conflicts with the interests of
     the other and may have to cease acting for both. Both parties must be

content to proceed on this basis, be competent to do so and give their consent in writing. However, if any doubt remains, the solicitor would be advised not to act for both parties.

Further reading

Gordon R Ashton, *The Elderly Client Handbook: The Law Society's Guide to Acting for Older People*, (Second edition, 2000) The Law Society

Gordon R Ashton, *Elderly People and the Law,* (1995) Butterworths

Gordon R Ashton (Ed) *Butterworths Older Client Law Service,* (1998 loose-leaf) Butterworths

Clements L, *Community Care and the Law,* (Third edition, 2000) Legal Action

The Law Society, *The Guide to the Professional Conduct of Solicitors* (Eighth edition, 1999), The Law Society

Age Concern Fact Sheets available from Age Concern England, FREEPOST, (SWB 30375), Ashburton, Devon TQ13 7ZZ. Tel: 0800 00 99 66

No 10*Local authority charging procedures for residential and nursing home care*

No 11*Financial support for people in residential and nursing home accommodation prior to 1 April 1993*

No 38*Treatment of the former home as capital for people in residential and nursing home care*

No 39*Paying for care in a residential or nursing home if you have a partner*

No 40*Transfer of assets and paying for care in a residential or nursing home*

Appendix A

CAPACITY TO MAKE A GIFT

The relevant test of capacity to make a gift is set out in the judgment in Re *Beaney (Deceased)* [(1978) 1 WLR 770]. In that case a 64-year-old widow with three grown up children owned and lived in a three-bedroom semi-detached house. Her elder daughter lived with her. In May 1973, a few days after being admitted to hospital suffering from advanced dementia, the widow signed a deed of gift transferring the house to her elder daughter. The widow died intestate the following year, and her son and younger daughter applied success-fully to the court for a declaration that the transfer of the house was void and of no effect because their mother was mentally incapable of making such a gift. The judge in the case set out the following criteria for capacity to make a lifetime gift:

> 'The degree or extent of understanding required in respect of any instrument is relative to the particular transaction which it is to effect. ... Thus, at one extreme, if the subject matter and value of a gift are trivial in relation to the donor's other assets, a low degree of understanding will suffice. But, at the other, if its effect is to dispose of the donor's only asset of value and thus, for practical purposes, to pre-empt the devolution of his estate under [the donor's] will or ... intestacy, then the degree of understanding required is as high as that required for a will, and the donor must understand the claims of all potential donees and the extent of the property to be disposed of.'

It is arguable that, when someone makes a substantial gift, a further point should be considered, namely, the effect that disposing of the asset could have on the donor for the rest of his or her life.

[Adapted from British Medical Association/Law Society, *Assessment of Mental Capacity: Guidance for Doctors and Lawyers,* (1995) BMA.]

Appendix B

PAYING FOR RESIDENTIAL AND NURSING HOME CARE

Charges

Individuals who can afford to pay for a place in a residential care or nursing home may arrange this independently, though it is advisable to seek a 'needs' assessment prior to entering residential or nursing care in order to achieve continuity if local authority funding may be needed in future:

- if met with a refusal to assess in advance, point out that the assessment of need for care provision does not depend upon the need for funding;

- it may also be wise to ensure that the particular home is willing to accommodate residents on local authority funding.

Local authority

Those who enter such a home through an arrangement made by the local authority must pay or contribute to the cost, whether the authority provides or buys in the accommodation:

- each authority must fix a standard weekly charge for its own homes which should represent the true economic cost of providing the accommodation – many have a standard scale of fees geared to their eligibility criteria;

- where the authority purchases a place from an independent home the weekly charge to the resident should represent the cost of the place to the authority;

- residents must generally contribute in accordance with their resources up to the appropriate charge, but no one will be required to pay more;

- the authority either:

  — pays the full fee to the home and collects the resident's contribution; or

  — pays its share whilst the resident and any third party pay the balance

- a contract with the authority or the home should state what is included in the charge and what are extras.

Health authority

Where a health authority arranges a place in a nursing home under a contractual arrangement the individual remains an NHS patient and no charge is made but social security benefits may be withdrawn or reduced.

It is important to ascertain whether a move from hospital to a private nursing home also involves a transfer of responsibility from the health authority to social services.

Means-testing

When the resident cannot afford the full charge an assessment is made of ability to pay and this is reviewed annually but a resident should ask for re-assessment at any time if this would be beneficial:

- the assessment relates to both income and capital:

  — since April 1993 assessment has been brought largely into line with that for income support, though local authorities retain some discretion

  — the capital cut-off point is £16,000 but capital above £10,000 will result in a tariff income (an attempt to apply a lower financial threshold before acknowledging need failed in *R v Sefton Metropolitan Borough Council, ex p Help the Aged* ([1997] 1 CCLR 57, CA)

  — *notional capital* and *notional income* rules apply as for income support

- assessment relates only to the means of the resident (unlike for income support where spouses and partners are generally assessed together):

  — there is no power to oblige a spouse/partner to take part *but* spouses are liable to maintain each other (National Assistance Act 1948, s 42) and court action may be taken against a liable relative (s 43)

  — jointly owned property may be deemed to be owned in equal shares (but query whether it has a value if a home is occupied by the joint owner)

  — since 1996 one-half of occupational and private pensions of the resident are re-routed back to the non-resident spouse

- the value of the resident's home is disregarded during a temporary stay or:

  — if occupied by a spouse/partner, or a relative who is aged 60 or over or incapacitated

  — if occupied by someone else and the local authority exercises its discretion

- there is a minimum charge payable by all residents and the assessment determines what should be paid above this, but all residents retain a personal expenses allowance (revised annually):

  — to be used by the resident for expenditure of personal choice such as stationery, personal toiletries, treats (eg sweets, drinks, cigarettes) and presents

  — the authority has a discretion to increase the amount, but it should not be used for top-up to provide more expensive accommodation

- authorities should carry out a benefits check because they have an incentive to ensure that people in homes are receiving maximum state benefits:

  — this should only be with the informed consent of the resident

  — income support will include a *residential allowance* (not for local authority homes)

Power to charge?

In two main situations (see *R v North and East Devon Health Authority ex p Coughlan* [1999] 2 CCLR 285; *R v Borough of Richmond ex p Watson* [1999] 2 CCLR 402) no charges may be made for the care of an individual:

- where, following discharge from detention under one of the longer treatment sections of the Mental Health Act 1983 (usually s 3 or s 37), he or she requires residential or nursing home care as a result of mental disorder:

  — no charge may be made for care as this is deemed 'aftercare' service provision under Mental Health Act 1983, s 117

— that section places a joint duty on the health and local authorities to provide the services required free of charge, unless it is decided by both that the person is no longer in need of these by virtue of their mental disorder

• (only applicable to placements in nursing homes) where his or her need is primarily a health care need:

— the health authority must fund the entire cost of the placement and the local authority has no power to purchase such care and pass the costs to the client

— the only exception is where the nursing care is 'merely ancillary or incidental to the provision of the accommodation' in a nursing home. This will depend on the level and type of care. Most nursing homes placements will be the responsibility of the NHS because a client will not be placed there unless their primary need is for nursing care, ie health care

Regulations and guidance

National Assistance (Assessment of Resources) Regulations 1992 *as amended*

Circular LAC (99)9 *'Charging for Residential Accommodation Guide' (CRAG)* (copies available from the Department of Health, PO Box 777, London SE1 6XH; Fax: 01623 724 524; e-mail: doh@prologistics).

[Adapted from Gordon R Ashton, The Elderly Client Handbook: The Law Society's Guide to Acting for Older People, (Second edition, 2000) The Law Society]

Index